THE POLITICAL ECONOMY
OF POLICY-MAKING

COMPARATIVE POLITICAL ECONOMY AND PUBLIC POLICY SERIES

Volume 4: The Political Economy of Policy-Making

THE POLITICAL ECONOMY OF POLICY-MAKING

Essays in Honor of
Will E. Mason

edited by

MICHAEL P. DOOLEY
HERBERT M. KAUFMAN
RAYMOND E. LOMBRA

foreword by
ROBERT W. CLOWER

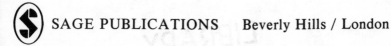 **SAGE PUBLICATIONS** Beverly Hills / London

For information address:

SAGE PUBLICATIONS, INC.
275 South Beverly Drive
Beverly Hills, California 90212

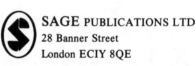

SAGE PUBLICATIONS LTD
28 Banner Street
London ECIY 8QE

Printed in the United States of America

Library of Congress Cataloging in Publication Data

Main entry under title:

Political economy of policy-making.

(Comparative political economy and public
policy series; 4)
Bibliography: p.
1. United States—economic policy—1961-
—Addresses, essays, lectures. 2. Economic stabilization—
Addresses, essays, lectures.
I. Dooley, Michael P. II. Kaufman, Herbert M.
III. Lombra, Raymond E.
HC106.7.P737   339.5'0973   78-25960
ISBN 0-8039-1238-2
ISBN 0-8039-1239-0 pbk.

FIRST PRINTING

CONTENTS

PART III: POLICY-MAKING IN AN OPEN ECONOMY

FOREWORD

Will E. Mason, in whose honor the present collection of essays is published, retired officially in 1977 after a long and distinguished teaching career that included more than twenty years as Professor of Economics at Pennsylvania State University. I say "retired officially" because, in Will's case, retirement from active teaching has meant little more than a change from part-time to full-time scholarly research and writing. Those have always been Will's primary interests. He is now in a position to pursue them single-mindedly.

Popular opinion to the contrary notwithstanding, there is no conflict or, indeed, any real distinction between scholarship and teaching. Will Mason aptly illustrates their compatibility. Known to his students as a dedicated, stimulating, and vigorous teacher, he is noted among his professional colleagues as perhaps the most knowledgeable, and surely one of the more provocative and insightful present-day interpreters of contemporary and traditional variations on historical themes of monetary theory and history. However, to students and professional colleagues alike, Will is viewed more as a man of thought than of action—a purveyor of ideas rather than a propounder of policies. So he appears, in truth, as a living example of the kind of "academic scribbler" to which Keynes paid tribute at the end of his *General Theory*.

> The ideas of economists are more powerful than is commonly understood. Practical men, who believe themselves to be quite exempt from any intellectual influence, are usually the slaves of some defunct economist. Madmen in authority, who hear voices in the air, are distilling their frenzy from some academic scribbler of a few years back.

Of course Keynes was wrong. The ideas of academic scribblers, at least in their original form, are not powerful in themselves. They become powerful, if at all, only through being successfully "brokered" by successive generations of students and other admirers. Fortunately, there is no Gresham's Law in this area of free enterprise. On the contrary, good ideas tend to drive out bad, for only good ideas continue to attract effective brokers.

To insinuate that the authors of the essays that follow are mere brokers of ideas would, of course, not only do less than justice to them but also to Will Mason. For what Will Mason has most effectively done for his students and professional colleagues is to make them aware of the highly unsettled and uncertain state of contemporary intellectual understanding of forces governing the coordination of economic activities in the world in which we actually live. At first glance, that may not seem like much. In a world where economists appear to be taken ever more seriously not only by "madmen in authority" but also by themselves, however, Will Mason's insistence on detached agnosticism surely is not misplaced. Certainly its importance has not been overlooked by any of the contributors to this volume. Each attacks a distinct policy-making problem in his own way. Each arrives at conclusions that are anything but preconceived. There is, indeed, no obvious unifying theme to link the essays that follow. Yet one clear message does emerge from the collection as a whole, namely, that it will be time enough for economists to bring light to the world when they have reason to believe seriously that they are not themselves still fumbling around in the dark. That seems to be a message worth learning.

Robert W. Clower
University of California at Los Angeles

INTRODUCTION

There is a growing restiveness within the economics profession. Some economists see the problem as reflecting the increasing irrelevance of economic theory. Alfred Eichner puts it this way:

> Economic theory has become increasingly more elegant as a set of axiomatic statements about resource allocation under competitive market conditions. The precision with which assumptions are stated, the subtlety with which the logic is then pursued, and the rigor with which a proof is finally adduced all seem to support the claim of economics to be the Euclidian geometry, if not the physics, of the social sciences.

> At the same time, economic theory has become less and less useful to anyone hoping to understand phenomena of the real world. . . . It is this contrast between its elegance and its relevance that underlies the current crisis in economics ["Post-Keynesian Theory: An Introduction," *Challenge* (May/June 1978):4-5].

Other economists apparently see the problem in quite a different light. In assessing the state of macroeconomics, Assar Lindbeck states:

> The present "crisis" in the Western economies is not, I think, mainly a "crisis in economics". . . . The main problem is not that we are unable to understand analytically what is happening, but rather that the institutional changes and the discretionary policies that are necessary for macroeconomic stability seem to be politically difficult to implement ["Stabilization Policy in Open Economies with Endogenous Politicians," *American Economic Review* (May 1976):18].

These alternative explanations of the "crisis" in economics need not be viewed as mutually exclusive. Orthodox theory usually abstracts from government behavior, implying that the latter can be viewed as an exogenous force superimposed on an invariant structure of behavioral relationships. However, recent work in the theory of public choice and in the factors affecting the formation of expectations, to cite two examples, emphasize the interaction between, and the economic rationale for, government actions and the behavior of other agents. Along similar lines, a theme which motivates many of the issues discussed in the following essays is that the apparent inability of economic theory to explain reality may be in part a reflection of both the failure to extend economic theory to the behavior of governments and the failure to recognize the interdependencies between the public and private sectors.

This volume, as the title indicates, examines various political and economic issues surrounding the formulation and implementation of policy (mainly in the United States). The implied disorientation of economic theory on the one hand and policy-making on the other, points to the need for a concerted effort to close the gaps between economic theory, economic policy, and economic performance. The analysis of a multitude of micro and macro (domestic and international) policy problems addressed in the following essays is directed toward this end.

Michael P. Dooley
Herbert M. Kaufman
Raymond E. Lombra

PART I
ECONOMIC INSTABILITY
AND STABILIZATION POLICY

Chapter 1

POLICY ADVICE AND POLICY-MAKING:
ECONOMIC, POLITICAL, AND SOCIAL ISSUES

RAYMOND E. LOMBRA
Pennsylvania State University

INTRODUCTION

An evaluation of the performance of the economy over the past decade leaves little doubt that the macroeconomic goals policy makers presumably were trying to achieve have proved elusive. The inflation rate has continued its upward secular drift and has been quite volatile relative to earlier periods. The economy suffered its worst recession since the Depression and the unemployment rate, like the inflation rate, displayed considerable downward inflexibility. In addition, the fixed exchange rate system broke down, the U.S. experienced record trade deficits, and the international value of the dollar exhibited considerable instability.

Such overwhelming circumstantial evidence, along with the fact that economists held many of the key policy-making positions over the period, is thought by many to warrant a summary judgment that the "science" of economics is intellectually bankrupt. Put less dramatically, the economy's performance must have at least initially been puzzling to the millions of former principles of economics students who learned what the goals were and how the proper dose of fiscal policy (given the multiplier) or monetary policy (given velocity) could cure some, if not all, of the economy's ills.[1] Some of these neophyte keynesians or monetarists might enjoy hearing their now older (wiser?) professors explain what went wrong. It is likely the responses, regardless of the professor's professional background, would have much in common. Many would argue their analysis was basically correct—it was just that policy makers did the wrong things! Doubters are referred to a recent discussion of monetary policy where Benjamin Friedman noted that tendency for economists (whether monetarist or keynesian) to think that the Federal Reserve does exactly the opposite of what they would personally recommend (Friedman, 1977:345). Leaving aside the questions of logic raised by such

AUTHORS' NOTE: I want to thank James Herendeen, Will E. Mason, Mike Wasylenko, and Nancy Wentzler for their very helpful comments on an earlier draft.

tendencies, Friedman's observation nicely illustrates a central problem in political economy; it is virtually impossible to convict one of error and usually quite difficult to convince one of error (Davidson, 1972:ix-x).

The aim of this chapter is to first provide a discussion of the issues which appear to underly policy advice from economists, and second to relate these various issues to the actual formation and implementation of policy by the policy makers. The general theme developed is inherently pluralistic—political, social, and economic judgments form the basis of policy advice and govern the choices policy makers make. The specific focus is on the notion that the economic instability we have experienced is *not* primarily the result of either our lack of knowledge about how the economy operated or policy-making that reflects errors in judgment or irrational behavior by the policy makers. The alternative hypothesis offered is that the interaction of individual and group "enlightened" self-interest in the public and private sectors moves the economy like an "invisible hand" along a dynamic time path characterized by considerable instability.

THE EVOLUTION OF STABILIZATION POLICY

The predominant economic paridigm governing U.S. policy-making until the Depression had been fashioned by classical (e.g., Smith, Mill, and Ricardo) and neoclassical (e.g., Fisher and Pigou) economists. At the risk of extreme over simplification, the prevailing view was that the economy was inherently stable in the sense that economic disturbances (or shocks) would set in motion natural forces which would tend to restore equilibrium at full employment. The hypothesized, internal self-correcting mechanisms resulting from the assumed flexibility of wages, prices, and interest rates (e.g., the real balance effect) provided an economic rationale for a laissez-faire, hands-off approach to government policy-making. In this connection it is important to note that when the Federal Reserve System was formed in 1913 there was virtually no understanding of the contemporary notion of stabilization policy. This being the case, Congress saw no need to provide any more guidance on what the Federal Reserve should do other than specifying the need "to furnish an elastic currency." As Milton Friedman and Anna Schwartz point out:

> The Federal Reserve therefore began operations with no effective legisla-
> tive criterion for determining the total stock of money. . . . These men were
> not even guided by a legislative mandate of interest. . .and were hardly
> aware of the enlarged powers and widened responsibilities the change in

circumstances had thrust upon them. Little wonder, perhaps, that the subsequent years saw so much backing and filling, so much confusion about purpose and power, and so erratic an exercise of power (Friedman and Schwartz, 1963b:193).

The Great Depression, which stimulated the work of Keynes, Kalacki and others, substantially altered the received paridigm. The new view pointed to inelastic expectations, animal spirits, pervasive uncertainty, and rigidities in the price-wage system, and argued that such factors would in the "short-run" swamp any self-correcting, natural forces which might operate following a disturbance to the economy. The hypothesized result was a tendency for the economy to settle at a less than full-employment level of activity—a state usually referred to as a persistent disequilibrium. This "revolution" in economic thought provided the intellectual and philosophical basis for a new more activist role for the government. As Lindbeck has stated: "Stabilization policy has since Keynes been based on two main premises: that macroeconomic fluctuations are largely a result of instability in market behavior; and that national aggregate demand management. . .is the basic means of overcoming these fluctuations" (Lindbeck, 1976:1). Following this watershed in political economy—which simultaneously gave birth to the modern notions of macroeconomics and stabilization policy—the question was not whether the government should intervene, but rather how, when, and to what degree.

The peak in optimism regarding the government's ability to "control" the economy with monetary and fiscal policy probably could be dated in the mid-1960s, following the passage of the 1964 tax cut. The business cycle was now viewed by many as passé—the government could be relied on to counter the instabilities in the economy.[2] Further, fiscal policy, as opposed to monetary policy, was generally viewed as the senior stabilization partner in terms of effectiveness.

The euphoria was short-lived: "credit crunches" of 1966 and 1969, the accelerating inflation rate, and the monetarist counter-revolution ushered in an era of reexamination of the premises which had contributed to the premature burial of business cycle analysis. The intellectual about-face was vividly demonstrated by the title of a session at the annual meeting of the American Economic Association in late 1971—"Have Fiscal and/or Monetary Policies Failed?" (American Economics Association, 1972).[3] As is usually the case, economists participating in this session were not of one mind regarding the reasons for the purported policy failure. In fact, the leading monetarist, Milton Friedman argued that "monetary policy did not fail in the past three years in the relevant scientific sense. The drugs produced the effect to be expected, though the wrong drug was administered" (Friedman, 1972:17). Such critiques of policy-making became progressively more pervasive and a massive volume of research was aimed at resolving various aspects of the controversy over the economic bases for particular approaches to policy-making. In this regard, the monetarist critique and some of the reactions to it are worthy of special attention.

A VIEW OF THE MONETARIST CRITIQUE

Few would deny that the monetarist view has gained considerable currency (no pun intended) over the past decade. As Franco Modigliani, a leading neokeynesian, has said: "the revaluation of the role of money has. . .resulted in a notable reduction in the cleavage of views concerning the importance and workings of money—largely, but not entirely, through the nonmonetarists moving toward the monetarists" (Modigliani, 1975: 181). Despite this admission, it should be recognized that an important impediment to any major synthesis has been a tendency for the combatents to over emphasize the differences in views, and for observers to misrepresent the essential aspects of the various controversies in order to facilitate pedogoçic discussions. Attempts to make inherently complicated issues simple should be encouraged, but if our principles of economics texts are used as a guide, many students may have come away from their study of "the dismal science" with a seriously deficient view of the rationale for alternative policy prescriptions. The purpose of this section is to point out some of the essential aspects of the ongoing debate between monetarists and nonmonetarists (usually referred to as keynesians or neokeynesians), recognizing that it too may be an oversimplification.[4]

Perhaps the most highly visible aspect of the debate has been the apparent disagreement over various aspects of the transmission mechanism for monetary and fiscal policy. In its more sophisticated form, the monetarist critique emphasizes the alternative judgments about the slopes and stability of the various functions underlying the Hicks-Hansen IS-LM model, and the need to distinguish carefully between real and nominal magnitudes. This analytical approach is supplemented with empirical work which purports to demonstrate: the money supply, as opposed to the nominal interest rate, is a superior intermediate target for the Federal Reserve to aim at; fiscal policy is accompanied by "crowding out" and thus over time has no lasting impact on economic activity; the Phillips curve is vertical at the "natural" rate of unemployment in the "long" run; and monetary policy is "neutral" in the "long" run in the sense that changes in the money supply, although reflected in the inflation rate, have no lasting effect on real output.[5]

While it is tempting to examine each of the above premises, there is considerable risk of getting bogged down in analytic details which may not be essential to understanding policy advice and policy-making. A more productive route may be to focus on the key economic, social, and political aspects of the monetarist critique and the reactions to it.

THE RELEVANT TIME FRAME

The first major issue concerns the time horizon or time frame to which monetarist and keynesian analysis applies. The issue has been summarized neatly by Modigliani:

> There is reason to believe that at present monetarists and nonmonetarists largely agree, at least qualitatively, about both the *short-* and *long-run* effects of monetary and fiscal policy. But this agreement may be somewhat misleading. For in the monetarists view, the *long-run* is around the corner and, therefore, what happens in the fleeting short-run is of little relevance. By contrast, for the nonmonetarists it is the long-run which is irrelevant because it is far away, and the short-run response is the only one that matters. It is this difference—plus a related difference in assessing the quantitative impact on demand of changes in exogenous variables other than monetary (and fiscal) ones—which, despite broad agreement of principle, would still lead, say, Friedman and myself to advocate much of the time, including right now, very different monetary and fiscal policies (Modigliani, 1975:181).

The qualitative agreement Modigliani mentions refers in part to the proposition that in the "long" run the Phillips curve is very steep or vertical and policy has negligible lasting effects on real variables, whereas in the "short" run the Phillips curve is negatively sloped (i.e., there appears to be a trade-off between inflation and unemployment) and policy can effect real variables.[6]

The monetarist critique has generally revolved around the notion that short run policy effects are difficult to predict. Friedman has said: "We cannot predict at all accurately just what effects a particular monetary action will have on the price level and, equally important, just when it will have that effect" (Friedman, 1968:15). The unpredictability of the "long and variable lag" (Friedman, 1961) is itself a reflection of considerable uncertainty about the structural relationships which guide behavior in the short run: "We have little confidence in our knowledge of the transmission mechanism, except in such broad and vague terms as to constitute little more than an impressionistic representation rather than an engineering blueprint" (Friedman and Schwartz, 1963a:55). Given the uncertainty over the short-run effects, the monetarists argue that pursuing an activist, discretionary policy geared toward short-run developments will often result in economic instability that is policy-induced. Instead, they emphasize the certainty attached to longer-run, steady-state effects and would accordingly recommended policy "rules," that are geared toward achieving desired long-run outcomes.

As Modigliani noted a central issue has always been how "long" is the "short" run and how far away is the "long" run in historical calendar time (as opposed to analytical time). With early work on the quantity theory usually pointing towards several decades for the proportionality between money and prices to hold,[7] it is little wonder Keynes argued that "in *the long run* we are all dead" (Keynes, 1924:80). Even Friedman, perhaps unwittingly, has admitted that the quantity theory hypothesis regarding the proportional relationship between money and prices may only hold in the historical long run: "this is an average relationship, not a precise relationship that can be expected to hold in exactly the same way in every month or year or even *decade*" (Friedman, 1974:535, emphasis added).

The relegation of the quantity theory to the historical long run made it easier for policy makers interested in the short run to ignore the monetarist message. Recognition of this fact and perhaps an a priori belief that the long run was considerably shorter than previous empirical work had suggested, provided impetus for the development of the recent literature on rational expectations (Shiller, 1978; Poole, 1976; Sargent and Wallace, 1976). In general, this literature suggests that the long run is indeed "right around the corner."[8] Tobin's response is typical of the keynesian reaction to this work:

> They are all inspired by faith that the economy can never be very far from equilibrium. Markets work, excess supplies and demands are eliminated, expectations embody the best available information, people always make any and all deals which would move all parties to preferred positions. With such faith the orthodox economists of the early 1930's could shut their eyes to events they knew *a priori* could not be happening. With such faith their successors of the 1970's can tell us that the very persistence of high unemployment and excess capacity reveal them to be the voluntarily preferred state of affairs. Keynes might say this is where he came in (Tobin, 1977:461).

THE WELFARE COSTS OF INFLATION AND UNEMPLOYMENT

The second major issue that conditions policy prescriptions by monetarists and their critics concerns their differential assessment of the costs to society of inflation as compared to the costs of unemployment. Unfortunately, the social costs of unemployment are much more visible, and therefore, more amenable to measurement than are the costs of inflation. The latter, which are mostly hidden and distributed over time, require considerably more ingenuity to locate, identify, and measure. As a result, sizing up the *net* cost or benefit to society of particular rates of inflation and unemployment has not progressed very far.

The welfare costs of inflation—which the monetarists emphasize—depend critically on whether the inflation is fully anticipated or not. To the extent that an inflation is unanticipated there are several potential redistributive effects. Within the *private* sector income and wealth can be redistributed. For example, debtors gain at the expense of creditors. If the rate of inflation is not fully anticipated, the interest cost to the borrower, and therefore the return to the lender, will be lower in real terms than expected at the time the loan contract was consummated. In addition, if wages lag behind prices, real wages fall and firms benefit. More generally, as an unanticipated inflation progresses, the resulting changes in relative prices are associated with a redistribution of income and wealth. If the inflation were fully anticipated we would expect wages and interest rates to reflect such anticipations, thereby limiting the extent of inflation-induced redistribution in the private sector.[9]

Unanticipated inflation can also generate distributive effects between the private and public sectors. Given the government's debtor status, inflation reduces the real value of the outstanding debt. In addition, the progressive nature of our tax system and the inadequate nature of current accounting practices regarding the valuation of the capital stock, depreciation, inventories, and so forth, results in an increase in real tax rates when prices and nominal income rise. Finally, inflation (even if anticipated) serves in effect as a government tax on the private sector's holdings of cash balances. Assuming a given demand for real cash balances, the nominal money supply will need to rise at the same rate as prices to satisfy demand. However, the issuer of cash balances—the government—will receive real resources in return. Thus the government can raise revenue by "inflating."[10]

In addition to the redistributive consequences of inflation it is also thought that the production of goods and services can be adversely affected. On the demand side, the accounting deficiencies mentioned above can discourage investment, uncertainty generated by inflation can increase savings and lower consumption, real balance (or wealth) effects can lower spending, net exports can decline, and so forth. On the supply side, resources are wasted in economizing on cash balances, gathering information more frequently, changing price lists, and so forth. More generally, the advantages of a stable unit of account are sacrificed.

Taken together it is usually argued that these many costs tear away at the fabric of society, making the economic system less efficient, inducing institutional and social pressures, and increasing government intervention. This is viewed as a highly unstable environment. Friedman argues: "It will either degenerate into hyperinflation and radical change, or institutions will adjust to a situation of chronic inflation." (Friedman, 1977:470).[11]

Many keynesians are not convinced. Commenting on the work on the social costs of inflation, Tobin has said: "Economists' answers have been remarkably vague, even though the prestige of the profession has reinforced the popular view that inflation leads ultimately to catastrophe" (Tobin, 1972:15). On the macro level the existence of a trade-off between inflation and unemployment in the short run is taken as a given by the keynesians, and thus they usually emphasize the billions of dollars of output forever lost when actual output falls short of potential output—that is, when the actual unemployment rate exceeds the unemployment rate thought to be a proxy for "full" employment. Assessing high costs of unemployment (and relatively low costs of inflation) is also often the result of what might be called a humanistic approach to the problem: "The question is not simply how much more unemployment we can stand, but whether we can stand, through deepening unemployment, a deepening of the race and class divisions that are already threatening to tear our society apart" (Liebow, 1970:2).[12] Liebow is even more specific: "behind much of what presents itself to us as family instability, dependent women and children, violence, crime, and retreatist life styles, stand men and women, black and white, who cannot support themselves and their families" (Liebow, 1970:11). Notice the similarity between Friedman's prognosis of the *ultimate* costs of inflation to society and the ultimate costs of unemployment presented here.[13]

THE ROLE OF GOVERNMENT IN SOCIETY

As discussed above, keynesians generally view the need for government intervention as self-evident. In the words of Heller: "We now take for granted that the government must step in to provide the essential stability at high levels of employment and growth that the market mechanism, left alone, cannot deliver" (Heller, 1967:9). For a variety of reasons monetarists remain unconvinced. This is the third key issue which separates monetarists and keynesians. Okun recognizes clearly the implications of disagreement over the issues discussed both here and in the previous section: "Most of the key policy controversies among economists [and policymakers] reflect different philosophies about the government's role in the society and the economy, and about the relative priority attached to various objectives that we all value to some degree" (Okun, 1970:19, brackets added).

The monetarists tend to espouse the principles of government that in recent times have charaterized the political philosophy associated with the "conservatives." Two broad principles are usually embraced: (1) the scope of government must be limited; and (2) government power must be dispersed (Friedman, 1962:2-3).[14] For Friedman and others the key issue is preserving freedom:

> The free man will ask neither what his country can do for him nor what he can do for his country. He will ask rather "What can I and my compatriots do through government" to help us discharge our individual responsibilities, to achieve our several goals and purposes, and above all, to protect our freedom? And he will accompany this question with another: How can we keep the government we create from becoming a Frankenstein that will destroy the very freedom we establish it to protect? Freedom is a rare and delicate plant. Our minds tell us, and history confirms, that the great threat to our freedom is the concentration of power. Government is necessary to preserve our freedom, it is an instrument through which we can exercise our freedom; yet by concentrating power in political hands, it is also a threat to freedom. Even though the men who wield this power initially be of good will and even though they be not corrupted by the power they exercise, the power will both attract and form men of a different stamp (Friedman, 1962:2).

Not surprisingly, an intimate link between economic and political freedom is perceived by embracers of the conservative view:

> Economic arrangements play a dual role in the promotion of a free society. On the one hand, freedom in economic arrangements is itself a component of freedom broadly understood, so economic freedom is an end in itself. In the second place, economic freedom is also an indispensable means toward the achievement of political freedom.
>
> Viewed as a means to the end of political freedom economic arrangements are important because of their effect on the concentration or dispersion of power. The kind of economic organization that provides economic freedom directly, namely competitive capitalism [i.e., a free enterprise economy], also promotes political freedom because it separates economic power from political power and in this way enables the one to offset the other (Friedman, 1962:8-9, brackets added).[15]

The logical result of these philosophical premises, along with the view that the private economy is basically stable, is that economic intervention by the government is to be carefully circumscribed. Friedman, for example, argues (1962, Chapter II) that the government's role should be limited to making rules, acting as umpire, and dealing where necessary with technical monopoly and neighborhood effects (so-called externalities). This, of course, leaves little room for discretionary stabilization policy.[16]

Such philosophical and economic justifications for the monetarist-conservative position calling for less rather than more government intervention, are reinforced by their acceptance of the notion of long and variable lags discussed earlier and by the perceived instability of the political process. The latter deserves special attention. Friedman argues: "There is still a tendency to regard any existing government intervention as desirable, to attribute all evils to the market, and to evaluate new proposals for government control in their ideal form as they might work if run by able, disinterested men, free from the pressure of special interest groups" (Friedman, 1962:197).

Simply put, monetarists and others argue that recommendations for an activist stabilization policy reflect a basic asymmetry in analytic approach; instabilities and imperfections in the private sector are emphasized and those in the political-administrative system are neglected (Lindbeck, 1976:11). A more *balanced* approach views macroeconomic fluctuations as resulting from "a complicated interaction between market forces and government behavior, i.e., as an interplay between the economic and political systems" (Lindbeck, 1976:1).[17]

Explanations for the instability of government actions are not hard to find. Among the most popular are the so-called political models of the business cycle (Nordhaus, 1975; MacRae, 1977), which are decendents of earlier work by Kalecki (1971), and more recently by Downs (1957) and Bartlett (1973). In general, this research involves an explicit analysis of the interactions between politics and economics.

Instead of being idealistic guardians of the public good that are guided by the desire to maximize social welfare, government and political parties are viewed as vote maximizers, just as producers are profit maximizers and consumers are utility maximizers. In such a world, "Government faces a production function for votes which depends on the programs it initiates and the information it provides to voters" (Bartlett, 1973:132). Since consumers and business are interested in minimizing the costs of government programs and maximizing the net return (i.e., the increases in real income) they individually will experience, there is an obvious incentive to engage in influence production (i.e., lobbying). Such pressure or influence manifests itself by interested parties providing the government with selective information concerning the benefits or costs of various programs.

> By providing selective, subsidized information those agents with a strong enough incentive, and also sufficient means to produce influence, will affect the decisions that the government makes. . . . Once made, the government must then provide consumers with information which is designed to increase their perceived utility from the purchasing program. All decisions made by the vote-maximizing collective body must either be obscured or justified (Bartlett, 1973:64).

With the interested parties usually providing political and financial support in return for favorable action, "enlightened" self-interest on the part of politicians and therefore maximization of their own welfare will, in general, override any idealistic societal concerns. This follows, in part, because influence production is costly and only well-organized special interest groups, who need not be representing society's concerns, have the resources necessary to produce influence.[18]

The discussion of the interaction between the political and economic systems provides a general longer-run framework within which to view the motivation for short-run policies actually pursued by the government. It is these policies (both monetary and fiscal) which often contribute to economic instability.

THE INSTABILITY OF MACRO POLICY

Among the many implications researchers have drawn from their analysis of the relationship between the political and economic systems is the notion that vote-maximizing government behavior contributes to macro policy stimulation and economic expansion as an election approaches and, inevitably, inflation and policy correction after the votes have been tallied. The electorate is presumed to suffer from myopia, and thus fails to give appropriate weight to the latter (Nordhaus, 1975; MacRae, 1977).

Layered on top of such government-induced cyclical instability is what appears to have been a related secular deterioration in the ability of fiscal policy makers to take account of and deal with the longer-run macroeconomic consequences of their shorter-run microeconomic policies. A misconception embedded in many undergraduate macroeconomics texts is that fiscal policy (i.e., policy regarding taxes, transfers, expenditures, and regulation) is *primarily* motivated by macroeconomic considerations. Taking as given the view that elected politicians in general try to maximize votes, it is unreasonable to assume that they will pursue what could be called "trickle-down" policies—i.e., policies designed to achieve "full" employment and "reasonable" price stability *and also* achieve some allocative or distributive objectives. The special interest groups, government agencies, and congressional committees are for the most part interested in specific problems and naturally seek out specific solutions. Roundabout or trickle-down macropolicies seem distinctly inferior on an intuitive level to direct, micro, problem-specific policies. As Okun points out: "The man in the street knows the penicillin designed to cure his sore throat is not injected into his throat; but he does not have similar experience with the flow of economic medicine through the body politic" (Okun,1970:5).

In general most changes in tax, transfer, expenditure, or regulatory policy are directed toward allocative or distributive goals (which may or may not be explicit). Examples abound: price supports for agricultural commodities, barriers to trade, welfare, social security, health insurance, minimum wages, housing subsidies, and so forth. The continuing attempt to "do good" by aiding or regulating specific sectors or groups in the economy, can be viewed as a supply response by the government to the demands of special interest groups and the public. With reference to government regulation of credit, Kane argues: "The very existence of this demand creates a 'political' market for regulation and establishes incentives for politicians and bureaucrats to supply regulation services" (Kane, 1977:56).[19]

The ever-expanding demands on the government's revenue base, along with the political costs associated with raising taxes, contribute to chronic budget deficits which in turn have macro effects (Buchanan and Wagner, 1977).[20] Unfortunately, the longer run macroeconomic implications of these policies have been largely ignored.

Does the senator from the Midwest know or care that raising price supports for agricultural commodities, acreage restrictions, and various import restrictions, which raise the price of food and farm income, pushes up the consumer price index which in turn raises payments tied to the "cost of living"—wages, pensions, food stamp allotments, and so forth? Do the representatives on the House Banking Committee recognize that the attempt to offset the unintended distributional effects of monetary policy on housing may, in fact, contribute to greater economic instability? If, in general the answer is no, then the proposition that fiscal policy is often destabilizing merits more attention. Put more strongly, given the short run, micro orientation of fiscal policy makers and their desire to maximize votes, the possibility of periodic loss of control over economic activity as the longer-run, macro effects of micro policies cumulate would seem quite high.

In theory the Federal Reserve, insulated by its "independence," is supposed to have the luxury of taking the "long view" and thus leaning against the destabilizing short-run exigencies of the President, the Congress, and the government bureaucracies. In practice this does not appear to be the way things have in fact worked out.[21] The Fed's failure or inability to consistently contribute to economic stability would seem to be the product of two factors: political pressures which severely circumscribe their independence; and a preference function characterized by considerable risk aversion.

As is well known, since 1970 the Fed has given some weight to the growth of various monetary aggregates in formulating and implementing policy. Within this strategy (described in detail by Lombra and Torto, 1975), the Fed has also continued to give heavy weight in the short run to stabilizing short-term interest rates. The money supply is an abstract concept that the public, the Congress and the President do not identify with. Interest rates, on the other hand, are highly visible and, when they rise, the Fed is immediately identified as the culprit. Understandably then, whenever monetary growth is, for example, exceeding the Fed's target, there is a tendency to moderate or postpone any slowing in the growth of reserves and the upward movement in interest rates which would result.

In justifying this approach political arguments are usually eschewed. Frontal attacks are not suprisingly avoided whenever possible. Instead, it is generally argued that the money supply data (as well as nonfinancial data) are quite erratic, and thus frequently do not provide a clear, unambiguous indication (or signal) of what direction the economy is moving in.[22] This leads policy makers to delay their response to *apparent* changes in the money supply until more monetary data (and nonfinancial data) are available to *confirm* that such changes are in fact *meaningful*. The resulting myopia, and inevitable passage of time until corrective action is taken, is widely viewed as a force tending to exacerbate, rather than dampen both cyclical swings in the economy and the secular rise in the rate of inflation.

Policy makers generally recognize that a lag exists between a policy action and its impact on economic activity. Yet as Pierce (1974) and others have pointed out, policy makers tend to discount forecasts heavily and instead give considerable weight to the latest data, when and if a policy move is considered. To illustrate, if the incoming data suggest inflation is running high, while the unemployment rate is reasonably close to the "full" employment rate, then regardless of how many economic forecasts are suggesting a recession six to twelve months down the road, the policy maker generally cannot be convinced to pursue stimulative policy now despite their recognition of the lag in policy effects. Implicitly, the tendency is to extrapolate current conditions into the indefinite future.

Although the economic literature on optimal policy under uncertainty provides some support for gradual policy adjustments (Brainard, 1967), and forecasters have been humbled from time to time over the past decade (McNees, 1977), the Fed's extreme risk aversion produces policy paralysis at critical junctures, the latest episode being the last half of 1974.

In its behalf, the Fed usually argues that irresponsible fiscal policy over the long run seriously disrupts economic activity, and makes it virtually impossible for the Fed to achieve even moderate success in attaining various macroeconomic objectives (Burns, 1976). Since monetary policy is so poorly understood by the public at large, and unfortunately, even by many congressmen charged with overseeing monetary policy,[23] the Congress can conveniently argue with equal veracity that it is, in effect, the independent Fed who is irresponsible (Kane, 1975:42). Regrettably, the Fed has often projected a degree of elitism in response—the image being that monetary policy is too complicated for mere mortals to comprehend. The Fed will also frequently argue that telling the public too much about monetary policy could in and of itself be destabilizing.[24] In this regard, Sherman Maisel, a former member of the Fed's Board of Governors, has stated: "The Fed has always resisted being too specific about [its] methods and its goals, clothing its operations in a kind of mystique that left it more freedom to maneuver" (Maisel, 1973:26). While the Fed is reluctant to specify its procedures too explicitly in order to protect its freedom of action, "its attempt to protect itself from both outside critics and internal disappointment . . . weakens its ability to improve its performance" (Maisel, 1973:311).

The confluence of uncertainty and political pressure encourage the Fed to focus on the short run and, like fiscal policy makers, to ignore the longer-run cumulative effects of policy decisions. In addition, ambiguity (or lack of specificity) in planning, executing, or evaluating policy is encouraged: "A bureaucracy tends to write its own laws of inertia in self-defense against public criticism" (Okun, 1970:117). As Will Mason points out the inevitable result is that: "experts cannot even individually decide, much less collectively agree, as to what it is they are talking about" (Mason, 1963:6)[25] The unfortunate consequence is the "disorientation" of policy advice and policy making.[26]

IS AMBIGUITY A VIRTUE?

While many policy makers and policy advisors would probably agree that discussions regarding "ends" and "means" are quite ambiguous, it is perhaps surprising to find that some think this lack of specificity is a necessary ingredient to the policy making process. For example, Rein and White have argued:

> We have a polical process precisely because people have multiple goals that somehow must be reconciled into a single course of government action. This resultant course of action may be called a policy, but that term is misleading if it is regarded as implying one mind, one will, and one theory. Legislation *requires* ambiguity in the statement of goals so that coalitions can be formed in support of it, and each group can believe that the legislation serves its own special purposes (Rein and White, 1977:123, emphasis added).

Even Charles Schultze, the current chairman of the Council of Economic Advisors, agrees:

> The first rule of the *successful* political process is, "Don't force a specification of goals or ends." Debate over objectives should be minimized partly because *ends and means are inseparable.* More important, the necessary agreement on particular policies can often be secured among individuals or groups who hold quite divergent ends (Schultze, 1968:47, emphasis added).

Lest you think this is idle theorizing, reflect on Maisel's view of the monetary policy strategy pursued by the Fed: "A possible side *advantage* of this strategy is that it can be followed even though it might be impossible to get agreement among the members of the FOMC either as to ultimate goals, or the form or level of an intermediate monetary variable, or as to how to define what strategy is being followed." (Maisel, 1969:154, emphasis added).

It would, of course, be naive to suggest that "good" policy procedures require everyone to agree on everything and all discussions to be models of clarity and logic. Nonetheless, economists should ask themselves whether or not a vague, nonspecific approach to policy-making is in effect one of the major problems tending to contribute to poor policy maker performance and poor policy advice. As Mason argues: "Federal Reserve authorities have shifted about among various criteria of monetary management—such as 'sound business conditions,' 'orderly government security market,' 'prevention of inflation,' etc.—until the policy referent at any particular time has become utterly unidentifiable" (Mason, 1963:108).[27] Even an activist like the late Senator Humphrey saw the problem: "it has been a little difficult for the Fed or any other agency of government to target its efforts toward goals when we are so ambiguous ourselves as to what we want" (Humphrey, 1975:107). It seems difficult to disagree with Mason: "policy determination—without guidelines or direction signals—will continue to be anarchical, inconsistent, and, to some extent, self-defeating" (Mason, 1963:105)

WHERE ARE WE HEADED?

It is easy to be pessimistic about the ability of policy makers to improve their performance, and thereby improve the performance of the economy. Even if the various political problems are abstracted from, the quality of policy advice received from economists, since that advice depends on a mixture of political, economic, and social value judgments, leaves much to be desired. The ambiguity already embedded in policy discussions is accentuated by the frequent failure of economists to separate means and ends, political vs. economic issues, macro vs. micro issues, the long vs. short run, and so forth. One suspects there is more agreement on these issues than has yet been revealed to policy makers and the public.

Congress, for its part, has already taken some important first steps in a belated effort to improve the performance of macroeconomic policy. In 1974 the Congressional Budget and Impoundment Control Act was passed. This legislation requires the Congress to select federal budget targets that are consistent with the objectives of national economic policy. Standing budget committees in both the House and Senate and a Congressional Budget Office were established, and explicitly charged with the task of formulating fiscal policies that would contribute to economic stabilization. Now the macro effects of micro policies are carefully scrutinized and the longer-run implications of various policy actions are analyzed. It is, of course, too soon to tell if these new procedures will make fiscal policy less destabilizing (more stabilizing?). However, the machinery is now in place and this itself is an impressive beginning.

The Congress has also acted on the monetary front. The provisions of Current Resolution 133, now codified in the Federal Reserve Reform Act of 1977, require the Fed to report quarterly to Congress on its plans regarding monetary policy over the coming year. The dialogue on monetary policy has to some degree improved understanding of policy and its impacts over the short and long run, and has begun to unravel the mystique surrounding the Fed's operations. While the results to date have been disappointing,[28] the "opening up" of the policy process is itself an important step forward.

To the extent that the above developments represent more form than substance, it may be true that raising the economic literacy of the policy maker and the electorate is the only way to improve policy making. The system of political accountability might also be altered, but this seems much less likely to occur. Unfortunately, increased understanding may only occur after a long, continuing series of policy errors that even ordinary citizens can recognize.[29] Lindbeck has clearly diagnosed the nature of the macro policy problem we face in the interim: "The main problem is not that we are unable to understand analytically what is happening, but rather that the institutional changes and the discretionary policies that are necessary for economic stability seem to be politically difficult to implement" (Lindbeck, 1976:18).

Economic policy depends on the underlying political base of support for the policy makers. Policy will be dominated by the special interests—public and private—as long as the political power structure is dominated by such interests. Ultimately, it may be that economic reform will require political reform. In the meantime the "enlightened" self-interest of the various agents will result in considerable economic instability. If Adam Smith's "invisible hand" was visible, the prognosis might be better.

NOTES

1. The Phillips Curve always made things more complicated pedogically, but this was often finessed by arguing that while absolute price stability was probably unachievable, "reasonable" price stability, say, an annual inflation rate of 2-3 percent, could be traded off for "full" employment. Belief in a stable Phillips Curve has virtually disappeared in recent years.

2. The study of business cycles within graduate econmics programs waned, and one would guess that the seminal work on cycles by Arthur Burns (who became chairman of the Federal Reserve in 1970) and Wesley Mitchell (1946) accumulated dust on library bookshelves.

3. While a reexamination was probably needed, it should be remembered that the effects of the Vietnam war—political and economic—contributed to macro policy paralysis.

4. One must be cognizant of the danger of erecting straw men. Use of the terms monetarist and keynesian to describe schools of thought can be misleading, because there is a considerable diversity of opinion within these camps. To maximize understanding, a first approximation of what constitutes monetarism is taken from Karl Brunner (1970). He argues the important building blocks are: the price-theoretical nature of the transmission mechanism; the stability of the private sector's internal dynamics; the dominance of monetary impulses; and the relative unimportance of allocative effects in the analysis of aggregative forces. A lengthier list of monetarist propositions and characteristics is developed by Thomas Mayer (1978). Keynesians, as discussed below, usually take issue with one or more of these tenets. For a recent example, see the thought provoking papers by James Tobin (1977; 1978).

5. The quotation marks around some of the words in the above passage are used to denote key terms which appear regularly in the literature and often carry implicit or explicit meanings subject to considerable ambiguity.

6. It should be noted that keynesians and monetarists would probably explain the existence of, and implications of, a negatively sloped, short-run Phillips curve quite differently. The latter would appeal to unanticipated inflation and the instability of the apparent trade-off, while the former would lean on the existence of contracts and so forth, which would encourage quantity adjustments rather than price adjustments in the short run.

7. See, for example, the work of Irving Fisher (1922), especially his discussion of transition periods (Chapter 4).

8. This literature is based on the premise that rational economic agents will use all available information in forming their expectations about the future behavior of policy makers, prices, wages, interest rates, exchange rates, and so forth. Such information would include the systematic response of policy makers to economic events and any autocorrelation in the past behavior of the economic system. The implication of this view is that slow, gradual adjustment of prices, wages, and interest rates distributed over time to, say, a permanent increase in the growth rate of the money supply, is irrational. Therefore, rational economic agents do not "adapt" slowly over a long period of time to a policy change. They respond quickly and the steady-state, long-run result is reached in a reltively short period of calendar time. Even in its weak form, which takes account of costs of information and existing contracts, the rational expectations hypothesis implies the economic system adjusts within five years.

9. Of course, the unorganized and/or those on fixed nominal incomes would still suffer.

10. See (Laidler and Parkin, 1975:786-794; Barro and Fischer, 1976:143-146; and Ackley, 1978) for shorter surveys, and (Phelps, 1972) for a more in-depth discussion of the costs of inflation.

11. Friedman goes on to say that the government could reform its ways by intervening less and pursuing less inflationary policies (e.g., the monetary rule). However, he is not sanguine about this latter possibility. Interested readers are also referred to the many congressional appearances by Arthur Burns when he was chairman of the Federal Reserve. He regularly lectured the Congress on the "evils" of inflation.

12. Liebow is an anthropologist. It is notewrothy that Okun, a leading keynesian, selected Liebow's essay as the lead paper in his edited volume (1972) on unemployment.

13. For Tobin there is no question about what "costs" society more: "It takes a heap of Harberger Triangles to fill an Okun gap" (Tobin, 1977:468). The "old" monetarist response (discussed in the previous section) was that there was no exploitable trade-off between inflation and unemployment in the long run, hence assessing relative costs over time was beside the point. The "new" response is that the Phillips Curve is positively sloped—inflation causes unemployment (Friedman, 1977).

14. Interested readers are referred to many of the publications of the American Enterprise Institute for elaboration.

15. Hayek's classic (1944) is highly recommended for further development of these notions.

16. In this connection, George Shultz (then Secretary of the Treasury) has said: "As a subject of considerable technical virtuosity, modern economics often obscures this relationship between personal freedom and economic behavior in a tangle of assumptions and computations. . . . Thus, in my judgment, economists have a particular responsibility to relate policy decisions to the maintenance of freedom, so that, when the combination of special interest groups, bureaucratic pressures and congressional appetites call for still one

more increment of government intervention, we can calculate the costs in these terms" (Schultz, 1974:330).

17. Lindbeck emphasizes that it is equally unbalanced to argue the extreme Chicago view "that we live in a highly stable market system which from time to time is upset by destabilizing actions by governments" (Lindbeck, 1976:11).

18. All of this is compounded by the fact that the government bureaucracies are interested in maximizing their security or survival. Such an objective is most easily achieved by attempting to maximize the size and rate of growth of the agency's budget: "budgetary decisions are really initiated within the bureaucracy and are then consolidated and finally passed on to the government for review and approval. . . . The bureaucracy in its pursuit of security, will provide selective information to the government which reinforces the decisions it has made at a lower level. These decisions will reflect a desire to find as many 'justifiable' and 'essential' expenditures as possible" (Bartlett, 1973:70-71).

19. See also the classic paper by Stigler (1971) and the recent monograph by Kaufman (1977).

20. The government even has a term to describe this process; certain expenditures (perhaps 80-90 percent of the total) are "uncontrollable."

21. See the paper by Weintraub included in this volume.

22. That is, the "signal to noise" ratio is low.

23. Doubters are urged to read the dialogue between the Chairman of the Fed and various members of the House and Senate Banking Committees each time the Fed is asked to testify on monetary policy.

24. The latter is the standard argument used by the Fed to justify not immediately releasing the decisions reached at monthly policy meetings. Speaking of Fed independence and all that it entails, Canterbury has stated: "The basic premise behind this independence is so obvious—or embarrassing—that it is seldom mentioned: the general public is either too ignorant or too immoral to be trusted with money management" (Canterbury, 1975:45). Kane (1975:41) argues that Congress is not equipped to deal with the Fed: "the ponderous multilayed structure of congressional decision-making and the economic naivete of the great preponderance of its members provide the most effective limitations on Congress' ability to dominate a reluctant Fed."

25. As noted earlier, see Friedman (1977:345) for a recent example of such disagreement by the experts.

26. This theme has been long put forth by Will E. Mason (1963). My appreciation of its paramount significance is entirely due to his untiring efforts to disentangle the semantics and substance of the never ending debates over monetary policy.

For completeness it should be added that instability also exists in private sector policy-making (regarding the setting of wages and prices, decisions that focus on the short run, pleas for protection from "unfair competition," and so forth). Such instability can be transmitted to the government sector through the activity of special interest groups, for example, who will argue that it is in the government's interest to take compensatory action. Pursuing this complex relationship lies outside the scope of the present paper. See (Herendeen, 1975, Chapters 2, 13) for a thoughtful discussion of some of the above issues.

27. In a similar vein Kane argues: "To work for the common good, one must know what the 'common good' is. Since this definition is not written daily in the clouds, Fed officials must assess the interpretations offered by interacting political groups interested in their policies." (Kane, 1974:743).

28. See the paper by Weintraub included in this volume.

29. Speaking of regulatory controls, Kane states: "Customarily a network of controls continues to expand unless and until the budgetary cost, social inconvenience, economic

waste, and distributional inequity associated with the system become painfully obvious even to the ordinary citizen" (Kane, 1977:64).

REFERENCES

ACKLEY, G. (1978) "The Costs of Inflation." American Economic Review (May):149-154.

AMERICAN ECONOMICS ASSOCIATION (1972) "Have Fiscal and/or Monetary Policies Failed?" American Economic Review (May):11-30.

BARRO, R. and FISCHER, S. (1976) "Recent Developments in Monetary Theory." Journal of Monetary Economics (April):133-167.

BARTLETT, R. (1973) Economic Foundations of Political Power. New York: Free Press.

BRAINARD, W. (1967) "Uncertainty and the Effectiveness of Policy." American Economic Review (May):411-425.

BRUNNER, K. (1970) "The 'Monetarist Revolution' in Monetary Theory." Weltwirtschaftliches Archiv Band 105, Heft 1, 1-30.

BUCHANAN, J. and WAGNER, R. (1977) Democracy in Deficit. New York: Academic Press.

BURNS, A. (1976) "The Independence of the Federal Reserve System." Challenge (July/August):21-28.

_____ and MITCHELL, W. (1946) Measuring Business Cycles. New York: National Bureau of Economic Research.

CANTERBURY, E. (1975) "The Awkward Independence of the Federal Reserve." Challenger (September/October):44-48.

DAVIDSON, P. (1972) Money and the Real World. New York: Wiley.

DOWNS, A. (1957) An Economic Theory of Democracy. New York: Harper and Row.

FISHER, I. (1912) The Purchasing Power of Money. New York: Macmillan.

FRIEDMAN, M. (1961) "The Lag in Effect of Monetary Policy." Journal of Political Economy (October):447-466.

_____ (1962) Capitalism and Freedom. Chicago: University of Chicago Press.

_____ (1968) "The Role of Monetary Policy." American Economic Review (March):1-17.

_____ (1972) "Have Monetary Policies Failed?" American Economic Review (May):11-18.

_____ (1974, 1976) "Letter on Monetary Policy to Senator Proxmire." Pp. 532-538 in Current Issues in Monetary Theory and Policy, ed. by T. Havrilesky and J. Boorman. Arlington Heights, Ill.: AHM Publishing.

_____ (1977) "Nobel Lecture: Inflation and Unemployment." Journal of Political Economy (June):451-472.

_____ and SCHWARTZ, A. (1963a) "Money and Business Cycles." Review of Economics and Statistics Supplement (February):32-78.

_____ and SCHWARTZ, A. (1963b) A Monetary History of the United States, 1867-1960. National Bureau of Economic Research. Princeton: Princeton University Press.

FRIEDMAN, B. (1977) "The Inefficiency of Short-Run Monetary Targets." Brookings Papers on Economic Activity (2):293-346.

HAYEK, F. (1944) Road to Serfdom. Chicago: University of Chicago Press.

HELLER, W. (1967) New Dimensions in Political Economy. New York: W.W. Norton.

HERENDEEN, J. (1975). The Economics of the Corporate Economy. New York: Dunellen Publishing.

HUMPHREY, H. (1975) "Midyear Review of the Economic Situation and Outlook." Hearings before the Joint Economic Committee, U.S. Congress (July).

KALECKI, M. (1971) Selected Essays on the Dynamics of the Capitalist Economy, 1933-1970. Cambridge, England: Cambridge University Press.

KANE, E. (1974) "The Re-Politicization of the Fed." Journal of Financial and Quantitative Analysis (November):743-752.

_____(1975) "New Congressional Restraints and Federal Reserve Independence." Challenge (November/December):37-44.

_____(1977) "Good Intentions and Unintended Evil—The Case Against Selective Credit Allocation." Journal of Money, Credit, and Banking (February):55-69.

KAUFMAN, H. (1977) Red Tape—Its Origins, Uses, and Abuses. Washington, D.C.: Brookings Institution.

KEYNES, J. (1924) Tract on Monetary Reform. New York: Harcourt Brace.

LAIDLER, D. and PARKIN, J. (1975) "Inflation—A Survey." Economic Journal (December):741-809.

LIEBOW, E. (1970, 1972) "The Human Costs of Unemployment," in The Battle Against Unemployment, ed. by A. Okun. New York: W.W. Norton. Pp. 1-11.

LINDBECK, A. (1976) "Stabilization Policies in Open Economies with Endogenous Politicians." American Economic Review (May):1-19.

LOMBRA, R. and TORTO, R. (1975, 1976) "The Strategy of Monetary Policy." Pp. 422-443 in Current Issues in Monetary Theory and Policy, ed. by T. Havrilesky and J. Boorman. Arlington Heights, Ill.: AHM Publishing.

MAISEL, S. (1969) "Controlling Monetary Aggregates." Pp. 152-174 in Controlling Monetary Aggregates. Federal Reserve Bank of Boston.

_____(1973) Managing the Dollar. New York: W.W. Norton.

MacRAE, C. (1977) "A Political Model of the Business Cycle." Journal of Political Economy (April):239-263.

MASON, W. (1963) Clarification of the Monetary Standard. University Park: Pennsylvania State University Press.

MAYER, T. (1978) The Structure of Monetarism. New York: W.W. Norton.

McNEES, S. (1977) "An Assessment of the Council of Economic Advisor's Forecast of 1977." New England Economic Review, Federal Reserve Bank of Boston (March/April):3-7.

MODIGLIANI, F. (1975) "25 Years after the Rediscovery of Money: What Have We Learned?—Discussion." American Economic Review (May): 179-181.

NORDHAUS, W. (1975) "The Political Business Cycle." Review of Economic Studies (April):169-190.

OKUN, A. (1970) The Political Economy of Prosperity. Washington, D.C.: Brookings Institution.

_____(ed.) (1972) The Battle Against Unemployment. New York: W.W. Norton.

PHELPS, E. (1972) Inflation Policy and Unemployment Theory: The Cost-Benefit Approach to Monetary Planning. New York: W.W. Norton.

PIERCE, J. (1974) "Quantitative Analysis for Decisions at the Federal Reserve." Annals of Economic and Social Measurement (March):11-19.

POOLE, W. (1976) "Rational Expectations and the Macro Model." Brookings Papers on Economic Activity (2):463-505.

REIN, M. and WHITE, S. (1977) "Can Policy Research Help Policy." The Public Interest (Fall):119-136.

SARGENT, T. and WALLACE, N. (1976) "Rational Expectations and the Theory of Economic Policy." Journal of Monetary Economics (April):169-183.

SCHULTZE, C. (1968) The Politics and Economics of Public Spending. Washington, D.C.: Brookings Institution.

SHILLER, R. (1978) "Rational Expectations and the Dynamic Structure of Macroeconomics Models: A Critical Review." Journal of Monetary Economics (January):1-44.

SHULTZ, G. (1974) "Reflections on Political Economy." Journal of Finance (May): 323-330.

STIGLER, G. (1971) "The Theory of Economic Regulation." Bell Journal of Economics and Management Science (2):3-21.

TOBIN, J. (1972) "Inflation and Unemployment." American Economic Review (March): 1-18.

_____(1977) "How Dead is Keynes?" Economic Inquiry (October):459-468.

_____(1978) "Monetary Policies and the Economy: The Transmission Mechanism." Southern Economic Journal (January):421-431.

Chapter 2

THE FEDERAL RESERVE MONEY SUPPLY ROLLER COASTER

ROBERT E. WEINTRAUB
Staff Director, Subcommittee on Domestic Monetary Policy,
Committee on Banking, Finance and Urban Affairs,
U.S. House of Representatives

INTRODUCTION

The U.S. economy has been riding on the "Federal Reserve money supply roller coaster" since 1914. The ride was more violent before World War II than it has been in the years since 1945. But lately the rolls have become increasingly undulant and the ride more unnerving and upsetting. The inflation swells and production and employment dips have been occurring in rapid fire succession, and so close together than one motion begins before the other ends. The result on the economy is called stagflation. This chapter explores why the Federal Reserve has allowed this to happen. I contend that the Federal Reserve can control money growth but that its policy makers have been more concerned about keeping order in money markets, and have let our money supply emerge as a byproduct of their money market strategy. I then present evidence showing that the Federal Reserve's money market strategy is myopic even in the context of interest rate goals.

BRIEF RECAPITULATION OF MONEY SUPPLY CHANGES

Conceptually, as Mason (1976) argued in a brilliant and decisive essay, money must be defined to include all items serving society as exchange media and only such items. I adhere to this tradition. I measure the growth of the U.S. money supply by percentage changes in M1 from one year to the next.

As shown in Table 2.1, from the end of World War II, M1 growth has rolled up and down in both short cycles and long waves. The timing of the rolls has been irregular and their size uneven. The short cycles have been imposed on three distinct long period waves.

Table 2.1: Percent Change in M1 from One Year to the Next

Year	Percent Change	Year	Percent Change	Year	Percent Change
1945	16.3	1954	1.5	1964	4.0
1946	7.3	1955	3.2	1965	4.3
1947	5.0	1956	1.2	1966	4.7
1948	0.5	1957	0.5	1967	4.0
1949	− 1.0	1958	1.2	1968	7.2
1950	2.7	1959	3.8	1969	6.0
1951	4.5	1960	− 0.1	1970	3.9
1952	5.0	1961	2.1	1971	6.7
1953	2.5	1962	2.2	1972	7.1
		1963	2.9	1973	7.5
				1974	5.5
				1975	42.
				1976	5.1
				1977	7.2
Period Mean	4.8		1.9		5.5

The first long period covered the years 1945-1953, from the last year of World War II to the last year of the Korean War. It was dominated by a sharply declining money growth rate from 1945 to 1949. M1 growth plunged from 16.3 percent in 1945 to 7.3 percent in 1946, 5 percent in 1947, 1/2 percent in 1948 and −1 percent in 1949. In 1950, it rose to 2.7 percent and then accelerated to 4.5 percent in 1951, and 5 percent in 1952. In 1953, M1 growth again dropped, falling to 2.5 percent.

The second long period covered the next ten years, 1954-1963. It was marked by three rapid rolls of M1 growth imposed on low average growth. Yearly M1 growth peaked in 1955 and 1959 and bottomed in 1954, 1957 and 1960. During this period, year to year M1 growth averaged only 1.9 percent and never exceeded 4 percent. At the end of the second long period, in 1963, M1 grew 2.9 percent.

The third long period covers the years from 1964. During this period average annual M1 growth nearly tripled. It jumped to 5.5 percent as the Federal Reserve money supply roller coaster angled sharply upward. Both troughs and peaks of the short period rolls in M1 growth tended to rise after 1964. Yearly M1 growth bottomed at 4 percent in 1967, at 3.9 percent in 1970, and 4.2 percent in 1975. It peaked at 4.7 percent in 1966, 7.2 percent in 1968, and 7.5 percent in 1973. Since 1975, M1 growth has again been rising. In 1977, it was 7.2 percent.

MONETARIST ANALYSIS, COUNTERARGUMENT AND TWO MONETARIST QUESTIONS

Monetarists assert that both the short cycles and long period waves of M1 growth delineated above had important effects on our economy's performance during the past thirty-two years. The cycles in M1 growth occurred in phase with cycles in economic activity. We suffered recessions in association with half cycle decelerations of M1 growth in 1949, 1954, 1957, 1960, 1967 (a mini recession), 1970, and 1974-1975. Monetarists argue that the short period downturns in money growth not only exacerbated every decline in economic activity we have experienced since 1947, but also caused some of them.

Monetarists also argue that the long sharp fall in M1 growth, which we experienced since the end of the World War II, shaped our inflation record since 1947. They assert that the declining trend in M1 growth during the immediate post-World War II years broke the inflation that followed termination of wartime price and wage controls in 1946. They argue further that low average money growth kept inflation under control from the end of the Korean war to the mid-1960s. Finally, they observe that inflation returned after 1963 when the trend in money growth turned up. As shown in Table 2.2, the Korean war period aside, since 1947 the current year percentage change in the CPI (consumer price index) has tracked the percentage change in M1 from two years ago reasonably well. The record is mapped in Figure 2.1 for the period since 1956. The substantial gap that occurred in 1974 reflects the sharp rise in import prices that year.

On the other hand, many assert that money supply is an endogenous variable, that the tilts and rolls in M1 growth were caused by concurrent trends and cycles in economic activity, and therefore, the monetarist argument is neither valid nor useful. But lest we get bogged down in "chicken or egg" economics, we must be careful to distinguish what has been from what could have been, and what is from what could be. The first monetarist question is whether the Federal Reserve *can* control M1 growth, not whether it does.

It is conceivable that U.S. post-World War II M1 growth emerged as the unavoidable consequence of trends and cycles in economic activity. In this case, the monetarist argument would have to be rejected. But it also is conceivable that the tilts and rolls in M1 growth, though historically tracking the economy's tilts and rolls, could have been avoided and, in turn, dampened the tilts and smoothed the rolls in economic activity. Thus, we must ask whether the Federal Reserve can closely control M1 growth.

Table 2.2: M1 Growth and Inflation

Year	Percent Change in M1 Lagged 2 Years	Percent Change in CPI	Year	Percent Change in M1 Lagged 2 Years	Percent Change in CPI
1947	16.3	14.5	1965	2.9	1.6
1948	7.3	7.7	1966	4.0	3.0
1949	5.0	− 1.0	1967	4.3	2.8
1950	0.5	1.1	1968	4.7	4.2
1951	− 1.0	7.0	1969	4.0	5.4
1952	2.7	2.3	1970	7.2	5.9
1953	4.5	0.8			
1954	5.0	0.4	1971	6.0	4.3
1955	2.5	− 0.3	1972	3.9	3.3
			1973	6.7	6.2
1956	1.5	1.5	1974	7.1	11.0
1957	3.2	3.4	1975	7.5	9.1
1958	1.2	2.7			
1959	0.5	0.9	1976	5.5	5.7
1960	1.2	1.5	1977	4.2	6.5
1961	3.8	1.1	1978	5.1	
1962	− 0.1	1.2	1979	7.2	
1963	2.1	1.3			
1964	2.2	1.3			

In discussing the first monetarist question, a caveat is in order. Monetarists do not argue that short-run growth in M1, for example, from one week or month to the next, can be closely controlled. Their argument is only that over the longer run, surely from one year to the next, M1 growth can be closely controlled. Accepting that it can be, the next monetarist question is why, as an historical matter, the Federal Reserve Board and Open Market Committee have chosen not to do so. Why, instead, have they chosen to react to economic developments in ways that have tied M1 growth to ongoing trends and cycles in production, employment, and prices? This is the central question of this essay. It is discussed immediately following discussion of the first monetarist question. Can the Federal Reserve control M1 growth reasonably closely over the longer run?

CAN M1 GROWTH BE CONTROLLED?

The specter of our monetary authorities being unable to control M1 growth haunts the literature, statements, and debates about monetary

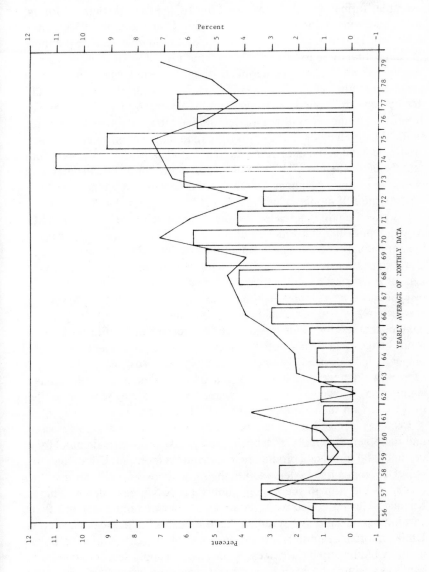

**Figure 2.1: Year to Year Percent Change Bar Chart is C P I
Line is M1 Money Supply Lagged 2 Years**

policy. Federal Reserve chairmen are foremost among those who raise doubts about the Federal Reserve's power to control money growth. For example, former Federal Reserve Board Chairman Arthur F. Burns, while testifying before the Senate Banking Committee in 1975, stated that "I am glad to have the opportunity to say right now that I do not think we have the power to achieve this or that rate of grwoth of the money supply—no matter how you define it—within a period of three months, or even six months" (U.S. Congress, 1975:47). Note he did not say it could not be done from one year to the next. More recently, current Reserve Board Chairman G. William Miller told the House Banking Committee that, "In an environment of briskly expanding economic activity and credit demands, the monetary aggregates also tended to grow more rapidly last year (1977). The public's demand for M1—currency and checking account balances—strengthened considerably, and growth in this measure of money accelerated" (U.S. Congress, 1978).

His assertion that increases in money demand dictate increases in M1 growth is puzzling. It is a misapplication of the theory of the firm. True, by logical deduction from this element of economic theory, it can be said that, given negatively sloped demand with respect to price, profit maximizing firms in a competitive industry will try to increase their rates of production in response to increases in demand. Further, assuming constant returns to scale and no externalities, it can be asserted that demand dictates the industry's long run output. In final equilibrium, there is no change in the firm's minimum average cost or price. Hence, industry output is fully demand determined. Applying this analysis to the money supply, we deduce that if for any reason money demand rises, money supply rises. However, it is totally inappropriate to use the theory of the firm to explain the supply of money. This is why.

If money demand increases, banks try to expand their earning assets and thereby their supply of deposit money, just as a rise in demand for a certain good impels its producers to expand their output. But though the impulses from a rise in demand are the same, here the application of the theory of the firm to the money supply process breaks down. This is because, viewed collectively, commercial banks cannot expand their earning assets unless they either have or can obtain excess reserves. Unlike the goods sector, where producers generally can obtain additional input by bidding up input prices, in the money supply sector commercial banks as a group can obtain incremental excess reserves (their input) only if the Federal Reserve supplies them. Thus, the theory of the firm is not an appropriate point of departure for analyzing the production of money. The money supply process is more appropriately analyzed by focussing on the Federal Reserve's supply of so-called base money, which includes reserves.

At any point in time, the quantity of money, M, no matter how defined, can be expressed as identically equal to the product

$$B \cdot m$$

where B denotes so-called base money, and m is the base money multiplier. The multiplier m, is not observed directly. It is computed by dividing observations of M by concurrent observations of B.

The Federal Reserve produces base money, which consists of coin and currency held by the public, including amounts held in bank vaults, plus member bank deposits in Federal Reserve Banks. The Federal Reserve can supply *base* money at any rate it chooses. It is not constrained by the profit motive. Nor, since elimination in 1965 and 1968 of the gold backing requirement behind Federal Reserve deposits and notes, has it been bounded legally in its ability to supply base money by any statutory provision.

If it desired to accelerate the growth of base money, the Federal Open Market Committee need only instruct the system's account manager to buy U.S. government securities at a faster rate. If it desired to decelerate the growth of B, the manager need only slow additions to the system's securities portfolio. The portfolio can even be reduced if desired. Although other factors affect the supply of base money, the Federal Reserve's open market powers are ample to control it very closely.[1]

In turn, control of base money gives the Federal Reserve reasonably certain and close control over M1 growth, even in the face of unexpected and undesired changes in the base money multiplier, m. The base money multiplier might fall when the Federal Reserve is trying to increase M1 growth. This would happen if the public increased its holdings of currency or time deposits relative to its demand deposits, or if banks increased their holdings of excess reserves. If not offset, decreases in m which occur because of these changes would decrease M1 growth. On the other hand, m might rise because the public decreased its holdings of currency and time deposits relative to its checking deposits, or because banks decreased their excess reserves. Increases in m from these changes would increase M1 growth, if they were not neutralized by Federal Reserve actions.[2]

Before the Federal Reserve can take action to offset undesired changes in m, it must know they have occurred. This is not a trivial problem. Because m is observed by dividing M by B, the Federal Reserve cannot know that m has changed in some undesired and unexpected way until after M is observed not to be growing as targeted (or projected). Moreover, because complete data on nonmember banks' deposits, which in the case of demand deposits comprise about 30 percent of the total, now are available only for the Federal Deposit Insurance Corporation's call dates at the end of each quarter, current information about m, as reflected in M, can be wrong.[3] However, in terms of M1 growth from one year to the next, the information problem does not appear to be very serious. Call data are available quarterly, and sample data are available on a weekly basis. Thus information errors are not likely to be substantial.[4]

USING B TO CONTROL M

The Federal Reserve Board's power to change reserve requirements (within statutory limits) can be used to counteract or reduce the size of any undesired change in m. More importantly, the Open Market Committee can completely offset and even overcompensate for changes in m by ordering a change in its input of base money B. Thus if changes in the preferences of banks for excess reserves, or the public for currency and time deposits, are operating to hold M1 growth below the desired or target rate, the committee can direct the system's account manager to increase the input of base money by whatever amount per week or month it takes to raise M1 growth up to the target rate.

As I have argued elsewhere (Weintraub, 1969; 1970, Chapters 9 and 10), some input of base money would do the job, provided however, that the target growth rate is reasonable and that incremental B is not totally absorbed or "trapped" in excess reserves, time deposits or currency. As indicated by the second proviso, the argument is not airtight. The first or direct effect of incremental purchases of government securities by the Federal Reserve is to bid market interest rates down. In turn, lower market interest rates impel banks to increase their holdings of excess reserves, and the public to hold more savings deposits relative to demand deposits. Because all extra inputs of base money B, might be absorbed in new excess reserves or time deposits, we cannot be certain that there is a rate of growth of B which will cause M1 growth to rise to the desired rate. This possibility makes monetarist claims that the Federal Reserve can increase M1 growth an empirical question. But the facts support the monetarist position. There never has been a time when an incremental input of base money has been fully absorbed in traps of any kind—currency, time deposits, or excess reserves. The historical evidence indicates that M1 growth can be accelerated to whatever rate is desired.

One further aspect of the issue of money supply control remains to be clarified. Can the Federal Reserve prevent runaway M1 growth in the face of rising money demand? The answer is an unqualified "yes." If slowing the input of base money into the money supply process by a certain percent does not produce a desired slowdown in M1 growth, the Open Market Committee need only tell the system's account manager to try slowing the input of B even more. As a matter of logic, it is inconceivable that a policy of slowing base money growth (contracting B if necessary) would not succeed in slowing M1 growth to any desired rate, regardless of the preferences of banks in regard to excess reserves and the nonbank public for currency and time deposits. In the extreme case, B could be reduced to approach zero, though I cannot envision the necessity of doing so. Thus, although we cannot be 100 percent certain that the Federal Reserve's power to control the growth of base money gives it the power to make M1 grow faster, there is no doubt whatever that it can prevent it from accelerating. Specifically, M1 growth can be increased or decreased to the rate commensurate with our economy's potential to increase production and maintained at that rate, if there is a will on the part of the Federal Reserve to achieve this result.

WHY HAS M1 GROWTH BEEN ALLOWED TO ROLL AND TILT AS IT HAS?

Throughout its history the Federal Reserve has been more concerned about money market conditions than about M1 growth. Its commitment to orderly money markets has caused money growth to behave procyclically for protracted periods and then to swing too far in the opposite direction. In interviews which I (Weintraub, 1974) conducted with Federal Reserve bank presidents and members of the Board of Governors a few years ago, I was often told that the Federal Reserve sometimes allowed M1 growth to stray from the optimal long run path while concentrating on "fighting fires" and "keeping order" in money and financial markets.

Coldwell (Dallas):

Well, I think we need to look at what are to be the actions of the Federal Reserve. Is the Federal Reserve to have its eye only on a target eighteen months out, or is it to respond to short-run fire fights and other things which develop in the economy and internationally?

Governor Bucher:

I also think there are times when we have to vary from paths. There are circumstances, such as the Penn-Central situation, and others, which are beyond our control. In these cases, we have to leave what would normally be a desirable path as far as money growth and other conditions are concerned.

Winn (Cleveland):

You know, I would agree that if you set controlling money supply as a single objective, and you were not concerned about the behavior of any of the other variables, you probably could control it much closer than you are able to do at the moment. But I think what happens is, is to your willingness to let some of the other elements fluctuate.

Later, returning to this theme, President Winn indicated that holding a steady monetary growth course could bring substantial money market rate changes. In specific, Winn said:

I'm contrasting this now in terms of the policy you're proposing. And you know, I know what we got in this period with what we did—what would have been the results if this had been different. And you know, what would 15 to 20 percent Federal funds rate mean?

Governor Sheehan:

During the first quarter of 1973 the money supply as defined by M1 grew very modestly, it shrank in January, and grew just a little in February and March. Then, in the second quarter it grew at a rate of between 10 percent and 11 percent. We got it back down again in the third quarter. Well, you sit in the Open Market Committee Meeting debating this, and you are in the middle of the second quarter and money is growing faster than you want it to grow, so you turn to the staff and say, "Staff, if we move against this high growth, what do you think the Federal funds rate is going to do?" The staff says, "If you want to get it down to within our proposed limits, during that three-month period, you have to be willing to accept a Federal funds rate in the range of 20 to 25 percent for eight to ten weeks." And then you say, "Well, is that all right with Friedman, just control the money stock, to hell with the interest rate. Can we ignore the stress this puts on S & L's all over the country and the financial system as a whole? It's just impracticable to completely neglect interest rates.

Hayes (New York):

There were times in '72 when I would have wanted to slow the rate of growth of money somewhat more than the System did. But . . . I suspect that a 4 percent growth in the money supply would have brought some awfully sharp market reactions because of wild interest rate moves.

Governor Brimmer:

Would I just aim for some growth rate in the money stock? The answer is no. There would be a great risk in setting our policy target in terms of the narrowly defined money supply and then sticking to that target.

There are, unhappily, also risks in allowing money growth to emerge as a byproduct of trying to keep order in financial markets. For example, the commitment under the New Economic Plan, from mid-1971 to mid-1973, to keep interest rates from rising required following open market policies which greatly accelerated M1 growth, especially in 1972 and the first half of 1973. The adoption of policies to slow money growth and fight inflation was delayed until after inflation began to accelerate rapidiy. When the reversal came it was exceptionally sharp. M1 growth plummeted from 8.6 percent in the twelve months ending in June 1973 to 3.2 percent in the twelve months ending in February 1975, and during the last eight months of that period, from June 1974 to February 1975, yearly M1 growth was only 1.2 percent. The sharp deceleration of M1 growth was a major contributing factor to the 1974-1975 recession, our worst since the 1930s. Moreover, because it takes about two years, on average, for money growth to impact on prices,[5] inflation continued to accelerate during the early stages of the recession, under the influence of the policies which had greatly accelerated money growth in 1972 and the first half of 1973.

Critics have long understood the harm that is done by the Federal Reserve's focus on money markets. In hearings before the Subcommittee on Domestic Finance of the House Banking Committee in 1964, Harry Johnson put it this way:

> Because it concentrates on money market and banking phenomena, rather than the effects of its policies on the quantity money and economic activity, and because the effect of monetary policy on the economy operates with a substantial lag, the central bank is extremely likely to push its policy too far and too fast before it realizes that the policy has taken effect and begins to consider moderating it; and because the realization of effectiveness comes late, it is likely to reverse its policy too sharply (U.S. Congress, 1964:971).

But though the danger was pointed out by Johnson and others, the Federal Reserve continued to pursue open market policies which generated roller coaster money growth after 1964. Moreover, as noted earlier, average M1 growth, which had been low (1.9 percent per year) from 1954 through 1963, was increased to 5.5 percent per year in the 1964-1977 period.

THE FEDERAL RESERVE'S MYOPIA AND TRADITIONAL STRATEGY

The subordination of moderate and stable money growth to orderly money markets results from the Federal Reserve's myopia, a condition in which things are seen clearly only when nearby. George Mitchell, formerly Vice-Chairman of the Federal Reserve Board, put it this way:

> But I think the easiest effects to perceive, and maybe the effects that we are over-influenced by, are the ones that you see immediately (Quoted by Weintraub, 1974:64).

Immediately, Federal Reserve policy makers fear changes in the federal funds rate, which is the rate of interest on funds borrowed overnight in the intrabank market and the shortest interest rate of all. In the proximate sense, the funds rate is determined by the supply and demand for reserves. The Federal Reserve has considerable power to influence the short-run behavior of the funds rate through the leverage its open market powers give it over the supply of reserves. Under its traditional strategy, the Federal Reserve has used its power to supply or withhold reserves to resist market pressures for the funds rate to change. Money growth has emerged as a byproduct of this strategy. As put by Lombra and Torto:

> An important characteristic of this approach is that it results in the supply of reserves and money being perfectly elastic at the targeted level of the interest rate R and the volume of reserves and money, therefore, being demand determined (Lombra and Torto, 1975:8).

Stable money growth can occur only as a happy accident under this strategy. If the demand for credit increases exogenously, there will be pressure for the federal funds rate to rise. Resisting it can require the Federal Reserve to supply new base money at a rate fast enough and for a period long enough to accelerate M1 growth near term, and inflation long term. Resisting downside pressure can require decelerating the input of base money, or even contracting B, below the rate consistent with the maintenance of M1 growth at the rate commensurate with our potential to increase production. In that event, recession results.

ASSUMPTIONS OF THE STRATEGY

As I (Weintraub, 1974:63-71) pointed out in my report to the House Banking Committee on Federal Reserve policy, the argument for taking these risks in regard to M1 growth rests on three assumptions. First, it assumes that random or exogenous money market pressures can be distinguished from endogenous procyclical pressures. Second, it assumes that all or a major part of an unresisted random exogenous increase in interest rates would last long enough and be large enough to cause disintermediation and other financial disruptions, and depress housing, inventory and other investments. If the change was not large enough or did not endure long enough, it could be ignored.

Third, the argument assumes that a small increase in the money supply induces a large fall in money market rates for a period which is long enough to permit the extraneous pressures to decay, and yet short enough to allow the Federal Reserve to achieve desired long run M1 growth. Figure 2.2 is used to illustrate what this assumption involves. It plots the rate of interest vertically and M1 growth horizontally.

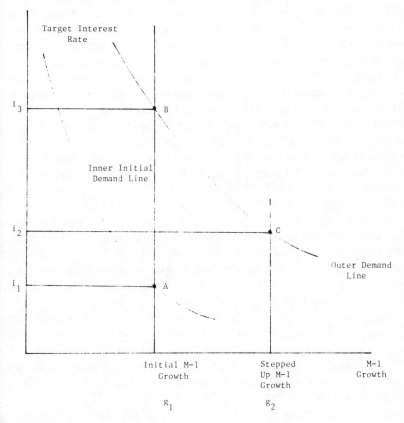

Figure 2.2

Assume that the inner demand line prevails initially and that the system is in equilibrium at the point on that locus where the Federal Reserve wants to be, which is point A. M1 growth equals g_1 and the rate of interest is i_1. Now assume that random extraneous forces pull demand up to the outer line. If M1 growth is not changed, the system is pulled to point B, which implies a much higher interest rate i_3. The Federal Reserve need not accept this solution, however. The system can be anywhere along the new (outer) demand line. Following its traditional strategy, the Federal Reserve would choose instead to go to a point like C; accepting an increased M1 growth but holding down the interest rate rise. C is assumed to be a temporary solution which is accepted on the assumption that the extraneous demand pressures will decay quickly enough so that we can return to point A before the higher money growth, g_2, becomes embedded in spending and investment decisions.

In evaluating this scenario two caveats are in order. First, unless it can be shown that the interest rate elasticity of money demand is extraordinarily low in the appropriate period, resisting random extraneous upward money market pressures can succeed only by generating excessive and probably irreversible M1 growth. In this regard, the Pierce-Thomson (1974) Federal Reserve monthly model indicates that a 100 basis point change in the federal funds rate is associated with a change in the annual growth rate of M1 of only 0.3 percentage point over a one-month period. Over a six-month period the associated change in the annual rate of M1 growth is 1 percentage point. If these results are accurate estimators of the statistical properties of money demand, there is virtually no direct cost of resisting a rise in the funds rate by accelerating money growth. Preventing a 100 basis point increase in the funds rate, requires M1 to increase to a level only $75 million above the level that would otherwise obtain at the end of the first month of any period during which a resistance policy was in force, and only $1.5 billion after six months; using $300 billion as the initial or "otherwise would obtain" money stock. But, although the interest rate elasticity of money demand may be low enough, the resistance strategy can involve substantial indirect costs. This brings us to the second caveat.

Even if an extremely low elasticity prevails, we cannot be sure that leaving the desired long-run M1 growth track would succeed in holding interest rates down in any meaningful sense because feedback from the effects of accelerating money growth on prices, production, and employment reduces the Federal Reserve's power to resist interest rate changes in the short run and overwhelms it in the long run. Because of the feedback, much larger increases in M1 may be required to prevent the federal funds rate from rising than are implied by accepted elasticity estimates, even over periods as short as three to six months.

As taught by Irving Fisher, accelerating money growth has three effects on interest rates. First, the acceleration creates unexpected incremental liquidity which is used at least in part to purchase securities, and thereby causes interest rates to be bid down. Second, the acceleration causes step-ups in the rates at which consumption and investment are rising, and as a corollary the rate of rise of income. In turn, the acceleration of income growth raises money demand and thereby acts to increase interest rates. In principle, the liquidity and income effects cancel one another, leaving interest rates unchanged. However, there is a third effect on interest rates from accelerating money growth. The acceleration in money growth also tends to accelerate both inflation and the expectation of inflation. The rise in expected inflation makes lenders more reluctant to lend and borrowers more willing to borrow. As a result, interest rates ultimately rise above initial levels following acceleration of money growth.

In summary, other things do not remain the same when M1 growth is accelerated. Regardless of the interest elasticity of money demand, any fall in interest rates which results from the liquidity effect of a step-up in M1 growth will be *small and short lived* because of feedback from the income and price effects of the acceleration in money growth. There would appear to be little point to accelerating money growth by way of attempting to hold down interest rates. Furthermore, regardless of the interest rate elasticity of money demand, there also would appear to be little to fear from gradually moderating M1 growth, say 1/2 percent per year every nine months, when it has been excessive. For example, with an elasticity as low as .1, and assuming the federal funds rate is 6 percent, a 2 percent decrease in the annual rate of M1 growth, which was carried out in four equal installments over three years, would produce at worst a short lived 30 basis points rise in the funds rate. With other things the same, each 1/2 percent drop in money growth would produce a 5 percent rise in the funds rate. With a 6 percent funds rate this works out to a 30 basis points rise for 1/2 percent drop. But although each 1/2 percent deceleration will produce its own 5 percent rise in the funds rate, their effects are not cumulative. As discussed next, in six to nine months feedback reverses the direct effect.

EVIDENCE

In this latter regard, Cagan (1972) studied changes in the commercial paper rate that occurred in the wake of step-ups in money growth in the United States in the 1910-1965 period. His results cover both the feed-in or direct effect and the feedback from money supply changes. Extraneous influences are ignored. Thus, Cagan's results shed light on the size and duration of the initial interest rate "bang" which we can expect from changing money growth, and on the longer-run effects as well.

Cagan's findings on the M1/commercial paper rate nexus in the 1953-1965 period are plotted in Figure 2.3. The results were obtained by regressing the commercial paper rate on lagged values of money growth rates, using first differences of quarterly data. He found that following a step-up in M1 growth of 1 percentage point per year, the commercial paper rate at first falls and later rises. However, the initial decline lasts less than one quarter and reaches only 7 basis points. In the third quarter the commercial paper rate is higher than initially and after 2½ years it is 40 basis points higher. Cagan's results tend to confirm Fisher's scenario.

In this regard, it is important to keep in mind that there was virtually no inflation in the 1953-1965 period. This is because, as discussed next, as Fisher's analysis suggests, increases in inflation are translated into increases in interest rates, approximately percent for percent.

Using a reduced form approach, I also found evidence that the initial response of short-term interest rates to changes in M1 growth is negative but trivial and short lived. My regressions show that the initial or direct effect is quickly offset by feedback from the effects of the money supply change on the state and thrust of the real economy, and later is swamped by feedback from the inflation effects of the money supply change.

My approach focuses on the federal funds rate and perceives its determination in the context of economic trends and pressures which affect the willingness of transactors to borrow and lend for a day or so.

Specifically, I assumed the following to be important for understanding the behavior of the funds rate:

(1) The season of the year

(2) The state of the real economy

(3) The thrust of the real economy

(4) The expected rate of inflation

(5) The thrust of monetary policy

Using standard regression techniques, I fitted quarterly averages of the daily effective federal funds rate to proxies for these pressures and trends, as follows:

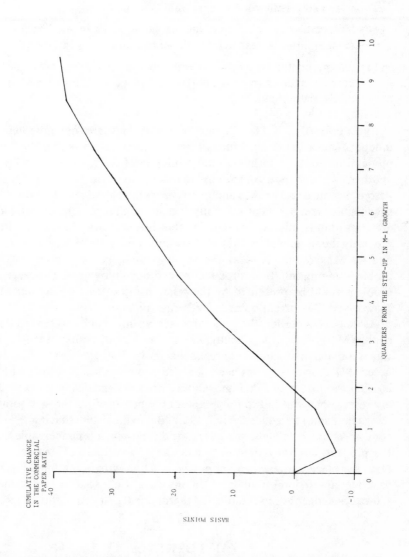

Figure 2.3: Cumulative Change in the Commercial Paper Rate in Response to a Step-Up in M-1 Growth of One Percent Per Year, 1953-1965 Data

(1) The Census Bureau's X-11 program for seasonal adjustment

(2) The average rate of unemployment in the current quarter for the state of the real economy

(3) The percentage change in real GNP from the same quarter a year ago for the thrust of the real economy

(4) The percentage change in the consumer price index from the same quarter a year ago for the expected rate of inflation

(5) The percentage change in M1 measured as an annual rate in the current quarter from a quarter ago to capture the thrust of monetary policy.

Except for the X-11 program, my variables are not completely independent of the federal funds rate. My assumption is that they are predetermined, or determined independently of the funds rate and one another. Though not completely realistic, the assumption is hardly heroic. Because real growth and inflation are measured over four quarter spans and unemployment normally lags other changes, these variables are at most only minimally related to the current quarter funds rate. For precisely the same reason, they also are only minimally related to current quarter M1 growth. Nor, as the results reveal, is multicollinearity a problem among inflation, production, and unemployment. However, a problem could be presented by the relationship of current quarter M1 growth and the current quarter funds rate average.

As discussed earlier, the Federal Reserve's myopia has often led it to change M1 growth procyclically, i.e., in the same direction as the funds rate is moving in an attempt to resist that move. But, again as was earlier noted, M1 growth also has been changed contracyclically, albeit with a lag. To the extent that M1 growth has been systematically procyclical, my regressions will fail to fully capture the power of M1 growth (other things the same) to reduce the funds rate. But to the extent that it has been contracyclical, my results will overstate this power. It is conceivable that the pro and contracyclical elements cancel one another, leaving my results unbiased estimates of the power of M1 growth (other things equal) to reduce the federal funds rate. In any case, I chose to regard money growth as exogenous in running the regressions included in this chapter.

MY HYPOTHESES

I did not know what I would find with respect to the X-11 program. I had definite ideas about the other variables. First, in theory interest rates are low when the economy is in a depressed state. Hence, I expected to find a negative relationship between the funds rate and unemployment, showing the funds rate falling as the unemployment rate (the manifestation of recession) rises.

Second, economists hypothesize that interest rates will rise as the economy moves ahead. Thus, I expected the results to show the federal funds rate rising as the growth of real GNP increases.

Third, followers of Irving Fisher assert that interest rates contain an allowance for inflation equal to the rate of inflation which is expected during the interest period. Following Fisher, I expected to find the federal funds rate rising approximately in proportion to the rate of inflation over the past year. Some may wonder about this; about how the overnight rate could contain an inflation add-on. But of course it should. If inflation has been 5 percent per year, and is expected to continue at that rate indefinitely, then 5 percent is the expected *annual* rate of inflation for the next thirty years, ten years, the next year, next month, and even tomorrow. In fact, if 10 percent inflation is expected all next year and 5 percent thereafter, rates on securities with maturities of a year or less will contain a higher inflation premium than longer rates.

Finally, at least since Keynes, economists have hypothesized that other things the same, especially prices, increases in the money supply act to decrease interest rates. The new money is used first to buy securities which bids rates down. Thus, I expected my results to show the federal funds rate declining as M1 growth increased, holding constant, as the regression procedure does, unemployment and rates of real GNP growth and inflation. Of course, the regression coefficient measuring the relationship between M1 growth and the federal funds rate measures only a fictional impact. We must also consider feedback from the effects of money growth on real GNP growth, unemployment, and inflation in assessing the Federal Reserve's money market strategy.

THE REGRESSIONS

I was not disappointed in any of my prior expectations. I regressed the quarterly average of the federal funds rate on my five independent variables for the periods 1955-1977 and 1970-1977. The results are set forth in Table 2.3. The coefficients on both my measure of tomorrow's expectation of inflation, that is the latest four quarter change in the CPI, and real GNP growth are remarkably stable. For the regressions beginning, respectively, in 1955 and 1970, the coefficients on real GNP growth were .17 and .20; and on inflation .875 and .878. The latter results

Table 2.3: Regressions on Quarterly Averages of the Federal Funds Rate,
1955-1977 and 1970-1977

	1955-1977	1970-1977
Constant term	−.1.441*	4.011
	2.007	1.291
Seasonal Factor	6.028	4.745
	1.963	1.076
Unemployment, average current quarter	− .685	− 1.194
	.073	.077
Real GNP growth from four quarters ago	.173	.201
	.042	.042
Inflation rate (CPI) from four quarters ago	.875	.878
	.044	.058
M1 growth current quarter annual rate	−.022*	− .176
	.039	.059
R^2 adj, for df	.862	.943
Standard Error	.874	.539
No. of observations	92	32

Coefficients are given above standard errors. Nonsignificant coefficients are starred.

are especially gratifying, as they provide strong evidence of Irving Fisher's contention that nominal interest rates, even short rates, contain add-ons roughly equal to the expected (here recent) rate of inflation.

The results also show a strong seasonal in the federal funds rate. Other things the same, recent experience indicates that on the average, there is a 105 basis points swing in the federal funds rate between the first and third quarters; up in the current year and back down between this year's third quarter and next year's first. The seasonal factor reduces the first quarter funds rate average nearly 53 basis points below the full year average, and the second quarter average 10 points. In the second half of the year, the seasonal tends to raise the average 53 basis points above the yearly level in the third quarter, and 10 points in the fourth quarter.

The coefficient on M1 growth changed from an insignificant −.02 in the 1955-1977 run to a significant −.18 in the 1970-1977 regression. This would be disturbing except that the coefficient is significant and close to −.18 in regressions I ran to check this very point using time periods beginning in 1960 and 1965. Let me also add that the extra runs produced no significant changes in the inflation and real growth coefficients.

The coefficients on the unemployment rate and the constant term changed from −.69 to −1.2 and −1.44 to +4.01. These latter changes would appear to reflect, in part, the rise in the real return to capital since the mid-1950s when the real return still had not fully recovered from the Great Depression low. The higher the real return, the higher the constant term will tend to be, and also the larger the reduction in the observed rate, which a given increase in the unemployment rate will cause.

SUMMARY

Directly, increases in M1 growth reduce interest rates. But it is myopic to focus on this result. Indirectly, increases in M1 growth increase interest rates, and as time passes interest rates rise above initial levels.

First, increases in money growth act to increase real GNP growth. Results I reported over a year ago (Weintraub, 1976) indicate that real GNP growth rises in the same year three-quarters of 1 percent for each 1 percent increase in M1 growth. Plugging this into my funds rate regression, I find that this first feedback would cancel the liquidity or direct effect of increasing money growth on the funds rate by itself within a year.

Two further effects of accelerating money growth also feedback to raise interest rates. First, as real GNP growth rises unemployment declines. The improvement in the state of the economy helps to bolster confidence which increases credit demands and pulls up interest rates. Second, still later, inflation accelerates. This factor comes to dominate the behavior of all interest rates, short and long, and all rise above initial levels, roughly percent for percent with inflation.

CONCLUSIONS

Cagan's results are not conclusive. Nor are mine. But together they present a formidable empirical challenge to those who would use monetary policy to resist money market pressures, and who fear the interest rate effects of achieving stable M1 growth "commensurate with the economy's long-run potential to increase production," as called for by the Federal Reserve Act of 1977. The challenge to Federal Reserve policy makers' traditional attention to short-run interest rate considerations, as revealed in my interviews with Reserve bank presidents and Reserve Board governors, is especially important during periods of buoyant credit demands and inflation. In such periods, loan demands are high and credit market pressures work to raise interest rates. If the

Federal Reserve allows its traditional concern for "order" in financial markets to dominate its day to day actions, and tries to resist the pressures that are operating to increase interest rates, it could cause explosively inflationary growth in both base money B, and M1.[6]

As this is being written (May 1978), loan demand is high and there are pressures for interest rates to rise. If fighting money market fires and resisting extraneous pressures on interest rates requires M1 growth to shoot-up well above the desired long run growth path (as happened from mid-1971 to mid-1973, and again in 1977), then, unless it is quickly brought back down, all too soon the result will be still faster inflation, even higher interest rates, and graver money market crises. It would be appalling if this happened for no good reason; if accelerating money growth could not achieve a large and enduring restraining effect on interest rates, but only an effect that is either trivial or ephemeral. Both Cagan's result and mine indicate it may be both.

NOTES

1. Base money equals the algebraic sum of (a) the Federal Reserve's portfolio of government securities and agency issues, (b) its discounts and advances, (c) its holdings of gold and Special Drawing Rights, (d) float, (e) Treasury cash outstanding, and (f) miscellaneous Federal Reserve assets less minor adjustments for (i) deposits other than member bank—Treasury, foreign and others—with Federal Reserve banks, (ii) Treasury cash holdings and (iii) miscellaneous liabilities. At year end 1977, the volume of base money equalled $130.7 billion, item (a) equalled $111.3 billion, or 85 percent of the total volume of base money.

2. For a fuller discussion of the determinants and determination of m, see (Weintraub, 1970, Chapter 8).

3. Up to date information on nonmember banks' deposits could be obtained by requiring the Federal Deposit Insurance Corporation to collect it, and pass aggregated data through to the Federal Reserve on a daily or weekly basis. If necessary, the Federal Reserve could reimburse the FDIC and nonmember banks their costs. Legislation to provide the Federal Reserve data from nonmember bank depository institutions has been introduced and is considered non-controversial.

4. Use of year over year data has the added virtue of eliminating the need of seasonally adjust the data.

5. The relationship is mapped in Figure 2.1 for the post-Korean war period. Also, using regression analysis, I found that yearly changes in the CPI followed yearly changes in M1 with a lag averaging two years in the 1947-1977 period, excluding the Korean war period. (For further details, see Weintraub, 1976.)

6. The danger is exacerbated by the current procedure under which member banks compute their required reserves against deposit liabilities of two weeks ago. Under this procedure, in periods when loan demands are high, banks often make loans, creating deposits in the process, without having the required reserves behind the new deposits. Later, in the next two weeks, they try to find the necessary reserves. In this search, they tend

to bid up the federal funds rate. Given its strategy of resisting changes in the funds rate, the Federal Reserve passively supplies the new required reserves. M1 growth is thus accelerated. Though the Federal Reserve in this case ratifies rather than promotes the acceleration, it is not less responsible for the rise.

REFERENCES

CAGAN, P. (1972) The Channels of Monetary Effects on Interest Rates. New York: Columbia University Press (National Bureau of Economic Research).

LOMBRA, R.E. and TORTO, R.G. (1975) "The Strategy of Monetary Policy." Economic Review, Federal Reserve Bank of Richmond (September-October):3-14.

MASON. W.E. (1977) "The Empirical Definition of Money." Economic Inquiry (December):525-538.

PIERCE, J. and THOMSON, T. (1974) "Short-Term Financial Models at the Federal Reserve Board." Journal of Finance (May):349-357.

U.S. Congress (1964) The Federal Reserve System After Fifty Years, Volume II. Subcommittee on Domestic Finance, Hearings, 88th Congress, 2nd Session.

_____(1975) Monetary Policy Oversight, Hearings on S. Con. Res. 18. Senate Banking Committee, 94th Congress, 1st Session.

_____(1978) Federal Reserve Consultations on the Conduct of Monetary Poicy. House Banking Committee, Hearings, 85th Congress, 2nd Session.

WEINTRAUB, R.E. (1969) "The Time Deposit-Money Supply Controversy." Pp. 300-312 in K. Brunner (ed.) Targets and Indicators of Monetary Policy. San Francisco: Chandler.

_____(1970) Monetary Economics. New York: Ronald Press.

_____(1974) "Report on Federal Reserve Policy and Inflation and High Interest Rates." In U.S. Congress, 1974, Housing Banking Committee, Hearings, 93rd Congress, 2nd Session.

_____(1976) "The Impact of the Federal Reserve System's Monetary Policies on the Nation's Economy." In U.S. Congress, 1976, Subcommittee on Domestic Monetary Policy, 94th Congress, 2nd Session.

Chapter 3

A THEORY OF MONETARY INSTABILITY

THOMAS M. HAVRILESKY
Duke University

INTRODUCTION

Monetary policy makers seem increasingly to profess agreement with theories that contend that stability in the growth rate of the money supply is an important condition for economic stability. They frequently claim to be trying to control money supply growth. Despite these laudable assertions and the encouragement of Congress evinced by its Resolution 133, there is considerable evidence that money supply growth is no more stable than it was in the premonetarist dark ages of the 1950s and 1960s.[1]

Why is money supply growth not better controlled? A compelling case can be made that the preference function of the monetary authority is constrained by numerous arguments which reflect the short-term state of the economy, especially financial markets, and that the weights attached to such constraints vary considerably over relatively short periods of time. It is well known that the monetization of federal deficits (in the interest of temporarily postponing higher rates; see, for example, Poole, 1976 and Weintraub, 1978), and the validation of nominal wage and imported raw materials price increases through "easier money" (in the interest of forestalling any recessionary influences upon the economy) require a relaxation of commitment to specific money supply targets (Havrilesky and Boorman, 1978: Chapter 15). Statistical evidence of decay in the Federal Reserve's anti-inflationary militance during the 1968-1972 period,[2] suggests that accommodating forces such as these contributed to the upward drift toward ever higher rates of growth of the

AUTHORS' NOTE: I am grateful to Martin Bronfenbrenner, Thomas Ferguson, Joseph Spengler, Pieter Korteweg, and Ronald Rogowski for discussions during the formative stages of this work. Members of the Economics Departments of Duke University, the University of North Carolina, and North Carolina State University provided helpful comments during and after seminars in which earlier versions of this theory were discussed. Ray Lombra was a thought-provoking and patient editor, and David Hirschfeld rendered invaluable and untiring research assistance in the data-search and estimation stages of the work. Finally, a word of gratitude to Will E. Mason, who first taught me the subtle linkages between monetary theory and monetary policy.

59

money supply. Similar processes seem to be at work in the the late 1970s. Growing numbers of economists are attracted to the theme that a business cycle is initiated by steady erosion of money supply control, because of monetary accommodation, followed by intermittent, abrupt attempts at downward correction which generate recessions (Havrilesky and Boorman, 1978: Chapter 15). A special variant of this theme is the rather fanciful notion that in the United States a cycle is typically caused by presidential incumbents who, with the connivance of the monetary authority, can woo myopic voters by more or less deliberately exciting the economy in election years and contracting it shortly afterwards (MacRae, 1977:239-263).

In short, the erratic behavior of the money supply seems to be explained by the monetization of government deficits, and the validation of nominal wage and price increases. Nevertheless, the degree of monetary accommodation varies greatly among nations during any interval of time and within the same nation over time: wage and price hikes are not always fully validated and government deficits are not always completely monetized. Unfortunately, there has not existed a theory of monetary accommodation which would facilitate prediction of the extent of validation and monetization. This chapter will develop and test a theory of monetary accommodation. This theory may be used to predict the erratic behavior of the money supply because, as long as the monetary policy maker is even remotely concerned about excessive money supply growth and/or inflation, an accommodating acceleration of money supply growth in one month tends to be followed by a corrective deceleration of money supply growth in later months. Thus, when short-term variations in money supply growth are viewed over longer periods such as a year, a theory of monetary accommodation that explains these short-term variations may provide a scheme for predicting longer-term money supply instability. However, before the theory is presented, a digressive conjecture may be of interest.

THE POLICY ENVIRONMENT AND THE STRUCTURE OF THE ECONOMY

The argument is sometimes presented that stable money supply growth is suboptimal because of frequent and unpredictable changes in the structure of the economy. For example, labor markets are alleged to undergo drastic shifts in behavior (Humphrey, 1973; reprinted in Havrilesky and Boorman, 1976; and Friedman, 1977). In addition, several econometric studies report a shift in the demand for money in the

1970s.[3] If the behavior of economic agents is ever-shifting, steady money supply growth may have highly variable effects on the performance of the economy.

However, many believe that at least some of this alleged instability in the structure of the economy may be linked to the instability of the policy environment itself. Recent work suggests a systematic connection between the stability of the preference function of the policy maker and the structure of the economy. The rational expectations hypothesis[4] indicates that a regime of stable, and hence perfectly predictable, policy actions will generate a stable structure in which policy actions have no effect on output and employment—a neoclassical world; a regime of unstable, and hence imperfectly predictable, policy actions will generate an unstable structure in which policy actions have some, generally unpredictable, effect on output and employment and prices.[5]

Another possible linkage between the preferences of the policy maker and the structure of the economy may occur if an unpredictable policy environment persists over long periods of time. This would tend to foster greater uncertainty in the behavior of economic agents. Pervasive uncertainty about future prices, wages, and interest rates generates inelastic price, wage, and interest rate expectations, and it is these inelastic expectations that are the root cause of the highly wage elastic labor supply, highly interest elastic money demand, and highly interest inelastic expenditures functions that characterize a Keynesian economic structure. Inelastic expectations thus impede the ready adjustment of prices, wages, and interest rates to economic perturbations; that is, they result in "sticky" wages and prices.[6] In the face of excess demand, market decision makers will not know the "correct" market-clearing prices for commodities, services, and productive factors. Consequently, they will adjust the *quantities* they exchange rather than the *prices* at which equilibrium quantities are exchanged. In this fashion, an economy becomes more prone to quantity adjustments of production and employment to exogenous shocks (see, for example, Hines, 1971; reprinted, in part, in Havrilesky and Boorman, 1976).

The same crippling uncertainty may help to explain those volatile "animal spirits," that is, unstable expenditures and money demand relations and other esoterica that permeate the world view of today's unreconstructed Cambridge (England) Keynesians.

Thus, an unpredictable stabilization policy tends to generate quantity adjustments to "surprise" policy actions and, if persistent over longer periods, results in the pervasive uncertainty that "Keynesianizes" the structure of the economy.[7] If uncertainty is the philosopher's stone of Keynes' world view, then an unpredictable policy environment is the crucible in which it is refined. Conversely, a predictable monetary environment tends to generate a neoclassical structure of ready price adjustments to predictable policy actions and, over long periods, of relatively elastic price, wage, and interest expectations which promote wage-price flexibility.

This leads directly to the question: May there not be a systematic pattern in the way the structure of an economy behaves over time? There is considerable evidence that as macroeconomic policy activism creates a Keynesian structure, it is complemented by microeconomic policies that tend to help preserve that structure. As an example, we have already discussed how unpredictable macro policy leads to inelastic (or adaptive) expectations in the labor market. This results in a negatively sloped, perhaps even flat, long-run Phillips curve. Humphrey (1973) has argued that this type of Phillips curve, in turn, can be and has been used to rationalize a wide array of microeconomic government interventions in the market ranging from wage-price guidelines and controls (to "root out" inelastic expectations) to manpower policies (to shift the Phillips curve into a "more favorable" position). As another example, macro policy unpredictability can be shown to lead to high nominal market rates of interest arising from inflationary expectations and higher risk premia. Such high interest rates, in turn, serve to justify a wide variety of microeconomic government interventions in credit markets, ranging from ceilings on deposit rates of interest and regulations on mortgage rates of interest to restrictions on the assets and liabilities of financial intermediaries, and even direct credit allocation by government.

It is, therefore, rather ironic that government interventions in labor and credit markets would tend to perpetuate the kinds of price, wage, and interest stickiness upon which they are often predicated. Moreover, some of this stickiness can be attributed to the uncertainty generated by stabilization policy. *Consequently, there seems to be a remarkable complementarity between the unpredictable macro policy environment that generates a Keynesian structure and the concomitant micro policy actions that follow from that structure and, at the same time, help to perpetuate it.*

CAUSES OF MONETARY ACCOMMODATION

Having argued that complementarity between micro and macro policy actions will help perpetuate an economic structure, let us now reexamine some of the major sources of macro policy instability. Is there a systematic element in the process of monetary accommodation? In addition to the conventional problems of inflation, unemployment, and exchange rate fluctuations, factors such as the funding and refunding of the government debt, union contract negotiations, oligopolistic price increases, and the behavior of natural resource price makers seem to have had sporadic impacts on monetary policy. For example, during the early 1970s Federal Reserve officials claimed that the strength of the oil cartel made traditional antiinflationary militance even more untenable. At other times, during the late 1960s, they said that the size of the federal deficit and a related crisis in the housing sector, or excessive nominal wage increases and the related possibility of recession required an accommodating monetary policy. One is drawn to the conjecture that the apparent erratic element in the behavior of the policy maker, and hence the instability that bedevils the economy, arises from the effect of successive "special" forces. Moreover, it appears that these ostensibly uncommon circumstances have a common thread running through them: they reflect the systematic importance of distributional considerations in monetary policy deliberations. Whenever the monetary authority has altered its preferences, changed its conventional reactions to the state of the economy, and relaxed its commitment to a specific money growth target, it seems to have done so because of pressures on the economy or sectors of the economy arising ultimately from attempts by particular groups to improve their position in the distribution of national or world income.

Consider, for example, either the effect of a union wage settlement wherein nominal wage increases exceed productivity gains, or the effect of an international conflict whereby the price of an "essential" imported raw material rises. Either of these factors will increase costs of production to domestic business firms. Assume that business firms raise their prices in order to shift, in inverse relationship to the price elasticity of demand, part of that cost on to consumers. There then ensues a general upward movement in many nominal wages and prices as individuals endeavor to circumvent the loss in real income. The resulting increase in the general price level (the acceleration in inflation) would, *ceteris paribus*, reduce the real value of financial wealth in the economy and thereby drive interest rates upward and real aggregate demand downward. The decrease in aggregate demand is likely to persist until, depending on the source of the initial increase in costs, nonunion wages fall or both prices and wages in industries most independent of the imported raw material fall. Thus, the attempt by certain groups to gain higher income can, in the short run, reduce real aggregate income in the economy as a whole.

In this situation the monetary authority has a choice: it can wait for a corrective reduction in the price level (or a deceleration in inflation) to its full employment equilibrium level (or rate of change), or alternatively, the monetary authority can validate the new price level (or new rate of inflation) by increasing the money supply (or its rate of growth). The latter will forestall the necessity of an immediate corrective adjustment in real aggregate demand. The prevention of undesired variations in real aggregate demand is one possible justification for monetary validation.

Another justification, one that most concerns us, relates to the effect of monetary validation in temporarily concealing the redistribution of income that is taking place. By increasing the money supply (or its rate of growth) the monetary authority may prevent an *absolute* decline in any nominal wages or prices and thereby temporarily, and partially, mask the decrease of certain *relative* wages and prices.[8] We conclude that while the accommodating alternative is fruitless in the long run, because it cannot prevent the loss in real income that must occur in certain (nonunion or nonimported materials) sectors, it has two advantages in the short run: it ameliorates swings in real aggregate demand and it conceals the redistribution of income.

In the case of a growing bond-financed government deficit, the monetary authority has a similar choice.[9] It could allow interest rates to rise, consistent with a new equilibrium or, in order to ease the squeeze on credit and "cover up" the redistribution of resources that is taking place, it could try to temporarily sustain lower interest rates by monetizing the deficit with acceleration of the rate of money supply growth in the short run at the cost of further inflation and higher interest rates in the longer period.[10]

In each instance, the monetary authority can temporarily conceal redistribution with an accommodating policy. If persistent, an accommodating policy of ready validation of nominal wage-price increases and easy monetization of deficits results in an acceleration of inflation. Expected acceleration of inflation often causes a tightening of monetary policy, and these episodic anti-inflationary binges, if persistent, tend to bring on recessions.[11] Thus, much of the cyclical variation in the economy may simply be a side effect of the process of monetary accommodation. Moreover, because an accommodative acceleration of money supply growth in one month or a number of successive months tends to be followed by corrective decelerations in later months, where absolute values of monthly variations in money supply growth are averaged over longer periods of time such as a year, a theory of monetary accommodation may provide a scheme for predicting money supply instability.

Arthur Burns succinctly identifies the sources of monetary accommodation:

Every time our Government acts to enlarge the flow of benefits to one group or another, the assumption is made that financing will be available. A similar tacit assumption is embodied in every pricing decision, wage bargain, or escalator agreement that is made by private parties or by government . . . such actions in combination may be wholly incompatible with moderate rates of monetary expansion [Burns, 1977:778].

In short, it seems that under certain circumstances the government will promise or allow income redistribution on behalf of some groups without even a warning to others that they will have to accept less. The process may come to resemble an *Alice in Wonderland* caucus race in which "everyone has won, and all shall have prizes."

Monetary officials often assert that the distributional considerations that hamper their proper stabilization activity stem from the failure of elected officials, union leaders, and businessmen to resolve their distributional conflicts effectively and realistically. On the other hand, individuals and organizations learn from experience the probability that the central bank will try to protect the economy from any immediate adverse impact of their actions on production, interest rates and employment, and mask the redistribution that they are engineering. Given such an assessment, economic agents are accordingly willing to bet on a probable amount of monetary accommodation in their decisions. They obviously believe it highly unlikely that the monetary authority could absolutely refuse to monetize any part of a major deficit, or validate any portion of a sizeable and significant wage-price hike without strong congressional or presidential support. In addition, private and public decision makers apparently perceive that the monetary authority, as a bureaucracy, can be expected to be notably eclectic in its reflexive willingness to appear to "fine tune" the economy in response to shocks, including those arising from distributive problems. The monetary authority seems to have arrived at the conclusion that temporary monetary ease can mollify distributional conflict.[12]

Is the public really so shortsighted? Paul Samuelson's candor in a recent interview regarding the role of the economic policy advisor is most telling:

The American public always wants promises in its platforms. In order to sell you have to oversell a little bit. Supply and demand works beautifully here. There's a demand for conning and a supply of conners (Samuelson, 1977:31).

In such an ignoble policy environment, it would be fanciful to suppose that elected officials, union leaders, and businessmen will regularly reach "noninflationary" decisions. Even apart from the likelihood of monetary accommodation, their bargaining is often the focal point of ideological and social antagonisms that make "fair" and "realistic" resolution difficult. In addition, the monetary authority can often serve as a convenient scapegoat for the consequences of their failures.

Nonetheless, a policy of easy monetary validation of wage and price increases, and facile monetization of deficits is not particularly wholesome. To drag the monetary authority further into the distributional morass ultimately widens the impact of the distributional conflict, creates cyclical swings in the economy, damages the market system, and tarnishes the legitimacy of the central bank as an institution. In the interest of economic stability and perhaps its own institutional integrity, the Federal Reserve should reduce the degree to which it hedges the risks of parties to distributional conflict, even though it cannot totally avoid being drawn into the problem. This can perhaps be accomplished if the process of monetary accommodation is better understood.

Progress in the theory of economic policy requires an analysis of the circumstances whereby redistributive pressures generate monetary accommodation. A major lacuna in *all* theories of inflation—cost push, sociological, or demand pull—is that they fail to explain the process of monetary accommodation. Why does the monetary authority attempt to conceal a redistribution by accommodating at some times and not at others? Cost push proponents argue that monetary accommodation, in an attempt to soften or defuse social tensions, is a *symptom* of inflation rather than a *cause*. They seem to contend that the monetary authority is *obliged* to accommodate for fear of sociopolitical consequences.[13] Yet monetary accommodation appears most often to be a matter of degree. There are historical instances of fairly massive redistribution that generated very little monetary instability; conversely, there are examples of timid and tentative attempts at redistribution that ignited ruinous monetary chaos. Theories of inflation are in an unsatisfactory state, abounding with "special cases" of unexplained episodic aggressive wage behavior, "supply shocks," variations in central bank "independence," and so on. Thus, a theory of monetary accommodation will erect a bridge between cost push and monetary theories of inflation. It will also provide a missing element—a theory of the seemingly exogenous and erratic (monetary) perturbation—in the theory of the business cycle.[14]

THE DISTRIBUTION OF INCOME

To begin the theory, consider the overall distribution of income as having two dimensions, functional and collective. The functional distribution reflects the earnings outcome of market processes. In the functional distribution the traditional focus is on the breakdown of aggregate income (national income) into the board factor earnings categories: wage and salaries, profits, rent, and interest. Given the distribution of earnings, a second dimension of the distribution of income relates to the distribution effected by government through expenditures on public goods and services, that is goods and services that are collectively consumed.

Any distribution of income will tend to elicit opposition from groups that are unhappy with it. For example, a functional distribution that favors property income, *ceteris paribus*, evokes the displeasure of groups which depend more heavily on labor income. Depending on the relative size distribution of labor and property income, it may also disturb groups who favor a less unequal personal distribution of income as a matter of principle.

As another example, depending on the size distributions of collective consumption and private consumption, a low proportion of collective consumption to private consumption will upset groups with relatively little private consumption and groups that, as a matter of principle, favor either more collective consumption or a less unequal distribution of total consumption.

Groups that are unhappy with an observed distribution will "signal" their disaffection in order to bring about a correction. The type of signalling should depend upon the particular distribution involved. When an unsatisfactory level of collective consumption relative to private consumption is perceived, electoral signalling will be used, since this allocation is primarily the responsibility of elected officials. While new methods of signalling are continually evolving, information (protest) tends to be transmitted through formal channels such as surveys, polls, petitions, election results, and conceivably through various types of informal channels, such as letters, telegrams, telephone calls, "inside connections," demonstrations, marches, and riots. It is reasonable to propose that, to the extent that government is responsive over a fairly short period of time, the end result of this electoral signalling will be a tendency toward what I call *political instability*, marked for example by increased turnover of elected and appointed officials. Political instability is thus viewed as a concomitant of electoral signalling.

Where the functional distribution of income is involved, signalling is likely, but not exclusively, to occur in nonelectoral channels. These channels of signalling may very well include market substitution, but to the extent that the demand for the factor is inelastic in the short run, nonmarket signalling will be used. In any case, there should be evidence of resistance to the group whose share of national income is higher, relative to other groups. Resistance may, for example, occur in direct bargaining sessions, as in the case of union wage demands, or it may occur through organized boycotts, as in the case of input or product price increases that are thought to be excessive. The end result of such nonelectoral signalling will be a tendency toward varying degrees of what I shall call *civil unruliness*, marked by increased strikes, boycotts, protests, and so on. An increase in strike, boycott and protest activity could therefore be either a response to increased equality (resistance from propertied classes), or a reaction to increased inequality (resistance from lower income groups).

There may, of course, be some electoral signalling, and hence political instability, associated with the functional distribution of income as citizens appeal to elected officials to resist the demands of groups making claims on the national income that are perceived to be excessive. For example, elected officials come under considerable pressure from consumers to oppose the periodic demands of farmers for higher price supports. Similarly, there may be some nonelectoral signalling, and hence civil unruliness, associated with the allocation between collective and private consumption. (These conjectures are tested below.)

THE DISCORDANCE-INEQUALITY TRADEOFF

Political instability and civil unruliness will be labeled forms of *discordance*. The preceding discussion suggests a hypothetical relationship between the level of either type of discordance and the related measure of inequality in the distribution of income. In Figure 3.1 inequality in the distribution of income is dimensioned between zero and one on the horizontal axis, with unity representing complete inequality and zero representing complete equality. (The measurement of inequality will be specified below.) The related level of discordance is measured on the vertical axis.

It is reasonable to assume that a discordance-minimizing distribution of income exists at some positive level of discordance, and that a perceived change in the distribution away from this minimum toward either of the extremes of equality or inequality will generate increased discordance. The "flatter" the function the less the incremental discordance cost of any redistribution.

Although there may well be other, nondistributive, causes of discordance, such as war and ethnic strife, we consider here only the discordance cost of inequality. Society is viewed as being constrained to be at some point on the function at all times. Thus, the relation can be called the discordance-inequality constraint.

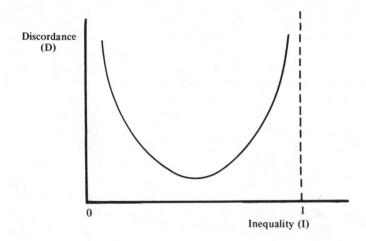

Figure 3.1: The Discordance-Inequality Constraint

Historically, we would expect to observe a discordance-inequality constraint with a higher discordance minimum in real world situations where one group has gained political power and is able to press for a redistribution in its behalf, and government is unable to withstand opposition from that group or is allied with it. In addition, we would expect to observe a more V-shaped constraint where government is too weak to finance benefits for one group by overtly allowing the income of other groups to be reduced. Such conditions may occur jointly. For example, circumstances such as these were present in many Central European nations following World War I. Relatively new democratic regimes give representation to working class parties, but could not afford to antagonize upper and middle income groups by overtly redistributing income away from them. In post-World War II Latin America, many regimes came to power on the basis of urban and rural lower class support, and yet could not overtly take resources away from upper income groups.

In contrast, a clamor for redistribution seems to arouse relatively little discordance (the discordance minimum is lower) where government can stand up to opposition from groups demanding a redistribution whether or not it has their support. Some of the more corporatist modern governments in Western Europe presently display this capability. In addition, one would expect to observe a more U-shaped constraint, where government can finance a redistribution by forthright transferring resources from other groups or allowing them to be transferred without worrying about the opposition giving rise to considerable discordance. The latter circumstance seems to have been present during the early years of the New Deal. At that time a substantial amount of redistribution occurred, but there appears to have been palpably little discordance in the form of political instability or civil unruliness.

Corporatism seems to be consistent with the sort of "solution" many individuals have in mind when they propose a "restructuring" of the government (and much of society) in order to reduce discordance and its side effects.[15] Corporatist societies feature elements of collusion in the symbiotic relationship between the state and various privileged interest groups; these interest groups tend to feature coercive membership and yet tend to be rather independent of member preferences. In contrast to a corporatist society is a pluralist society featuring more autonomous, overlapping, and voluntaristic interest groups that tend to be more sensitive to member opinion. In corporatist societies governments seem to have more success in getting interest groups to control or suppress signalling; discordance is less likely to erupt under these circumstances. This suggests a concomitant reduction in both the level and slope of the discordance-inequality constraint.

One would expect the discordance-inequality constraint to be fairly stable over short periods of time but to change rather slowly over longer intervals, reflecting learning and acclimatization to new norms and ideals of income distribution. For instance, increased signalling on the part of lower income groups would raise the discordance cost of *more* inequality, and increased signalling on the part of upper income groups would raise the discordance cost of *less* inequality, as in Figures 3.2 and 3.3.

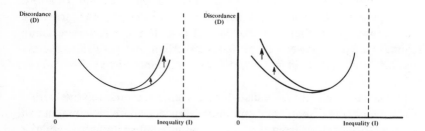

Figure 3.2: A Rise in the Discordance Cost of More Inequality

Figure 3.3: A Rise in the Discordance Cost of Less Inequality

An increase in signalling may reflect a reduction of corporatism in society. For example, as one reflection of a decline in corporatism in the United States, during the past thirty-five years the essential ruling government coalition of Southerners, labor, minorities, and urban political machines slowly but inexorably deteriorated and was not replaced by a new one. Instead, single interest constituencies increasingly fragment the political scene. One consequence of a decline in corporatism is that government becomes increasingly unable to reduce equality in the distribution of income without attracting considerably more flak from middle and upper income groups. Another consequence is that, regardless of attempts at redistribution, the overall level of signalling increased. In terms of the present model, the secular rise in signalling would slowly increase both the level and slope of the discordance-inequality constraint.

Assuming a purely egalitarian government, inequality and discordance will both be "bads." With decreasing marginal utilities of less inequality and less discordance, "social" indifference curves are downward sloping and concave in D,I space; bliss is obtained at the zero intercept, (0,0). This is shown in Figure 3.4.

For a purely inegalitarian government, equality and discordance are bads so that the indifference curves are upward sloping and convex; bliss is at (0,1) on the horizontal axis. This is shown in Figure 3.5.

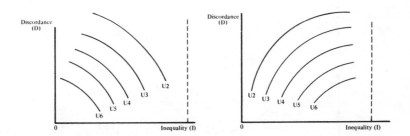

Figure 3.4: Indifference Curves of a Purely Egalitarian Government

Figure 3.5: Indifference Curves of a Purely Inegalitarian Government

It can be seen that for egalitarian governments under the above constraint, maximization of utility is possible only along the downward sloping portion of the constraint, the upward sloping portion being "inefficient." For inegalitarian governments, maximization of utility is possible only along the upward sloping portion of the constraint, the downward sloping portion being "inefficient." This suggests that, for a given constraint and shifting utility function, the slope of the observed reduced-form relationship between discordance and inequality will be negative for egalitarian regimes and positive for inegalitarian regimes. This is shown in Figures 3.6 and 3.7.

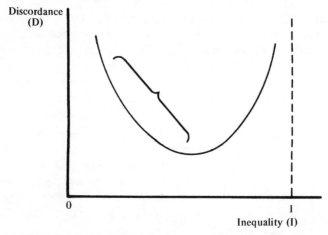

Figure 3.6: Efficient Locus of a Purely Egalitarian Government

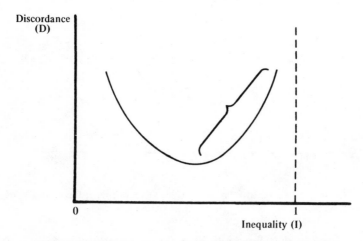

Figure 3.7: Efficient Locus of a Purely Inegalitarian Government

For given preferences and a changing constraint, the observed reduced-form trade-off between discordance and inequality cannot be so easily predicted. It might have a negative or a positive slope. For example, for egalitarian regimes a fall in the discordance cost of inequality could result in the choice of less discordance or more discordance by government depending on how "discordance averse" government is. This is shown in Figures 3.8 and 3.9.

As discussed above, we shall assume that the discordance-inequality constraint (broadly defined to include the strength of fundamental coalitions, the thrall of group loyalties and allegiances in society and the extent of their, often collusive, reinforcement by the state) shifts only

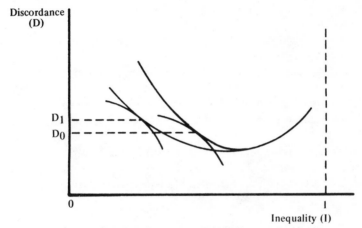

Figure 3.8: Increase in Discordance

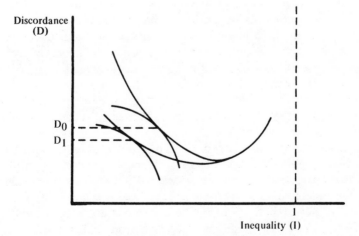

Figure 3.9: Decrease in Discordance

gradually over long periods of time. Over short intervals of a few years it is expected to be fairly stable. In contrast, the preferences of government can reasonably be expected to shift fairly frequently over short periods, modern governments being notoriously sensitive to domestic and international public opinion. In addition, the preferences of government can be expected to vary independently of the discordance-inequality constraint, the latter reflecting the effect of forces, such as the degree of corporatism, that are fairly slow to change.

Under the assumption that a government is egalitarian, any change in its preferences in favor of less inequality, where the discordance-inequality constraint is assumed given, will give rise to an increase in discordance. The steeper the slope of the constraint, the more sensitive is the regime to protests from the political right, and the greater the increase in discordance for any attempted reduction in inequality.

In short, under the reasonable assumptions that there exists a stable U-shaped relationship between the distribution of income and discordance, that an egalitarian government exists (one possessing a concave utility function in discordance-inequality space), and that this utility function shifts over time, there should exist a monotonic, negatively sloped tradeoff between discordance and inequality, that is, any reduction in inequality will be associated with an increase in discordance.

MONETARY ACCOMMODATION AND MONETARY INSTABILITY

Earlier we pointed out that monetary accommodation seems to be associated with attempts by groups, working through the market or through government, to improve their positions in the distribution of income and that the temporary acceleration of money supply growth seems to be used to conceal the distributive and aggregate employment and production effects of such attempts. Now we can place these observations in better perspective. In fact, the discordance-inequality tradeoff suggests a systematic relationship between distributive changes and monetary accommodation.

On the assumption that discordance is bad for the monetary authority, and the assumption that the effects of changes in the distribution of income can be, at least temporarily, concealed, it follows that *increases* in discordance based on redistribution which causes *less* inequality will be, temporarily, forestalled by an *increase* in monetary accommodation. Conversely, *decreases* in discordance based on redistribution which causes *more* inequality will generate a *decrease* in monetary accommodation.

At this point, it would be preferable to test directly the theory of monetary accommodation. Unfortunately, useful income distribution and discordance data are available only on a yearly basis, while the process of monetary accommodation seems to be a much shorter-lived phenomenon. Empirical testing is therefore only possible if the theory of monetary accommodation can be transformed into a theory of monetary instability.

Monetary instability is customarily regarded as the variation of the money supply about its long-term growth path. In order to use the theory of monetary accommodation to generate predictions about monetary instability, it is necessary to make an assumption concerning how the monetary authority responds in subsequent months to current discordance-induced accelerations and decelerations in money supply growth. We shall posit that the monetary authority is so disturbed by accelerations in money supply growth that discordance-induced accelerations in money supply growth tend to be followed by corrective decelerations in subsequent months. However, we shall further postulate that the monetary authority is *not* similarly concerned about decelerations in money supply growth. Discordance-induced decelerations in money supply growth shall be assumed not to be followed by corrective accelerations in subsequent months.

This lack of symmetry may at first appear rather queer. However, perhaps in sympathy with the swing in public opinion that occurred during the latter 1960s and 1970s in the United States, the monetary policy maker came to view the long-term trend in money supply growth as being excessive. In such circumstances it is reasonable to assume that the monetary authority will attempt to correct an accommodative acceleration, but will view deceleration in money supply growth as a respite from the usual climate of pressures for accommodation. The policy makers will seize these rare opportunities to try to return to more reasonable rates of money supply growth.

Monetary instability is measured as a yearly average of absolute values of monthly deviations of money supply growth about its trend. The assumed assymmetry in the monetary authority's response to discordance-induced acceleration and deceleration in money supply growth imparts a positive relationship between increases in discordance (less inequality) and monetary instability measured in this manner.[16] Our hypothesis is that *the greater the incremental discordance cost of a change in the distribution of income (a reduction in equality), the greater will be observed monetary instability over a period of time.*

The model is

$$D_{1t} = f(\underset{-}{I_{1t}}) \tag{1}$$

$$D_{2t} = g(\underset{-}{I_{2t}}) \tag{2}$$

$$M_t = h(\underset{+}{\triangle D_{1,t-j}}, \underset{+}{\triangle D_{2,t-j}}) \tag{3}$$

where D_1 = a political instability measure of distribution-induced discordance,

D_2 = a civil unruliness measure of distribution-induced discordance,

I_1 = private consumption as a percentage of total (collective plus private) consumption,

I_2 = property income as a percentage of national income,

M = monetary instability measured as the yearly average of absolute values of monthly deviations of money supply growth about its trend.

The algebraic signs beneath the variables show the expected signs of the partial derivatives. The $t-j$ subscripts denote an (unspecified) lead or lag relation).

ESTIMATION OF THE DISCORDANCE-INEQUALITY TRADEOFF

As a test of this theory, the discordance-inequality tradeoff and the monetary instability relation are estimated using yearly data for the United States for the 1960-1975 period. Two variants of the discordance-inequality tradeoff are estimated, one using a measure of political instability as the dependent (discordance) variable with a measure of collective consumption relative to private consumption as the explanatory (inequality) variable, another using a measure of civil unruliness as a dependent (discordance) variable with a measure of the functional distribution of income as the explanatory (inequality) variable.

As a measure of inequaltiy in the functional distribution, yearly property income (profits, rent, interest, and proprietary income) as a percentage of national income is used; as a measure of inequality in the breakdown between private and collective consumption, one minus "social expenditures" as a percentage of GNP is used. ("Social expenditures" being defined to include health, education, welfare, transfers, pensions, culture, and the like—excluding housing expenditures.)

An increase in property income as a percentage of national income is interpreted as an increase in inequality. While this is quite a crude measure, it is not an unreasonable gauge of inequality since property income is generally believed to have a more skewed personal distribution than labor income. An increase in the quantity one minus social expenditures as a percentage of GNP is also interpreted as an increase in inequality because private consumption is generally believed to have a more skewed distribution by size than collective, in this case "social," consumption.[17]

As a measure of political instability, the yearly turnover in congressional seats is used.[18] For nonelection years, values are interpolated. This crude measure overlooks turnovers resulting from the age composition of Congress and the size of congressional pensions. In addition, it places no additional weight on the shift of seats between political parties. Moreover, it ignores executive office instability, reflected, for example, in popularity polls as well as in turnover in executive appointments and precipitous discontinuities, such as attempted assassinations and other crises.[19]

As a measure of civil unruliness, man days lost from strikes per 1,000 workers per year is used. This measure captures the size, frequency and duration of one of the most continuously available measures of civil unruliness. Nevertheless, it does not directly reflect other types of civil unruliness such as sit-ins, protests, demonstrations, and riots.[20]

Yearly data for all four measures were gathered for the 1960-1975 period in the United States. The ordinary least squares results are reported in Table 3.1.

Given the rough and ready nature of our data, the results are impressive. The R^2's are surprisingly high, considering the ex post nature of the data (*expected* distributions and *threatened* distributions probably give rise to more discordance than can be measured directly), and considering the likelihood of omitted nondistributional variables having an influence on discordance. Indeed the low Durbin-Watson statistics in equations 2A, 2B, and 2C suggest the possible presence of some omitted systematic influence on the man-days-lost-from-strikes variable and prohibit interpretation of the t statistics in these equations. For equations 1A and 1B or 1C there are only six or five degrees of freedom respectively (because nonelection year values of the dependent variable were interpolated). Nevertheless, the negative estimates for the slope coefficients in equations 1A, 1B, and 1C are statistically significant at the .05 level, and do not falsify the hypothesis of a negative tradeoff between discordance and inequality. In addition, the negative estimates for the slope coefficients in equations 2A, 2B, and 2C further do not falsify the discordance-inequality tradeoff hypothesis.[21]

Table 3.1: The Discordance-Inequality "Tradeoff" YEARLY DATA, 1960-1975

EQUATION	DEPENDENT VARIABLE	CONSTANT	EXPLANATORY VARIABLES				R^2	DW
			(One Minus "Social" Expenditures) / GNP (I_{1t})	(Property Income / National Income) (I_{2t})	Mean Years of Formal Education	Lagged Monetary Instability		
(1A)	Turnover of Congressional Seats $(D_{1,t})$	1.872 (9.594)	-1.762 (-8.403)				.83	1.38
(2A)	Man Days Lost Per 1000 Workers From Strikes $(D_{2,t})$	1.834 (3.959)		-5.248 (-3.082)			.42	.95
(1B)	Turnover of Congressional Seats $(D_{1,t})$	1.441 (4.147)	-1.479 (-5.323)		0.0142 (1.472)		.86	1.58
(2B)	Man Days Lost Per 1000 Workers From Strikes $(D_{2,t})$	.2422 (.1711)		-3.780 (-1.808)	0.1009 (1.177)		.48	1.13
(1C)	Turnover of Congressional Seats $(D_{1,t})$	1.787 (9.632)	-1.674 (-8.367)			0.2531 (1.011)	.85	1.94
(2C)	Man Days Lost Per 1000 Workers From Strikes $(D_{2,t})$	1.927 (4.041)		-5.315 (-3.079)		-3.600 (-1.353)	.49	.91

t Statistics are in parentheses

Two sets of regressions were estimated using variables that did not relate to the distribution of income. As a test of the effect of the overall economic aspirations of the population on discordance, mean years of formal education were included as an additional variable in equations 1B and 2B. The hypothesis was that as years of education increase there will be considerably less complacency regarding distributive outcomes, and discordance will increase (Hibbs, 1973). The sign of the estimated coefficient was positive as expected. However, neither coefficient was statistically significant at any high level of significance.

Another interesting conjecture is that an increase in monetary instability makes the performance of the macroeconomy worse. (As discussed earlier, accelerations and decelerations of money supply growth rates are shocks to the economy and, according to the rational expectations hypothesis, as monetary "surprises" increase so too does the likelihood of quantity adjustments to these and other shocks.) Poor macroeconomic performance can reasonably be expected to increase discordance. To test this, lagged values of the monetary instability variables were introduced as explanatory variables. The results are reported in equations 1C and 2C of Table 3.1. Again the hypothesis is that monetary instability generates poor macroeconomic performance, and thereby aggravates (has a positive effect on) discordance in the economy. For the political instability-dependent equation, 1C, the sign on the monetary instability coefficient is positive as expected but the estimate is not statistically significant. For equation 2C, where man-days lost-from-strikes is the dependent variable, the estimate bears a negative sign. The latter result may be explained by the often observed fact that, while other measures of discordance may increase, during periods of poor macroeconomic performance strike action falls sharply.[22]

As a test of the effect of functional distribution on political instability and collective consumption on civil unruliness, multivariate regressions were run introducing both measures of inequality as explanatory variables.[23] These results are not reported in Table 3.1. In both cases, the additional variable did not improve the fit, prove statistically significant, or move the Durbin-Watson statistics out of the ranges in which they fall in Table 3.1.[24]

ESTIMATION OF THE
MONETARY INSTABILITY RELATION

In order to derive a measure of monetary instability, a percentage trend growth rate of the narrow money supply of approximately 4-1/2 percent per year was estimated in an equation using seasonally adjusted monthly money supply data for the 1960-1975 period. The yearly average of absolute values of annualized monthly deviations of money supply growth from that trend is our measure of monetary instability. Absolute values were used because one month's deviation from trend could be followed in later months by corrections to that deviation. As there seems to be no discernible trend in the resulting vector of observations, even in the early 1970s, no bias would appear to be imparted from the use of a single sixteen-year trend. (The presence of a trend in the observations would have suggested the use of a number of subtrends in calculating the monetary instability variable.)

First differences of fitted values from each of the discordance-inequality regressions (equations 1A and 2A in Table 3.1) entered the monetary instability equation in Table 3.2 as explanatory variables. Fitted values were used because they capture distribution-induced changes in discordance rather than changes in discordance from all causes.[25] Lead, contemporaneous, and lagged first differences were tried, Only lagged first differences yielded estimates that were statistically significant and R^2's that were not extremely low. The finding of a lag between discordance and monetary instability is consistent with the assumption that a current discordance-induced acceleration of money supply growth (increased monetary accommodation) is followed by a corrective deceleration in money supply growth in later months. By this assumption, current discordance could reasonably be expected to affect monetary instability with a one year lag. This finding implies that the process of short run monetary accommodation interferes with monetary stability over a rather extended period of time.

The overall results do not falsify the hypothesis that monetary instability is sensitive to incremental discordance. The positive and highly significant estimate for the political turnover variable indicates that political discordance generates monetary instability. The unexpected negative estimate for the "strikes" variable, significant at the .10 level, indicates that monetary instability varies inversely with the "strikes" measure of discordance.[26]

Contingent upon the validity of the assumption that an increase in monetary instability reflects an increase in monetary accommodation and that a decrease in monetary instability reflects a decrease in monetary accommodation, these results imply that the Federal Reserve is quite willing to use an accommodating policy to mitigate the discordance that is based on increased government expenditures, but assumes a hard-nosed unaccommodating stance toward the discordance that is

Table 3.2: The Monetary Instability Relation
YEARLY DATA, 1960-1975

EQUATION	DEPENDENT VARIABLE	CONSTANT	EXPLANATORY VARIABLES						R$_2$	D.W.
	Yearly Average of Absolute Value of Monthly Deviations Of Money Supply Growth from Trend (M_t)		Lagged First Differences in Turnover of Congressional Seats (Fitted Values) ($\Delta D_{1,t-1}$)	Lagged First Differences in Man Days Lost Dummy From Strikes (Fitted Values) ($\Delta D_{2,t-1}$)	Arthur Burns Dummy	Lyndon Johnson Dummy	Election Years Dummy	Lagged Dependent Variable		
(3A)		.0094 (2.863)	1.613 (3.756)	-.0968 (-1.603)					.57	1.80
(3B)		.0113 (3.278)	1.803 (4.143)	-.0959 (-1.654)	-.0074 (-1.361)				.66	2.29
(3C)		.0064 (1.769)	1.712 (4.225)	-.1012 (-1.797)		.0084 (1.584)			.68	2.25
(3D)		.0093 (2.647)	1.556 (3.005)	-.0940 (-1.454)			.0017 (.2278)		.58	1.75
(3E)		.0135 (2.978)	1.816 (4.067)	-.1185 (-1.941)				-.2826 (-1.268)	.65	1.64

t statistics are in parentheses

grounded in attempts by labor to increase its share of national income.[27] This interpretation suggests that monetization of government deficits rather than the validation of wage and price increases has been the principal source of monetary instability over the 1960-1975 period. The estimates indicate that Federal Reserve officials apparently stand up to the demands of organized wage—and price—setters but relent before the onslaught of big government. The main source of inflationary distress, as far as monetary policy-making is concerned, has been the spending of government.

As there could presumably be other nondistributional sources of monetary instability, a number of additional tests were performed. First, an intercept dummy variable was introduced with a value of one for the years of Arthur Burns' chairmanship of the Board of Governors of the Federal Reserve System, and a value of zero for all other years. The result, reported in equation 3B in Table 3.2, indicates a decrease in monetary instability over the Burns years that is statistically significant at the .05 level. This finding falsifies the view that during William McChesney Martin's tenure the Federal Reserve assumed a more stable "sound money" position than during the Burns era (cf. Maisel, 1973).

In recent years a new vogue in monetary policy research has centered around the widely discussed theory of the political business cycle. As a test of this theory, an intercept dummy was introduced with a value of one for all election years in the 1960-1975 period. Results are reported in equation 3C of Table 3.2. There is no statistically significant change in monetary instability in these years.[28]

Because the years of Chairman Martin's tenure were, except for 1969, also years of Democratic presidency, four separate regressions were estimated, each introducing a binary variable with a value of one for the term-in-office of a particular president, and a zero for all other years. The terms were those of Presidents Kennedy, Johnson, Nixon, and Ford (1961 through 1964 were treated as Kennedy years). Only the estimate for the years of the Johnson administration, 1965-1968, proved statistically significant and it is reported in equation 3D in Table 3.2. In this subperiod there was indeed a significant increase in monetary instability. This result corroborates the dramatic image of LBJ as an inveterate Federal Reserve arm-twister, successful in persuading the monetary authority to try to conceal through monetary accommodation the redistributive effects of the deficits associated with the Great Society and Vietnam war expenditures (Maisel, 1973).

Finally, as changes in discordance seem to have a lagged effect on monetary instability, it is reasonable to conjecture that the monetary policy maker might attempt to dampen that instability over time. To test for this, lagged values of the dependent variable were introduced as an explanatory variable. The hypothesis was that the monetary authority would respond negatively to a prior year's instability, that is, it would try to dampen fluctuations in money supply growth over time. The results are reported in equation 3E of Table 3.2 The lagged dependent variable has the expected sign but is significant only at the .10 level of significance.

CONCLUDING COMMENT

This chapter presents a theory of monetary accommodation. As such, it forges an elemental link between cost push and monetary theories of inflation, and offers a venue for further inquiry into the theory of monetary perturbations in the business cycle. While the empirical work must be cautiously interpreted, particularly as data limitations do not permit a true test of the theory of monetary accommodation or estimation of the temporal pattern of monetary accommodation, it may serve as the basis for further critical refinement. Work should continue if we expect to realize any palpable improvement in the management of money. In addition, perhaps the theory of monetary accommodation, as one part, indeed a major but heretofore undeveloped part, of the theory of economic policy, is an area where the parochial and ideological barriers to unified social system theory may begin to erode.

NOTES

1. For further discussion of this Resolution and the recent behavior of the money supply, see, for example, Pierce (1978) and Weintraub (1979).

2. Central banks, usually acting as agents of central government, are supposed to be able to control the supply of money. Economists have estimated reactions of the money supply and other variables controlled by the monetary authority to the state of the economy as measured by the actual and predicted rates of price inflation, levels of unemployment, and other indices of economic well being. The sign and direction of these monetary policy reactions roughly correspond to the implicit counter-cyclical mandate imposed on the central bank by government. Nevertheless, there is evidence that these reaction patterns are quite variable over time. See Havrilesky, Sapp and Schweitzer (1975), reprinted in Havrilesky and Boorman (1976).

3. A survey of empirical work in the demand for money appears in Havrilesky and Boorman (1978: Chapters 7 and 8).

4. This hypothesis suggests that economic agents will not discard, a priori, any means of developing more accurate expectations by investing in ways of predicting policy maker behavior. Thus, the behavior of individual economic agents, as estimated in the behavioral relations of any hypothetical model of the economic structure, may actually reflect expectations regarding the objectives and reactions of policy makers.

Thus, according to the rational expectations hypothesis, changes in the structure of the economy may not be unrelated to changes in objectives and reactions of policy makers. If the economy is in equilibrium and if changes in monetary policy objectives are anticipated, then economic agents will adjust their behavior so as to minimize the effect of anticipated monetary stabilization policy on their desired allocations of goods and factor endowments; equilibrium values of real variables and the estimated structure will be relatively stable over time. Only unexpected shifts in the policy maker's preferences, resulting in surprise variations in money supply growth, can generate unanticipated inflation, temporarily altering the perceived real wage and interest rates, thereby changing the structural responses of labor suppliers, labor demanders and asset holders to observed inflation, and consequently affecting output and employment temporarily.

Thus, in the long run, with all policy actions fully anticipated, the estimated structured is relatively stable. In the short run, if all policy actions are not fully anticipated, (unless estimators have accurate knowledge of how behavioral responses to unanticipated policy actions are formed) the estimated structure will not be so stable. The systematic interdependence between preferences and structure virtually eliminates the ability of policy makers to affect output and employment in the long run, and given the state of current knowledge, greatly diminishes their ability to predict the effects of imperfectly anticipated policy actions on output, employment and prices in the short run (see, for example, Sargent and Wallace, 1976).

5. Variations on this idea have been offered by Sims (1974) and Lucas (1976). Tests have been performed by Neftci and Sargent (1976).

6. The elasticity of expectations is the ratio between a percentage change in current price and the resulting percentage change in every expected future price (Hicks, 1939).

7. A paper, by Mullineaux (1977), indicates that uncertainty is greatest during periods of stabilization policy "surprises."

8. Ultimately, of course, some wages or prices will rise more than others. This is reminiscent of Charles Schultze's view of inflation: a shift in demand will drive prices up because the "rigid wages and prices" of industries from which demand is diverted fail to decline and may even rise a little. See Schultze (1959). One fault with "cost push" and "sociological" explanations of inflation such as Schultze's is that they ignore the importance of the accommodating alternative exercised by the monetary authority. Neither cost push, sociological or monetary theories of inflation explain in a general fashion the degree of monetary accommodation (except in the extreme case where, because capital is perfectly mobile internationally, the central bank can sterilize no part of the reserve inflows brought about by wage and price behavior).

9. For an expansion of the arguments presented here with regard to government deficits see Havrilesky (1979, 1978).

10. From time to time, Federal Reserve "insiders" have promoted and tried to justify "distributive constraints" upon Federal Reserve policy actions, constraints that define a feasible zone beyond which, for example, short-term interest rates cannot be pushed. See, for example, Maisel (1973). This, together with other attempts at concealment, are doomed to failure since monetary policy cannot, in the long run, normally effect relative prices, including real wages and real interest rates.

11. Wage, deficit, and commodity price shocks may, therefore, explain part of the apparent instability over time of the monetary policy reaction function as well as its occasional "perverse" estimates. The central bank may choose either to resist their stimulus to inflation by contracting or to conceal the redistribution of income by expanding. See footnote 2 above. Burns (1977).

12. Gottfried Habeler's (1976) analysis is apt here:

Looking at the whole picture—labor unions and other pressure groups trying to increase their share in the national product and the government itself increasing its demands steadily—one is led to regard inflation as society's method of reconciling and scaling down inconsistent claims of the various groups on the national product.

13. For examples of this view see Cobham (1978), Brown (1975) and Devine (1974). Among notable earlier analysis of the problem is Bronfenbrenner (1954).

14. Recent survey articles reflect the fact that something is indeed missing in the monetary theory of inflation (see, for example, Barro and Fisher, (1976), and Laidler and Parkin, 1975).

A good example of the disarray of the monetary theory of inflation is Gordon (1977).

Cost push theorists attempt to ignore money altogether, and look for direct links between price inflation and nonmonetary (often distributive) causes. Statistical fit is usually quite poor. For example, the relation of labor's share of national income to inflation is highly erratic over time and among countries (see Dirlam, 1976).

15. "The only way to solve the inflation problem would be to dissolve pressure groups and make the economy more competitive. But only a strong government can do that and democracy is likely to perish in the process" (Habeler, 1976:152).

Only the coercive intervention of the modern bureaucratic state "can collaborate in controlling citizen-initiated protest and in ensuring proper fiscal discipline and management" (Schmitter, 1977).

16. If a yearly average of *algebraic* values had been used, the rather strong assumption of assymetry would have been uneccessary to obtain a positive relationship. Hypothetically, the algebraic measure would vary positively with changes in discordance under all circumstances except when accommodatory accelerations and decelerations are completely corrected in subsequent months. The equations of Table 3.2 were all estimated using the algebraic measure but there was very little change in the results.

17. These are rather imperfect measures for several reasons. One is that the same level of a variable may imply different degrees of inequality over time. For example, a given ratio of property income to national income implies different degrees of inequality at different stages of the business cycle. Another source of imperfection resides in the fact that these are highly aggregative measures. For example, some aspects of collective consumption, such as expenditures for higher education, actually have quite a skewed distribution.

18. Other potential measures of political instability, such as political polls and major cabinet realignments, might also be useful and have been used in other aspects of my research. In fact these relations were estimated using political polls as discordance variable and very similar results were obtained.

19. As discussed earlier, government preferences are viewed as shifting quite independently of political turnover. Preferences can obviously shift considerably without much change in turnover when the incremental discordance cost of changes in the distribution of income is quite small.

20. Other potential measures of civil unruliness, such as police expenditures on civil unrest, are not available. For an important study of other causes of civil unruliness, see Hibbs (1973).

21. The absence of off year data probably imparts a negative bias to the estimates of equations 1A, 1B, and 1C in Table 3.1 because discordance is probably systematically less in nonelection years.

The absence of other explanatory variables in the strikes-dependent equations, 2A, 2B, and 2C, may impart a positive bias to the estimate. For example, strike activity and property income as a percentage of national income both tend to vary procyclically. Thus, the true relationship between strike activity and property income as a precentage of national income is probably more strongly negative than estimated here.

22. Contemporaneous values of the monetary instability variable were also tried but no statistically significant estimates resulted.

These experiments suggest that while monetary accommodation is used to mitigate distributional discordance over short intervals, and thereby leads to monetary instability over longer intervals, and that while monetary instability impedes the overall macro-economy, these impediments do not accelerate future political turnover or increase future strike activity in the economy. Rather current monetary accommodation, because of its adverse effects on the economy, may reduce future strike activity (Hibbs, 1978:153-175).

23. Schmitter argues that for many countries political instability and civil unruliness are not related. As a test we fitted political turnover as a dependent variable to our measure of strikes as an explanatory variable. The equation has an R^2 of only .12 with a positive but statistically insignificant estimate (Schmitter, 1977).

24. Because the discordance-inequality tradeoff could be convex, a quadratic form was tried for both relations. The R^2's were slightly lower and, although the signs were correct, estimates were not statistically significant.

25. Actual values of first differences in the discordance variables were also tried in the monetary instability relation with very little change in the overall results.

26. In a series of preliminary regressions, lagged first differences of the inequality variables were introduced directly as explanatory variables with the monetary instability variable as a dependent variable. Results in this reduced form estimation were consistent with those reported above.

27. The unexpected negative coefficients on the lagged first differences in strike action variable implies a surprisingly resolute Federal Reserve. The estimate, however, is probably biased in a negative direction to the extent that years of great instability are preceded by recession years, which are well known to be years of reduced strike action. See, for example, Maisel for an alternative view.

28. A similar binary variable was introduced with a value of one for all election and *preelection* years. Again, the results were statistically insignificant. Maisel, *ibid.*

REFERENCES

BARRO, R. and FISHER, S. (1976) "Recent Developments in Monetary Theory." Journal of Monetary Economics (April):133-168.

BRONFENBRENNER, M. (1954) "Some Neglected Implications of Secular Inflation." In K. Kurihara (ed.) Post Keynesian Economics. New Brunswick, N.J.: Rutgers University Press.

BROWN, E.P. (1975) "A Non-monetarist View of the Pay Explosion." Three Banks Review (March):115-130.

BURNS, A. (1977) "The Importance of an Independent Central Bank." Federal Reserve Bulletin (September):777-781.

COBHAM, D. (1978) "The Politics of the Economics of Inflation." Lloyd's Bank Review (April):178.

DEVINE, P. (1974) "Inflation and Marxist Theory." Marxism Today (March):32-41.

DIRLAM, J.B. (1976) "Inflation in France." In G. Means et al. (eds.) The Roots of Inflation. New York: Burt Franklin & Co.

FRIEDMAN, M. (1977) "Nobel Lecture: Inflation and Unemployment." Journal of Political Economy 85 (June):451-472.

GORDON, J. (1977) "World Inflation and Monetary Accommodation in Eight Countries." Brookings Papers on Economic Activity 2:409-468.

HABELER, G. (1976) "Some Current Suggested Explanations and Cures for Inflation." Pp. 143-165 in K. Brunner and A.H. Meltzer (eds.) Institutional Arrangements and the Inflation Problem. Carnegie-Rochester Conference Series on Pubic Policy 3. Amsterdam, North Holland.

HAVRILESKY, T. (1979) "Sources and Symptoms of Monetary Instability." In J.Q. Adams (ed.) Institutional Economics: Essays in Honor of Allan G. Gruchy. Leiden: Martinus Neijhoff.

———(1978) "The Distribution of Income and Monetary Policy." In T. Wilson and K. Boulding (eds.) Redistribution Through the Financial System. New York: Praeger.

———and BOORMAN. J. (1978) Monetary Macroeconomics. Arlington Heights, Ill.: AMH Publishing.

———(1976) Current Issues in Monetary Theory and Policy. Arlington Heights, Ill.: AHM Publishing.

HAVRILESKY, T., SAPP, R., and SCHWEITZER, R. (1975) "Tests of the Federal Reserve's Reaction to the State of the Economy." Social Science Quarterly (March): 835-852.

HICKS, J.R. (1939) Value and Capital. New York: Oxford University Press.

HIBBS, D.A. (1973) Mass Political Violence. New York: John Wiley.

HIBBS, D. (1978) "On the Political Economy of Long-Run Trends in Strike Activity." British Journal of Political Science 8(April):153-175.

HINES, A.G. (1971) On the Reappraisal of Keynesian Economics. London: Martin Robertson.

HUMPHREY, T. (1973) "Changing Views of the Phillips Curve." Monthly Review, Federal Reserve Bank of Richmond 58 (July):2-13.

LAIDLER, D. and PARKIN, M. (1975) "Inflation. . .A Survey." Economic Journal (December):741-809.

MacRAE, C.D. (1977) "A Political Model of the Business Cycle." Journal of Political Economy 85 (April):239-263.

MAISEL, S. (1973) Managing the Dollar. New York: W.W. Norton.

MULLINEAUX, D. (1977) "Inflation Expectations and Money Growth in the United States." Research Paper No. 28, Federal Reserve Bank of Philadelphia.

NEFTCI, S. and SARGENT, T. (1978) "A Little Bit of Evidence on the Natural Rate Hypothesis." Journal of Monetary Economics 4 (April):315-320.

PIERCE, J.L. (1978) "The Myth of Congressional Supervision of Monetary Policy." Journal of Monetary Economics 4 (April):363-370.

POOLE, W. (1976) "Benefits and Costs of Stable Money Growth." In K. Brunner and
   A.H. Meltzer (eds.) Institutional Arrangements and the Inflation Problem. Carnegie-
   Rochester Conference Series on Public Policy. Amsterdam, North Holland.

SAMUELSON, P. (1977) "Some Dilemmas of Economic Policy." Challenge (April):31.

SARGENT, T. and WALLACE, N. (1976) "Rational Expectations and the Theory of
   Economic Policy." Journal of Monetary Economics (April):169-183.

SCHMITTER, P.C. (1977) "Interest Intermediation and Regime Governability in
   Contemporary Western Europe." Unpublished paper presented at the 1977 Congress
   of the American Political Science Association, Washington, D.C.

SCHULTZE, C.L. (1959) "Recent Inflation in the United States." Joint Economic
   Committee, Employment, Growth and Price Levels, Paper No. 1.

SIMS, C.A. (1974) "Distributed Lags." In M. Intrilagator and D. Kendrick (eds.)
   Frontiers of Qualitative Economics. Amsterdam, North Holland.

WEINTRAUB, R.E. (1979) "The Federal Reserve Money Supply Roller Coaster." This
   volume.

Chapter 4

THE PERSISTENCE OF INFLATION

THOMAS M. HUMPHREY
Federal Reserve Bank of Richmond

Inflation will continue to be the *problem for some time to come. . . . [N]o longer merely cyclical or random—it is,* for the first time *in American History,* secular.

Will E. Mason (1958, pp. 153, 160, emphasis added)

INTRODUCTION

Among the most exasperating and puzzling of recent economic phenomena is the apparent intractability of the inflation rate. Once started, an inflation becomes difficult to subdue. It seems to develop a momentum of its own, independent of other basic economic conditions. It resists or at best responds only sluggishly to traditional restrictive policies. Its persistence in the face of high unemployment and excess capacity has resulted in the addition of the term *stagflation* to the economist's lexicon.

What accounts for the stickiness of the inflation rate? Why is it so policy-resistant and difficult to control? Why is it so slow to decelerate even when demand is slack? Many economists believe that the answers lie in the mechanism through which inflationary impulses are transmitted through the economy.[1] Embedded in this mechanism are certain delays or lags that may slow the spread of inflation over the total price structure and may also prolong its duration. Particular prices that lag behind general inflationary movements have to catch up later to reestablish their relative position in the price structure. This lag/catch-up characteristic of the inflationary transmission mechanism is offered by some as an explanation of why strong upward pressures on prices persist long after demand slackens.

The most important lags in the process through which inflation is diffused through the economy are the *price-adjustment lag* and the *expectations-formation lag*. The first refers to the delayed response of the rate of price increase to shifts in aggregate demand. Demand pressure

89

is transmitted to prices via a complicated and circuitous channel that runs from output to inputs to input prices to costs, and finally to product prices. The price-adjustment lag accounts for the time it takes for demand to affect prices through the channel of costs. It should be noted that many of these costs themselves adjust slowly, partly because they are influenced by sticky price anticipations. These sticky anticipations are described by the second lag, which refers to the slowness with which expectations of future inflation are revised when individuals realize that actual inflation has turned out to be different than was expected. For example, immediately following periods of rapidly accelerating inflation, expectations about the future behavior of prices continue to reflect the preceding price experience even though the current rate of inflation may be decelerating. Some analysts point to these lags as the reason that inflation is so persistent and hard to subdue, even in the face of high unemployment and excess capacity.

The purpose of this chapter is to examine the price-adjustment and expectations-formation lags, and to indicate how they may affect the speed, pattern, and duration of inflation. The chapter proceeds in the following manner. First, it identifies the location and describes the operation of the lags in the inflationary transmission mechanism. Second, it provides an explanation of the existence of the lags. Third, and most important, it analyzes the policy implications of the lags. Finally, the appendix contains a brief description of how the lags are treated in simple analytical models of the inflationary process.

SKETCH OF THE INFLATIONARY PROCESS

The first objective is to describe the operation of the lags in the inflationary mechanism. As a necessary preliminary, a brief description of the inflation process is offered, with emphasis on the time sequence or chronological order in which key economic variables (spending, output, costs, prices, expectations, and so on) adjust to inflationary pressures. The hypothetical example presented below may not conform to all of the inflationary episodes experienced in the United States, although it probably typifies most of them.

As a first approximation, the sequence of events in a typical inflation may be described as beginning with an increase in aggregate demand to a level in excess of the economy's capacity to produce.[2] Such a step-up in the rate of spending might stem from any of a variety of causes including: (1) an increase in the government's budgetary deficits; (2) an episodic expansion in private spending associated, say, with a major innovation;

and (3) an acceleration in the rate of monetary growth either actively engineered or passively permitted by the monetary authorities. Whatever the cause, the increased rate of spending, if it is to continue, must be supported by a sustained higher rate of monetary growth. Without this concomitant monetary growth, rising prices would simply reduce the real value of existing cash balances below the level that people desire to hold. In an effort to rebuild their price-eroded real balances, cashholders would cut expenditures, thereby bringing the inflation to a halt. An increased rate of spending cannot be maintained for long without the monetary expansion necessary to finance it. Assuming such expansion occurs, however, the corresponding increased rate of spending leads to a build-up of excess demands on the economy. Businessmen initially respond to this rising demand not by raising prices but rather by reducing inventories and expanding output. That is, their initial adjustments are to quantities; price adjustments come later—hence the so-called price-adjustment lag.

The stimulus to final output resulting from these quantity adjustments is transmitted back to earlier stages of production via increases in the demand for labor and material inputs, as well as for intermediate (semi-finished) products. Demand pressure passes downward to lower stages of production where prices—especially those of raw materials and other basic commodities—are particularly sensitive to increases in demand. These prices begin to rise almost immediately as do certain competitive (nonunion) wages whose adjustment is not delayed by long-term union contracts or collective bargaining agreements. Since the output of earlier stages of the productive process constitutes the input of later stages, these rising wages and prices pass back up through the interindustry structure in the form of increased costs. In short, demand pressure is transmitted downward, thus invoking cost increases that ripple upward until they finally reach the finished product stage. Here businessmen, operating with fixed percentage markups over costs, pass these cost increases on in the form of higher prices. These price increases induce workers operating under collective bargaining agreements to bargain for cost of living increases in the next wage contract. The resulting increases in labor costs are passed through into still higher prices. Such cost-induced price increases, of course, constitute the delayed price response to the prior shift in demand. These cost and price increases provoke further rounds of wage and price increases that add impetus to the inflation through the channel of costs.

It should be noted that the expectations lag is in operation throughout the early and intermediate stages of the inflation. Price anticipations are based on perceived trends and so do not change quickly. Because these trends are estimated largely from past experience, it takes time to adjust expectations to higher current rates of inflation. Thus, when the actual rate of inflation begins to rise, the expected rate is not immediately affected. Only after the actual rate has exceeded the expected rate for a time will the latter start to rise. But it will rise slowly at first because it continues to reflect the lower past rates of inflation. Eventually, however, the expected rate rises faster and faster as people become acclimated to the higher actual rate and adapt their expectations to it. Once aroused, inflationary expectations feed back into the current rate of inflation as firms and unions seek to raise prices and wages at the same rate as they expect prices in general to rise. At this stage of the inflationary process, where cost increases are passing through into price increases and the expected rate of inflation is rising to catch up with the actual rate, the main impact of the inflationary stimulus shifts from quantities to prices. The temporary output and employment effects diminish, and purely inflationary price effects dominate.[3] The lags, however, may be long; and the price system may take several years—years that may even encompass a business recession—to complete all adjustments. Particular costs and prices that have lagged behind the others will have to catch up in order to restore the equilibrium price relationships disturbed by the inflation. Also, at the end of a serious inflation, inflationary psychology may continue to exert upward pressure on wages and prices even after other basic pressures have begun to dissipate, since it takes time for expectations to catch up with the accelerating price movements of the recent past. This catch-up process may extend well into an ensuing recession, thus resulting in the anomaly of rising prices despite slackening demand.

In the process just described, the chain of causation or pattern of adjustment runs from spending to output to costs to prices to expectations, and back again to input and product prices. This sequential process is represented schematically in Figure 4.1, which also shows the location of the price-adjustment and expectations lags. It should be emphasized, however, than an important constraint exists to the continuous operation of this process. Specifically, the process cannot continue unless it is constantly refueled with additional supplies of money. A determined stand by the monetary authorities to deny this fuel will eventually bring it to a halt.

THE WINDING-DOWN PROCESS

The lags described in the preceding section continue to operate even after an effective program of monetary restraint is implemented. Spending slackens, output falls, and input demands decline; but prices nevertheless

THE INFLATIONARY TRANSMISSION MECHANISM

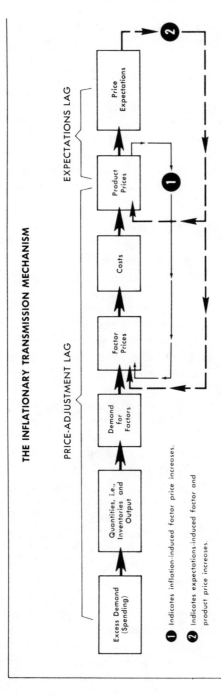

PRICE-ADJUSTMENT LAG   EXPECTATIONS LAG

❶ Indicates inflation-induced factor price increases.

❷ Indicates expectations-induced factor and product price increases.

The inflation process is set in motion by a rise in aggregate demand or spending to a level in excess of the economy's long-run capacity to produce. Businessmen initially respond to the excess demand by drawing down inventories and stepping up production. Output expands and the demand for resource inputs increases. The resulting upward pressure on resource prices pushes up unit production costs upon which product prices are based. Prices therefore rise. These price increases induce resource owners to bargain for cost-of-living pay increases to restore real earnings eroded by inflation. This feedback of product prices into resource costs generates additional rounds of inflation. The price-adjustment lag is the time it takes for demand pressure to affect product prices through the complicated channel of factor costs. If the inflation persists, it eventually induces upward revisions of expected future rates of inflation, which feed back into wages and prices to add further momentum to inflation. Slow to build up and hard to reverse, price expectations may keep wages and prices increasing long after demand slackens. The expectations lag accounts for the slow adjustment of the expected future rate of inflation to changes in the actual current rate.

Figure 4.1

93

continue upward because recent cost increases are still working their way through the system and because inflationary expectations continue to mount. But as demand pressures slacken throughout successive stages of production, the resulting weakening of costs eventually leads to an easing of prices of final goods and services. As the actual rate of price increase falls and remains for a time below the expected rate, expectations of further rises are gradually revised downward. Since the expected rate is a determinant of the actual rate, the decrease of the former will produce a further deceleration of the latter. But the price-adjustment and expectations lags draw out the winding-down process, and the actual rate of inflation will converge on its new equilibrium level only slowly.

FACTORS RETARDING PRICE ADJUSTMENT

What characteristics of a modern economy account for the lags described in the foregoing sections? In the case of the price-adjustment lag, the answer is fairly straightforward. The lag arises from institutional arrangements and behavioral practices that operate to make many costs and prices relatively unresponsive to short-run shifts in demand.[4] For example, long-term contracts fix some wages and prices for substantial intervals of time. In addition, regulated rates of public utilities can be changed only after lengthy administrative and judicial proceedings. Moreover, there exist a variety of legal restrictions on wage and price flexibility, including minimum wage laws, rent controls, oil price ceilings, interest-rate ceilings, and the like. There are also numerous government-sanctioned trade-restriction and price-fixing arrangements, such as production and marketing quotas for certain agricultural products, import quotas, licensing and other restrictions to entry of professions, and resale price maintenance agreements. All these contribute to the stickiness of the prices affected.

An important factor retarding price adjustment is the inflexibility of many wages. Owing to long-term labor contracts, delays in the adjustment of price expectations, and perhaps also workers' money illusion (i.e., failure to distinguish between nominal and real wage increases), some wages tend to lag behind inflation during certain phases of the business cycle. When inflation accelerates in the upswing, these wages are often slow to respond. In later stages of a sharp inflation, however, wage increases may outstrip price increases. Wages may then tend to rise ahead of prices to restore real earnings eroded by past price increases and to protect real earnings from anticipated future price increases. But the lag becomes noticeable again when inflation is subsiding as the rate of wage increase shows little tendency to decelerate, even though the rate of rise of other prices is diminishing.

Another important factor contributing to price rigidity is the price-setting behavior of large-scale firms operating in manufacturing industries. In the typical imperfectly competitive market, the price mechanism works in the long run as prices adjust to clear the market. In the short run, however, prices are relatively inflexible. Firms do not typically alter their prices in response to short-run shifts in demand. At least three explanations of this behavior have been offered.

According to the first, firms have difficulty distinguishing between real demand shifts specific to a particular industry and shifts in nominal aggregate demand for the output of all industries. Because they alter only the composition and not the overall level of aggregate demand, specific demand shifts may occur without inducing a corresponding rise in input prices. By contrast, an economy-wide demand increase leads to an equiproportional bidding-up of input prices. In the former case, industry cost and supply curves remain unchanged. In the latter case, however, cost and supply curves shift sharply upward, just matching the rise in demand. The rational entrepreneurial reaction to the former is a change in some quantity, whereas the rational reaction to the latter is a change in prices. But when aggregate demand alters there is a good likelihood that each producer will tend to regard the shift in demand for his product as special to him and so adjust quantity rather than price. Only later, when cost changes become widespread, will producers correctly perceive the demand shift as an economy-wide phenomenon. Then and only then will they start to change their prices. A second explanation stresses the administrative inconvenience and costs of frequent price changes—for example, the expense of printing and disseminating new price lists—as a reason for sticky oligopolistic prices.

Still a third explanation of price inflexibility in imperfectly competitive markets begins with the observation that in the complex and dynamic modern industrial economy there is always much uncertainty about the equilibrium or market-clearing price. Firms operating in this kind of environment try to avoid the market disruption, confusion, and perhaps even overt price warfare that could result if each sought individually to determine the equilibrium price. In order to prevent such confusion from developing, firms seek ways to coordinate price changes. Such coordination, if successful, will assure that firms raise prices in unison and that price changes will not occur when demand shifts are thought to be temporary and reversible. Firms have devised several techniques to facilitate price coordination. Infrequent price changes are perhaps the simplest of these. Price leadership constitutes another such technique. In this case, one firm—often the largest in the industry—initiates price changes, and the rest more or less automatically follow that price change. Perhaps the most widely used mechanism for coordinating price behavior, however, is to base selling prices on unit labor and material costs that are the same for all firms in the industry. This practice is accomplished by the use of so-called unit cost or mark-up pricing formulas.

Unit-cost pricing is thought to be characteristic of many of the large oligopolistic firms that operate in American industry. The mark-up technique of pricing involves setting prices on the basis of a constant percentage markup applied to production costs per unit of output at some standard level of plant operation or capacity utilization. The chief cost components are unit labor and unit materials costs. Included in the mark-up is the firm's profit margin per unit of output. This profit margin is usually set to provide a fixed target rate of return on equity. Since percentage markups or profit margins are treated as fixed constants in unit-cost pricing formulas, it follows that formula-based price changes are strictly cost-determined, that is they result solely from changes in unit labor and material costs. Prices respond to costs, not to demand. Moreover, since standard unit labor and material costs are roughly the same for all firms in the industry, unit-cost formulas insure that price changes will be uniform throughout the industry, thereby minimizing the risks of competitive price undercutting. Thus unit-cost pricing is consistent with the slow response of prices to shifts in demand, the dependence of prices on costs, and the coordination of prices in concentrated industries.

A SOURCE OF CONFUSION

The long delay in the adjustment of many prices to demand pressure makes it difficult to distinguish cause from effect in the inflationary sequence and contributes to confusion in popular understanding of the source of inflation. The sequence of cost-price response observed in concentrated industries, for example, may suggest that inflation is initiated by autonomous increases in costs. The use in such industries of mark-up or unit-cost pricing formulas, and the resulting dependence of prices on costs, means that firms do not raise prices unless there occurs a prior increase in costs. This cost-price sequence, with costs rising first and prices later, makes it appear that inflation is *caused* by rising costs when in fact excess demand is usually the culprit. For, as pointed out earlier, both the cost increase and the ability of firms to pass on this increase are due to a prior expansion in aggregate demand for final goods and services.

Similarly, the long lag in the response of oligopolistic prices to prior inflation pressures may make it appear that large firms in concentrated industries play an important independent role in generating inflation. Due to the price-adjustment lag, catch-up price increases in such industries are often delayed until well after the restrictive policies start to turn the inflation process around. The apparent perverse behavior of prices when markets are slack and unemployment is rising fosters the notion of giant firms arbitrarily exercising monopoly power by effecting autonomous increases in prices totally independent of economic conditions.[5] But it should be noted that the price increases in such situations can be interpreted as constituting a delayed reaction to prior economic conditions of expanding demand and demand-induced cost increases and a near perfect example of the price-adjustment lag. They might well be interpreted as a delayed manifestation of the effects of a general inflation rather than of inflation-initiating price behavior.

From this interpretation it follows that big firms are not inflation starters. Nevertheless they may play an important role in the working out of the inflationary process. Specifically, they may be inflation prolongers. It follows logically from the mere existence of the price-adjustment lag that administered prices do not usually initiate inflation. Instead they tend to slow it down. By doing so, however, they extend the duration of inflation and protract the period necessary for its reversal. Administered prices are a problem because they act to prolong inflation once it gets started, and because they delay the success and exacerbate the adverse side effects of anti-inflationary stabilization policy. Just as in an upward price spiral sticky administered prices retard the spread of inflation, so when the spiral is unwinding they delay its deceleration and impede the return to price stability.

THE EXPECTATIONS-FORMATION LAG

As noted earlier, the complicating effects of the so-called price-adjustment lag are reinforced by a comparable lag in price expectations, which tend to adjust slowly to the actual rate of inflation. Why does this expectations lag occur and what determines its length?

The expectations lag occurs because people have imperfect foresight and cannot predict the future with certainty. If the future were known with absolute certainty, there would be no forecasting errors and no expectations lag. Anticipations would adapt themselves instantaneously to realized outcomes, and the expected rate of inflation would always be the one that actually occurred. Although the future is emphatically uncertain, people nevertheless try to make informed guesses about it, often on the basis of analyses of the past. Thus, one longstanding explanation of the lag holds that price predictions are based on perceived trends as estimated from past price experience perhaps modified by current information.

Because they reflect the past, these trends and the predictions derived from them change slowly over time. Transitory deviations from the trend have little impact on expectations. Thus, if the current rate of inflation departs from the recent trend, the expected rate will remain unchanged for a time. It requires the cumulative influence of a sustained change, or at least a very large change, in the actual rate to produce a change in the expected rate. And even then the adjustment will not be instantaneous or complete. The expected rate will continue to lag behind the current rate. As time passes, however, and the new rate persists, it will eventually begin to dominate the trend. The price experience of the more distant past gradually will be forgotten and the expected rate will finally converge on the actual rate.

The length of time required for this convergence cannot be specified with any degree of precision. It depends on what interval or intervals of the past people consider in formulating their expectations and, in particular, on what relative weight they assign to the price experience of the more distant past. In general, the greater the weight assigned to the distant past, the longer will be the lag. The lag may indeed be quite long because people, in formulating their expectations, may look not merely at a chronological succession of prior years, but rather at the relevant phases of a succession of past inflation-recession cycles and at the public policy response to these episodes. Looking back at a succession of what might be regarded as stop-go policies, for example, people may expect the recession phase to be brief and to be followed immediately by an expansionary phase that experience suggests may bring new inflationary pressures. To use a popular expression, they may "look across the valley."

A second factor that may affect the length of the expectations lag is the *variability* of the rate of inflation about the trend. The greater the variability of the actual rate of inflation the greater is the financial incentive to forecast it more accurately, i.e., to predict the variations, not just the trend. Accordingly, forecasts of the inflation rate will be revised more frequently and will rely more heavily on current and recent information. The whole time frame employed in observing past price behavior and past forecasting errors will contract and shift toward the present. Correspondingly, the expectations lag will be shorter.

TIME LAGS AND DEMAND MANAGEMENT POLICIES

This chapter has focused on the role of time lags in the inflationary transmission mechanism. These lags raise several potential problems for demand management, i.e., monetary and fiscal, policy. First, if the lags are variable and hard to predict, policy makers may experience difficulty in accurately forecasting when their policy actions will take effect on the rate of inflation. In this case, discretionary policy-making becomes a potentially risky undertaking. That is, unpredictability of the lag effects of policy may render the latter destabilizing rather than stabilizing. For this reason, some analysts have advocated the abandonment of discretionary policy in favor of fixed policy rules. Other observers, however, argue that the lags are not so variable and unpredictable as to defeat effective policy forecasting and control. Actually, little is known about the variability of the lags. The evidence is simply not sufficient to settle the issues. Whether rules would be superior to discretion in the conduct of stabilization policy remains an open question.

Additional policy problems arise from the *length* rather than the variability and unpredictability of the lags. As previously mentioned, the price-adjustment and expectations lags extend the time it takes for a policy-induced change in spending to work its way through to the rate of inflation. Moreover, they influence the pattern of response of quantities and prices to inflationary stimuli. Specifically, they cause the quantity response to precede the price response. When spending changes, output and employment adjust first, prices only later. What are the policy implications of such consequences?

First, owing to the slow response of inflation to a spending change, anti-inflationary monetary-fiscal policy can be expected to produce observed results only after a corresponding lag. Quick monetary remedies for inflation are not likely to be found. Moreover, since the initial impact of a change in spending is on output and employment rather than on prices, a move to monetary restraint would almost surely entail a recession or at least a marked retardation in the rate of expansion of the economy. In short, a temporary but protracted period of unemployment, idle capacity, and sluggish growth might have to be endured if restrictive policy were to be successful in permanently lowering the rate of inflation.

Second, due to the difference in timing of the response of output and prices to a spending change, anti-inflationary policy may appear impotent or even perverse. Because inflationary movements tend to subside so slowly, prices may continue to rise long after output and employment have turned down. Thus inflation can persist even in slack markets, a condition variously known as inflationary recession, stagflation, or slumpflation. During such periods, monetary restraint may be wrongly blamed for causing both the slump and the accompanying inflation. At such times, monetary authorities, anxious to achieve quick and relatively painless results, may be tempted to abandon the policy of restraint as ineffective at best and harmful at worst.

Third, the same asymmetrical pattern of response—output first, prices only much later—may create the dangerous illusion that expansive policy in the upswing can achieve permanent gains in output and employment at the cost of little additional inflation. If inflation proceeds as described in the foregoing sections, this view may have unfortunate consequences. For it is virtually impossible to peg output and employment above their natural or equilibrium levels without continuously accelerating the rate of inflation. In any case, time lags may well compound the problem of curbing inflation by leading to the undue prolongation of expansive policy, thus increasing the momentum behind inflation when it finally occurs.

Indeed, these time lags together with society's commitment to full employment may bias monetary-fiscal policy toward inflation over the entire policy cycle. The lags cause output and employment to adjust before prices. Consequently, on the upside the desired output results of demand expansion occur before the undesired inflationary results, thus encouraging the prolongation of policy stimulus. On the downside, however, the painful effects come first as restrictive policy produces undesired and costly rises in unemployment with little initial effect on the rate of inflation. Not surprisingly, the appearance of painful rather than desired results leads to impatience with restrictive policies and often to their premature reversal. The policies are abandoned before they have a chance to eliminate the inflation generated in the preceding upswing. The net result is that restrictive policies reduce the inflation rate less than expansive policies raise it and inflation ratchets upwards.

DIRECT CONTROLS

If orthodox demand-management policies cannot curb inflation without causing painful rises in unemployment, then what other means can be utilized? One suggestion is to reimpose direct wage-price controls. Several arguments have been advanced in behalf of controls. The most naive is that controls can constrain the rate of inflation while the authorities pursue demand-expansion policies necessary to insure full employment. This argument assumes that the rate of inflation can be permanently pegged in the face of persistent excess demand. In fact, however, the rate of inflation tends to gravitate to an equilibrium level where excess demand is zero. Controls can delay the adjustment to that level but they cannot stop it. The equilibrium rate of inflation will inevitably be reached either via evasion, i.e., through black markets, or after the controls are lifted. In the final analysis, controls will have no effect on the equilibrium rate of inflation, which is determined by aggregate demand. It logically follows, therefore, that a decrease in aggregate demand, not the application of controls, is the *sine qua non* for the reduction of the inflation rate.

CONTROLS AND THE EXPECTATIONS LAG

A more sophisticated argument for controls calls for using them as a supplement to monetary and fiscal policy. The prescription here calls for first employing a monetary-fiscal policy sufficient to eliminate excess aggregate demand, then using controls to speed the actual rate of inflation to its new equilibrium level. In this view, a controls program properly coordinated with restrictive demand policy could help short-circuit the painful process of winding-down a stubborn inflation.

The foregoing argument rests on the belief that controls can exert an independent influence on otherwise sticky price expectations. Eradication of inflationary expectations is of course a prerequisite to the elimination of inflation, since the former is a determinant of the latter. The problem is how to dampen expectations. The orthodox method is to create slack (excess supply) in the economy, thus causing the actual rate of inflation to fall below the expected rate, inducing a downward revision of the latter. Owing to the expectations lag, however, this adjustment may be a slow process and a prime example of how sluggish price anticipations can impede the return to price stability. Direct controls are viewed as a means of speeding the expectations adjustment, and thus reducing the duration and severity of the economic slowdown necessary to bring inflation to its equilibrium level determined by aggregate demand.

How could controls influence expectations? Two mechanisms have been suggested. First, the mere announcement of controls might alter expectations in the desired direction. Second, by freezing prices or at least severely constraining their rate of rise, controls would cause the gap between the expected and actual rates of inflation to be greater than it would otherwise be. Assuming that the rate at which expectations are revised varies directly with the size of the gap, controls would thus accelerate the downward revision of expectations.

This view, however, probably overestimates the influence of controls. To have anything more than a temporary impact on price expectations, the controls must convince the public that the trend of prices when controls are in force is a reliable indicator of the likely future trend of prices after they are lifted. The public may be hard to convince, especially if the controls have failed to stop inflation in the past. Aside from this point, it is hard to understand why controls should have a stronger impact on expectations than, say, an announced policy of a permanent reduction in the growth rate of the money stock. What counts is not the means by which the government announces its determination to permanently reduce inflation but that those intentions be believed.

CONTROLS AND THE PRICE-ADJUSTMENT LAG

It should be noted, moreover, that even if controls *could* reduce the expectations lag, they would tend to lengthen the price-adjustment lag, and this would impede the return to equilibrium. The attainment of economic equilibrium requires that two conditions be satisfied. First, inflation must be correctly anticipated, i.e., the expected rate of inflation must equal the actual rate. Second, the equilibrium structure of relative prices must be restored. Lagging prices and costs must be allowed to catch up to and reestablish their equilibrium relationships with other prices that have already adjusted to inflation. Controls interrupt this catch-up process by arbitrarily freezing all prices and costs. As a result, catch-up adjustments are postponed until the controls are lifted and account for the observed tendency for prices to rise sharply when controls are terminated. Note that this problem would not arise if controls could distinguish between legitimate catch-up and unwarranted anticipatory price increases. In practice, however, the two are virtually indistinguishable and controls prohibit both. By forcing the postponement of catch-up price increases, controls probably protract the inflationary process and lengthen the interval required for the rate of inflation to reach its equilibrium level. In the interim, the controls-distorted price structure generates inefficiency, resource misallocation, and income redistribution. Clearly, in the context of the explanation presented here, controls offer no solution to the problem of sticky inflation.

OTHER PROPOSED SOLUTIONS

One of the more promising, and yet untried, solutions to the lag problem is indexation, i.e., the inclusion of purchasing power clauses in all contracts. With all contractual prices tied to automatic cost of living escalators, inflation would be transmitted more quickly and evenly throughout all markets, thereby permitting faster restoration of relative price equilibrium. On the downside, indexation could help reduce expectations more quickly, thus shortening the time required to remove inflation. Critics argue that indexation would intensify inflation. This criticism confuses the *level* of inflation with the *speed* with which inflationary impulses are propagated through the economy. There is no reason to believe that escalator clauses by themselves would have any effect on the rate of inflation. The speed of inflation would be increased, to be sure, but the level of inflation would not necessarily be any higher. Another partial solution to the lag problem would be to shorten the length of contracts. For example, trade-union collective bargaining agreements could be renegotiated more frequently as could long-term contracts for raw materials and energy supplies.

A distinction should be made here between reforms designed to increase the speed of response of inflation to changes in aggregate demand and reforms aimed at reducing the equilibrium rate of unemployment, i.e., the unemployment rate that, given the inevitable frictions, rigidities, and imperfections in the economy, is just consistent with zero excess demand and stable (nonaccelerating, nondecelerating) rates of inflation. Indexation falls in the former category while so-called structural reforms fall in the latter. Structural reforms refer to microeconomic policies directed at improving the efficiency of labor and product markets. True, these policies may increase the responsiveness of inflation by eradicating market imperfections that inhibit price flexibility. But their chief purpose is to reduce the equilibrium rate of unemployment at which the demand for and supply of labor are in balance and at which any stable rate of inflation (including a zero rate) is possible. By so doing, structural policies may make it easier in at least two ways to bring inflation under control. First, they may render the equilibrium rate of unemployment and the corresponding zero or other desired steady rate of inflation a more acceptable policy option. By bringing equilibrium unemployment down to a socially tolerable level, structural policies reduce the risk that political pressure will be put on the authorities to peg unemployment at even lower levels that can only be maintained by a constantly accelerating rate of inflation. Second, they reduce the severity of the recession necessary to achieve price stability. Since a dampening of inflation requires a temporary rise in unemployment above its equilibrium level, it follows that any policy that reduces the latter also reduces the transitional level of unemployment.

CONCLUSION

The policy implications stemming from the preceding analysis are straightforward. Admit that there are no quick and easy solutions to the inflation problem. Realize that any serious anti-inflation program faces the formidable obstacles of entrenched inflationary expectations and eroded public confidence in the government's ability and determination to fight inflation and to tolerate the resulting economic slack. Comprehend that, obstacles notwithstanding, the costs of removing inflation may be far less than the costs of accepting it as a permanent way of life.[6] On the basis of this cost-benefit analysis establish a permanent target rate of inflation. Rely on demand-management (i.e., monetary and fiscal) policies to bring inflation down to the desired target level. Assuming that level is zero, reduce the rate of monetary expansion and trim budget deficits until the growth rate of total spending (aggregate demand) is equal to the long-term trend growth rate of real output (aggregate supply). Eschew controls. Recognize that a reduction of inflation necessitates a transitional rise in unemployment above its equilibrium level with the extent and duration of the rise depending upon the speed with which inflation is to be removed. In other words, recognize that quick eradication of inflation requires high excess unemployment for a relatively short period, whereas slower eradiction requires a lower level of excess unemployment for a prolonged period. Choose the desired path to price stability always realizing that the choice is between higher excess unemployment for a short time or lower excess unemployment for a long time. Acknowledge also that the severity and duration of the recession necessary to eliminate inflation depends upon the responsiveness of wages and prices to deflationary pressure and upon the adjustment speed of price expectations. Use indexation, if possible, to increase the downward flexibility of wages and prices. Similarly, seek to influence expectations by preannouncing the inflation target and by adhering to a path consistent with achieving it. Once inflation is removed, maintain price stability by avoiding expansionary policies that generate excess demand. Balance the budget each year and maintain a money stock growth rate roughly equal to the long-term growth rate of real output. If society is unwilling to tolerate the equilibrium unemployment rate associated with price stability, design structural policies to lower that rate by improving the efficiency of labor and product markets. If society is still unwilling to accept that rate, face up to the fact that price stability may be impossible to achieve.

NOTES

1. See, for example, the studies by Cagan (1974, 1975a, 1975b), and Laidler (1973, 1974). See also the articles by Friedman (1975) and Selden (1975). The present chapter draws heavily from Cagan and Laidler.

2. In starting with demand, the example does not deny that supply shocks—crop failures, strikes, natural disasters and the like—may also play a role in inflation. Given the random, transient, and often reversible nature of these shocks, however, it is unlikely that they could produce a continuing (sustained) inflation. What they can do is to temporarily intensify an inflation generated by demand forces. This is the problem of price blips illustrated by the transient double-digit episode of 1974 when supply constraints caused inflation to deviate temporarily from its basic trend rate determined by excess demand. When the supply shocks abated, inflation returned to its basic path. Note also that supply shocks can be treated as an excess demand phenomenon, albeit one in which the excess arises from falling supply rather than rising demand.

3. Note that the expectations lag temporarily influences real economic activity by causing the nominal and real (i.e., inflation-corrected) prices of factor inputs to move in opposite directions. Put differently, the expected inflation component of nominal wage and interest rates may not adjust sufficiently to offset actual inflation, thus causing changes in the corresponding real (price deflated) values of those variables. For example, when an inflationary stimulus begins, nominal wages and interest rates adjust upward by the amount of the expected inflation. Because the expected rate of inflation lags behind the actual rate, however, the adjustment is incomplete and consequently real wages and interest rates fall. Businessmen take advantage of the falling real wage and interest rates by hiring more labor and borrowing from banks in order to expand production. These effects, together with decreases in the demand for money (and hence rises in spending) induced by higher nominal interest rates, result in a temporary rise in real output and employment. The stimulus ends, however, when expected inflation catches up with actual inflation. When this happens, nominal wages and interest rates fully reflect the actual rate of inflation and real wages and interest rates return to their initial levels. Similar real effects operate on the downside when actual inflation falls below expected inflation. In this case, the expectations lag results in a temporary rise in real wage and interest rates, and these rising real costs act to temporarily depress real economic activity below its equilibrium level.

4. Note that the rigidities or inflexibilities described in this section refer not to *levels* of particular prices and costs but rather to *rates of change* of those variables. The concept of rigid price levels, of course, implies the complete absence of price change, and is thus irrelevant to the analysis of inflation, which deals with continually rising, not constant, prices. The problem of sluggish inflation is not one of downward inflexibility of price levels, but rather the resistance of changes in prices from the established rate of increase.

5. This simplistic cost push view is implausible and at odds with the orthodox theory of monopoly behavior. According to the latter view, a monopolist sets a relative price for his product that maximizes profits in real terms and maintains that real price by adjusting his nominal price to allow for inflation. The logical implication is that given the degree of monopoly power, monopolists would have no incentive to raise prices other than to keep pace or catch up with inflation. With real prices already established at profit-maximizing levels, any further upward adjustment would reduce profits. On the other hand, if prices are being raised to exploit hitherto unexploited monopoly potential, the question arises as to why those gains were foregone in the past. In either case, rising real prices imply nonrational behavior. It is true that rising real prices would be consistent with profit-maximizing behavior if the degree of monopoly power were increasing. But there is little empirical evidence that monopoly power is on the rise.

6. A policy of accommodating permanent inflation is likely to lead to a pattern of accelerating and highly erratic (variable) inflation. Such inflation, by virtue of its variability and unpredictability, imposes substantial costs on the economy. Not only will there be repeated falls in output and employment whenever the inflation rate drops, but the very unpredictability of volatile inflation increases business uncertainty, makes capital investment decisions riskier, diverts energies and skills from industry and production into speculative activities designed to beat the inflation, and reduces the information content of market prices, thereby making the price system a less efficient mechanism for coordinating economic activity. All this makes for a wasteful and inefficient use of resources that results in a lower level of output than the economy is capable of producing. The costs of inflation can be measured in terms of this lost output. Similarly, the benefits of removing inflation can be reckoned in terms of the increased output that would result.

APPENDIX

THE TREATMENT OF LAGS IN SIMPLE ANALYTICAL MODELS OF THE TRANSMISSION MECHANISM

The inflationary mechanism and its constituent lags can be summarized in the form of simple analytical models.[1] Economists have long used such models to study how lags affect the speed and duration of inflation. More recently, such models have been employed to estimate the impact of lags on the effectiveness of anti-inflationary policy. These models specify the chief determinants of the current and expected future rates of inflation. They also specify the lags linking the variables and determining the pattern of their interaction over time. Comprising these models are a *price-adjustment equation* and an *expectations-formation equation*.[2] The price-adjustment equation explains how the current rate of inflation responds to inflationary expectations and to lagged excess demand—the lag on the latter variable representing the price-adjustment delay. The expectations-formation equation explains how price anticipations are generated and revised in the light of past price experience. As shown below, the latter equation expresses the lag between the expected and actual rates of inflation as an exponentially-declining weighted average of past rates of inflation.

A crude version of this two-equation model is presented in the following paragraphs.[3] It should be strongly emphasized, however, that the model constitutes a severe oversimplification of a complex process and should be interpreted with some skepticism. Presented solely as an illustration, the model purposely omits many of the variables and behavioral relationships that a more complex, sophisticated, and realistic model would contain.

THE PRICE-ADJUSTMENT EQUATION

Most models of the inflationary mechanism contain an equation that explains how the current rate of inflation is determined, i.e., the rate at which businessmen mark up their prices. One such equation shows the rate of price inflation p varying directly with lagged excess demand x_{-1} and with the expected rate of price increase p^e. The equation is written as follows:

$$p = ax_{-1} + p^e_{-1} \tag{1}$$

where p is the current rate of inflation (expressed as a percentage rate), x_{-1} is excess demand lagged one period, p^e_{-1} is the present period's expected rate of inflation forecast at the end of the preceding period, and a is a coefficient specifying how much each unit of lagged excess demand contributes to the rate of price increase. The excess demand variable x is measured in terms of real output since businessmen initally respond to changes in demand by altering quantity produced. More specifically, excess demand x is represented by the difference between actual and capacity real output. Actual output can exceed capacity output because that latter is defined not as the absolute physical limit or maximum ceiling level of output but rather as the output associated with the economy's normal or standard level of operation.

Equation 1 states that if aggregate demand and supply are equal so that there exists no excess demand (x = zero), then actual price inflation p will just equal expected inflation p^e_{-1}, i.e., businessmen will be raising their prices at the rate at which they expect other businessmen to be raising theirs. If, however, an expansion in demand raises x above zero, businessmen will eventually react to the excess demand by raising prices at a rate in excess of the expected rate of inflation. This price response, however, is not instantaneous. For a while, quantities rather than prices tend to absorb the impact of excess demand as businessmen temporarily expand output and perhaps allow their inventories to be depleted. These quantity changes affect demands for and prices of factor resources, and ultimately invoke cost increases that signal the desirability of raising the rate at which prices are marked up. Later, therefore, businessmen respond to the excess demand by raising prices. The same price-adjustment lag operates on the downside. Thus, if a subsequent slackening of spending causes excess demand x to become negative (i.e., a situation of excess supply), the actual rate of price increase p will eventually fall below the expected rate p^e_{-1}. The key word here is *eventually* because the lag prevents prices from responding immediately to shifts in demand.

THE PRICE-RESPONSE LAG

The one-period delay on the excess demand variable symbolizes the tendency for price adjustments to lag behind shifts in demand.[4] This price-adjustment lag is meant to account for the time it takes for demand pressure to work backward through the interindustry structure and for costs to work forward. To summarize, the association of the price-adjustment lag with the excess demand variable x implies that the impact of a shift in demand is initially registered on x. That impact is not immediately transmitted to prices, however. Instead it is transmitted first to quantities and subsequently to costs. Prices do not respond until rising costs induce them to do so.

THE EXPECTATIONS-FORMATION EQUATION

The second equation of the model is the expectations-formation equation. It is written as follows:

$$p^e = bp + (1-b)p^e_{-1} \qquad (2)$$

or, alternatively, as

$$p^e - p^e_{-1} = b(p-p^e_{-1}). \qquad (2a)$$

Equation 2a states that the change in the expected rate of inflation $p^e - p^e_{-1}$ is proportional to the amount by which the period's actual inflation p deviated from expected inflation as forecast at the end of the preceding period p^e_{-1} with the factor of proportionality b having a value between zero and unity.

Embodied in the equation is a particular theory—the so-called adaptive-expectations or error-learning hypothesis— of how inflationary expectations are formed. According to the error-learning hypothesis, people formulate expectations about the inflation rate, observe the discrepancy between the actual and anticipated rates, and then revise the anticipated rate by some fraction of the error between the actual and anticipated rates. Expectations are revised in proportion to the error associated with the previous level of expectations.

It can also be shown that the adaptive-expectations hypothesis is equivalent to the theory that people formulate price expectations from prior price experience by looking at a geometrically-weighted average of past rates of inflation with the weights diminishing exponentially as time recedes. This alternative interpretation of the adaptive expectations hypothesis is written as follows:

$$p^e = b \sum_{i=0}^{\infty} (1-b)^i \, p_{-i}. \tag{2b}$$

Here Σ is the *summation operator* indicating the mathematical operation of adding a succession or series of terms, in this case the weighted past rates of inflation. The *summation index* i represents each past time period starting with the most recent ($i=0$) and extending backward to the most distant ($i = \infty$). The variables p_{-i} are the past rates of inflation, one for each of the i periods stretching backward into time. Attached to each past rate of inflation p_{-i} is a corresponding *weight* that measures the degree of influence that each p_{-i} has on the formation of price expectations p^e. The weights are expressed as $(1-b)^i$, one for each of the i time periods. Since, as mentioned previously, the coefficient of expectations b is a fraction whose magnitude lies between zero and one, it follows that the term $(1-b)$ will also be a fraction. And since any given fraction raised to progressively higher integral powers yields successively smaller numbers, it follows that the weights $(1-b)^i$ must decrease as the exponent i increases, i.e., the weights must diminish the further back in time one looks.

Graphically, the weights are distributed along an exponentially declining curve whose slope reflects the speed of adjustment of expectations. A steep slope represents a short weighting scheme, implying swift adjustment, and conversely for a relatively flat slope. The slope itself is determined by the magnitude of the fraction $(1-b)$. A value of $(1-b)$ close to zero implies that the weights decline rapidly as time recedes, and so future price expectations depend primarily on recent experience. On the other hand, if $(1-b)$ is closer to one in value, rates of inflation from the more distant past enter the equation with higher weights, and recent price information is discounted more heavily. Econometricians who have attempted to fit equation 2b to the statistical data have found the fraction $(1-b)$ to be both significantly greater than zero and less than one. These findings imply that while people generally assign higher weights to more recent phenomena, these weights do not dominate the cumulative weight of all past price experience. In short, price anticipations continue to reflect past price experience which explains why the expected future rate of inflation does not adjust instantaneously to the current rate.

To summarize, equation 2b states that the expected future rate of change of prices is based on a geometrically declining weighted average of past rates of change of prices. The equation, therefore, constitutes a precise specification of the common sense notion that expectations are based on past experience with more emphasis given to recent, rather than distant, experience.

THE EXPECTATIONS LAG

The preceding discussion clearly implies that the length of the expectations lag can be defined in terms of the coefficient of expectations b. The coefficient b itself measures the speed of ajustment of expectations to experience, i.e., the quickness of response of P^e to realized actual rates of inflation p.

The average length of the expectations lag is the counterpart of the speed of adjustment. This lag is expressed as $(1-b)/b$. The closer b is to one, the shorter the lag. In the extreme case where b equals one, the lag is nonexistent, and the expected rate of inflation adjusts instantaneously to the current rate. Thus when b is set equal to one in the expectations-formation equation

$$p^e = bp + (1 - b)p^e_{-1}, \tag{2}$$

the equation collapses to $p^e = p$, i.e., anticipated and actual inflation are always identical.

On the other hand, the lag will be longer the closer b is to zero. In the extreme case where b equals zero, the lag is infinitely long, i.e., the expected rate of inflation never changes. This result can be demonstrated by setting b at zero in equation 2, which yields $p^e = p^e_{-1}$, showing that the expected rate of inflation always remains unaltered from the preceding period. In short, if b is zero, the lag is of infinite length and expectations never change regardless of what is happening to the actual rate of inflation.

One possible shortcoming of the adaptive expectations or error-learning model is that it regards the speed of adjustment or coefficient of expectations b as a fixed constant. And since b determines both the length of the expectations lag and the slope of the weighting pattern used to distribute the lag, it follows that the model, by implication, also treats these phenomena as given constants. This treatment is surely too restrictive. Some analysts think, contrary to the model, that the coefficient b is capable of being influenced by outside information and by the behavior of the rate of inflation itself. For example, it has been suggested that the sensitivity of price anticipations is greater and the corresponding adjustment lag shorter for high and volatile rates of inflation than for low and steady rates. Finally, some observers believe that the expectations coefficient can be influenced by government policy. In fact, this idea constitutes one rationale for direct wage and price controls.[5]

THE COMPLETE SYSTEM

Taken together, the price-adjustment and expectations-formation equations summarize the operation of the inflationary transmission mechanism. These two equations explain the mutual determination of actual and expected rates of price increase. They also indicate the iterative interaction process whereby the expected inflation rate influences the actual current rate, which in turn becomes a determinant of next period's expected rate, which feeds back into next period's actual rate, and so on. Moreover, the model demonstrates how inflationary expectations operate to lengthen the lagged adjustment of prices to short-run shifts in demand. This latter result is obtained by substituting the expectations-formation equation into the price-adjustment equation and then solving recursively for p. The resulting "reduced form" expression is:

$$p = ax_{-1} + ab \sum_{i=2}^{\infty} x_{-i} \tag{3}$$

where the second term on the right-hand side of the equation represents the delayed price impact of excess demand attributable to the operation of the expectations lag. Equation 3 states that once price anticipations enter into price-setting behavior, they tend to prolong the inflationary process. They cause current prices to respond not only to last period's excess demand but also to excess demand in the more distant past.

Finally, the model identifies excess demand as the proximate source of inflation. Specifically, the model implies the following casual chain.

(1) Inflation is determined by excess demand and inflationary expectations.

(2) Inflationary expectations are generated by previous inflationary experience and hence by previous excess demand.

(3) Therefore, excess demand—past and present—is the proximate cause of inflation.

The inflation-generating role of excess demand is made explicit in the reduced-form equation 3, where past levels of x constitute the sole independent variables. The model does not explain how excess demand itself is generated. Such an explanation would require an additional equation expressing the relation between excess demand and the independent variables that determine it. At a very minimum, the list of independent variables would include the money stock since excess demand cannot be long sustained without the monetary growth necessary to support it. Note, however, that there is at least one situation in which excess demand would properly be treated as an independent variable and the money stock as a dependent variable. Such would be the case if society were committed to a full-employment objective in excess of the natural or equilibrium level of employment. Here the policy makers would be expected to pursue the target employment rate (or level of excess demand), passively permitting the money stock and the rate of inflation to adjust so as not to inhibit attainment of the full-employment goal. In this case the level of excess demand would enter the system as a datum to determine the size of the money stock. Thus, depending upon the policy regime, excess demand may appear either as an endogenous or an exogenous variable.

NOTES

1. For a thorough review of inflation models see the article by Laidler and Parkin (1975), especially pp. 774-781 that describe models similar to the one presented in this appendix.

2. Some models of the inflationary process contain a third equation that explains how inflation-generating excess aggregate demand is determined.

3. The model presented here is adapted from similar models developed by Phillip Cagan and David Laidler. See Cagan (1975:94-6) and Laidler (1973, 1974). For an elementary description of Laidler's model, together with a diagrammatic illustration its dynamic properties, see Laidler and Parkin (1975:776-8).

4. More sophisticated models would express the delayed price adjustment as a distributed lag, i.e., a lag spread over a number of time periods.

5. The argument here is that by directly altering the expectations coefficient, controls could speed the downward adjustment of price expectations necessary for the removal of inflation. Of course controls might also speed the adjustment process simply by constraining the actual rate of inflation below the level that would otherwise occur at a given level of unemployment. In the latter case, controls would take the expectations coefficient as a given constant.

REFERENCES

CAGAN, P. (1974) The Hydra-Headed Monster: The Problem of Inflation in the United States. Washington, D.C.: American Enterprise Institute for Public Policy Research.

———(1975a) "Changes in the Recession Behavior of Wholesale Prices in the 1920's and Post-World War II." Explorations in Economic Research 2 (Winter): 90-96.

———(1975b) "Inflation and Market Structure, 1967-1973." Explorations in Economic Research 2 (Spring): 203-16.

FRIEDMAN, M. (1975) "Rediscovery of Money-Discussion." American Economic Review 65 (May): 178.

LAIDLER, D. (1973) "The Influence of Money on Real Income and Inflation: A Simple Model with Some Empirical Tests for the United States 1953-72." Manchester School of Economic and Social Studies 41 (December): 367-95.

———(1974) "The 1974 Report of the President's Council of Economic Advisors: The Control of Inflation and the Future of the International Monetary System." American Economic Review 64 (September): 535-43.

———and PARKIN, M. (1975) "Inflation: A Survey." Economic Journal 85 (December): 741-809.

MASON, W.E. (1958) "The 'New Inflation' and the Middle Class." In Problems of U.S. Economic Development, Vol. 2. New York: Committee for Economic Development.

SELDEN, R. (1975) "Monetary Growth and the Long-Run Rate of Inflation." American Economic Review 65 (May): 125-28.

PART II
EQUITY AND EFFICIENCY
CONSIDERATIONS
AND POLICY-MAKING

Chapter 5

PRICING DEVICES
TO AID THE INVISIBLE HAND

W I L L I A M   J.   B A U M O L
Princeton and New York Universities

INTRODUCTION

Students of Adam Smith are all well aware of his recognition of the imperfections of the market mechanism. Certainly he believed that the market should not be left in complete control of the allocation of resources. For example, he felt it entirely appropriate for government to supply public works which constitute no insignificant component of the nation's output. He even went so far as to argue the need for intervention in cases where there are present what we today call "externalities" (Smith, 1937:308).

Yet, despite Smith's unwillingness to place his stamp of approval upon everything that the market mechanism provides, he never considered it appropriate to appeal to the businessman's conscience to remind him of the "social responsibilities" of the firm. On the contrary, he repeatedly emphasized the untrustworthiness of "merchants and manufacturers" who are always ready to engage in a "conspiracy against the public" (Smith, 1937:128). For one of the basic conclusions of the *Wealth of Nations* is the unreliability of voluntarism as an instrument to secure a desirable allocation of resources. In one of its most famous passages, the book tells us that "It is not from the benevolence of the butcher, the brewer, or the baker, that we expect our dinner, but from their regard of their own interest" (Smith, 1937:14). And in the invisible hand passage the theme is repeated, with Smith telling us that "I have never known much good done by those who affected to trade for the public good" (Smith, 1937:423).

Modern economists have tacitly echoed these ideas and, in at least one way, carried them a step further. The price mechanism—the instrument of the invisible hand—does, it is admitted, have its defects. But the remedy is not to abandon that mechanism or to superimpose other instruments with which it is not readily cross bred. Rather, the obvious thing to do is to use prices themselves as the means to improve the workings of the price mechanism.

Perhaps the most noteworthy exponent of this idea was A. C. Pigou, whose proposal that taxes and subsidies be used to correct the behavior of the generators of detrimental and beneficial externalities represents precisely this sort of approach. It uses a price instrument to correct the imperfect behavior of market prices. Rather than seeking to affect the psyche of the businessman, it seeks to change the entries in his payoff matrix in such a way that when he pursues his own goals he unwittingly and automatically is led—by a strengthened invisible hand—to work toward those of the society, or rather, of the individuals who compose it.

After a brief reexamination of the Pigouvian proposal in light of recent experience, this chapter will describe several attempts by the author to follow in the same direction in other areas. Specifically, it will describe some recent work seeking to use the price mechanism to improve passenger railroad operations. It will examine three candidate procedures that were considered for this purpose, and will seek to evaluate the issues that arise in choosing among them.

EFFLUENT CHARGES IN LIGHT OF RECENT EXPERIENCE

As a dedicated advocate of effluent charges as an effective means to deal with environmental damage, I must concede, reluctantly, that their use no longer seems to me to be as straightforward as I had once imagined. Taxes upon polluters raise issues of distributive equity and political palitability which have often been noted. But their problems go well beyond this.

One of the main arguments of those who advocate effluent charges over a system of direct controls is the contention that the former benefit from the certainty of death and taxes—the fact that taxes are often collected more or less routinely and automatically—while direct controls depend upon the vigilance of the regulatory agency, its ability to catch the polluter who violates the rules, to gather the evidence needed to convict him, to carry the process of prosecution through successfully, and, finally, to get the courts to impose more than token penalties.

Unfortunately, this contrast is an oversimplification. Knowledgeable and sympathetic lawyers assure me that if and when effluent charges legislation is finally passed somewhere in the United States, one can be certain that it will be tied up in the courts for years. Those who are likely to suffer a financial burden as a result can be relied upon to seek relief by every available avenue. And the law provides grounds enough for the purpose. If, for example, the courts do follow Pigou in interpreting effluent charges as *taxes*, it is very likely that they will not permit a regulatory agency to play any role in setting the fees, since that would usurp a legislative perogative. More important, they would very likely reject geographic differences in the levels of these charges based on differences in damage done by equal emissions in different areas, for such differences in tax rates, either from one state to another, or within different areas of any one state, are likely to be considered discriminatory.

These barriers to effective use of effluent charges may be considered artificial—the product of defective human institutions. But there are other problems which arise directly out of the nature of the issue. Having been involved in the months of effort required to draw up a draft statute, I am painfully aware of the extent to which the task is impeded by the imperfection of our knowledge and our analysis. Water is polluted by a vast number of impurities. How many of them should be subjected each to its individual effluent charge? What relative rates should be set for the different pollutants, particularly when some of them are *suspected* of constituting serious threats to health, but for which the evidence is not reasonably conclusive (and, indeed, may never be). What does one do about emissions of agencies of federal, state and local governments, which sometimes spew forth the bulk of our waterways' pollutants?

Perhaps more serious still are the problems of continuous source monitoring. Some types of direct controls share with effluent charges the need for reliable information on the quantities of the different emissions of the individual polluter. After all, we can neither send the polluter his monthly effluent-charges bill nor can we apprehend him for violation of an emissions quota if we do not know how much he is spewing forth. However, it must be emphasized that this is *not* true of all methods of direct control. A law which requires the installation of smokestack scrubbers or the retrofitting of aircraft with sound absorption material can be monitored well enough by occasional checking of the equipment to verify that it is in place and in operating condition. Though this sort of control is anathema to most economists, it is clear that it does escape the need for metering.

This point is important because metering of most pollutants is still an extremely costly, time consuming, and primitive affair. No one has yet invented a meter with an electronic brain that can be attached to the end of the pipe through which the polluter emits effluent into a waterway (indeed, many emitters do not even know how many such pipes they have or where they are located). For example, perhaps the most talked of source of damage to waterways is BOD (biochemical oxygen demand). But to measure this, one must take samples by hand, using elaborate precautions to avoid contamination, and these samples must then be taken to a laboratory to undergo weeks of development and testing before the BOD content of an effluent can be evaluated.

Even noise pollution, for which the monitoring equipment is quick, accurate, and sophisticated suffers from a crucial shortcoming. Unless the noise is produced by a single, well-identified source, this equipment cannot apportion the responsibility for noise among those who generate it. Highways represent the extreme example. Their sounds can be a source of extreme annoyance, but the generators of the sounds are very large in number and extremely mobile, so that it is virtually impossible to track down the screeching motorcycle that passed at 2 a.m., or the loud truck that woke people again a half hour later. The erection of reflecting sound barriers, and the prohibition of particularly noisy retread truck tires, inefficient though they may be, have so far proved more effective means to deal with the matter.

None of this is intended to constitute an appeal to my colleagues to retreat from their predilictions for pricing instruments as the ideal means to strengthen the invisible hand. Rather, it is intended to point out to them at least the outer layer of complexities that can beset the approach, that they may be better prepared to deal with the resulting difficulties. It also is an appeal for further research on the means needed to make the approach work—research on metering techniques, research on practical criteria on which to base reasonable relative prices for different pollutants, research on the pertinent legal issues, and so on. This is one case in which the call for further research is not just a conventional platitude put forth to conceal the absence of substantial ideas. Here we *do* have a very good idea of what information we lack and, therefore, the problems effectively prescribe the sort of research that is required.

A MARKET INSTRUMENT FOR THEATRE SUBVENTION

However, not all market measures give rise to such formidable obstacles. In passing, I offer a brief description of one such measure which is perhaps a bit removed from the economists' usual areas of discussion. The program in question is a market device for the distribution of subsidies to the live performing arts.

This is not a place to discuss the pros and cons of such subvention. Rather, I take it for granted that the community has elected to provide some such funds. The problem is to decide upon their allocation among the many claimants upon these finances.

Virtually any procedure for the allocation of funds to the arts invites some degree of control of the activities of the recipients by the donating agency. Funding agencies, whether they like it or not, are likely to find themselves in the position of arbiters of tastes, both because they tend to provide funds to those applicants whose performance most closely accords with the donor's preferences, and because applicants are apt to modify their activities in ways that they think are likely to prove appealing to major sources of funds. In the process, the preferences of the audiences may be assigned a secondary influence.

There is another problem in this area. Consciencious donors have found the task of apportionment of their funds to be a time consuming and costly process. Particularly when it comes to the hundreds of experimental theaters and the dozens of innovative dance groups, each with its tiny budget, the administrative cost of the ordinary process of allocation is likely to be troublesomely high.

As an alternative, at one point I proposed a program under which the allocation of at least a portion of the funds going to the smaller performing groups would be carried out by the audience itself. This program was subsequently put into practice by the Threatre Development Fund, a nonprofit organization whose purpose is to help the live performing arts. The voucher program, as it is now called, involves the sale of books of tickets to students, union members, and other selected groups. Each such voucher costs one dollar to the purchaser and is useable for admission to any performance by any participating group (subject, of course, to availability of seats). However, when the organization turns its voucher in to the Theatre Development Fund, it receives in return, not the dollar that the attendee paid for it, but $2.50. That is, for every dollar contributed by the audience member, an additional $1.50 is contributed by the foundations which provide finances to the Theatre Development Fund.

The program has so far proved popular among experimental theatre groups, audiences, and others associated with it. Foundations, however, seem to have been reluctant to give up the control of the allocation of their funds to this market mechanism which has succeeded in cutting administrative costs to negligible levels, decreased the foundations' role as arbiters of aesthetic values, and contributed to the influence of the audience over the programming of the performing groups that participate.

Clearly, the aim of the market mechanism is not quite the same as the goals which concern us primarily in this chapter—the modification of the behavior of private enterprise to move it in directions which are preferred by the community. But those who believe in the social responsibility of business usually include financial support of worthy causes among that list of responsibilities. What this program has shown is that market devices can be useful in an administrative role in any such philanthropic program, whether financed by business, by individuals, or by the public sector.

MARKET METHODS TO IMPROVE QUALITY OF SERVICES PURCHASED BY GOVERNMENT

One of the persistent problems besetting governmental use of outputs supplied by the private sector is the control of quality of its purchases. This is a problem which has plagued the defense establishment, the space program, and other branches of government.

But perhaps nowhere was the issue as persistent and acute as in the purchase of passenger transport services from the railroads by Amtrak, a quasi public corporation established by congress to rehabilitate railroad passenger service. As I described in an earlier article on the subject, it is difficult to think of any arrangement better guaranteed to elicit service of the poorest quality than was the initial contract imposed upon Amtrak before it came into existence.

Oversimplifying somewhat, that contract required Amtrak to pay the railroads the avoidable costs of their passenger traffic, a sum which it was obligated to pay no matter how well or how badly the task was carried out. Amtrak's only effective recourse, if service standards deteriorated sufficiently, was to take the railroads to court, suing them for nonperformance of the (vaguely specified) contractual obligations relating to service quality.

Two features of the arrangement bear emphasis: First, the railroads had every incentive to drive passenger traffic away, since they received no share of passenger revenues, and since the payment of essentially no more than avoidable cost meant that in the long run it would pay the railroads to close down as many routes as possible, something they were unlikely to be permitted to do unless they could show that demand along such routes was sufficiently sparse. Second, it should be noted that the arrangement, in effect, amounted to an (essentially noncompensatory) cost-plus contract in which the railroads were literally offered no incentive for avoiding wasteful outlays which could be interpreted to fall into the avoidable-cost category. It is only surprising that under such a contract service did not deteriorate even further then it did.

When the time for renegotiation of the contract arrived, the railroads predictably asked for another cost-plus contract, but one based on "full cost" rather than avoidable cost, i.e., one which included the accountants' allocation of those costs shared with freight operations.

As a consultant to Amtrak, I strongly urged that this demand by the railroads be resisted and that, instead, they be paid only on the basis of performance, on terms under which quality of performance would make the difference between reasonable profits and substantial losses.

This was in fact done, and after about a year of negotiations the bulk of passenger traffic was indeed carried under new contracts in which payments were based heavily on quality of performance. This is not the place to go into the details of the contracts. It is sufficient to note that the performance characteristic emphasized most heavily, indeed, almost to the exclusion of the others, was promptness of arrival. Along each route a fee was fixed for each train arriving on time (within tolerance limits specified by the Interstate Commerce Commission) with a deduction from this total payment based on the amount of time by which late trains were actually delayed.

The reasons for the emphasis on promptness as the criterion of performance are somewhat complicated and not terribly interesting. But it is noteworthy that hindsight confirms the wisdom of this decision, given the fact that Amtrak has gradually taken over responsibility for marketing, operating condition of the cars and engines, cleanliness of the cars, and so on. In short, virtually the only option now in the hands of these railroads is the speed with which it gets the trains to their destination.

It may be noted that the statistics on the first year of operation do seem to confirm that the program of incentives has produced a significant improvement in the promptness of arrivals. We cannot be sure of this since at the same time the new contracts were negotiated there was some change in the scheduling of trains, generally giving them somewhat more time to get to their destinations. Moreover, during the same period, those railroads which had held out against the new incentive contracts also improved their performance on the average, but not by nearly as much as the railroads under incentive contracts.[1]

SOME PRINCIPLES FOR THE DESIGN OF PERFORMANCE INCENTIVES

The central issue I want to discuss in this chapter was brought to my attention very recently when the government of another country approached me about the design of a contract with the same objectives as Amtrak's, but one suited to its own circumstances.

In addition to the differences between the two countries, the ideas of my associates and my own were influenced both by the Amtrak experiences and subsequent reflections on the entire issue.

Three basic principles now seemed clear, though they do not always immediately recommend themselves to those who are directly affected by such an agreement:

(1) Quality of performance is generally a continuum. Twelve minutes late is better than fifteen and eleven is better than twelve. Thus, any "standard" which is set up as a borderline between "acceptable" and "unacceptable" performance is arbitrary and artificial, and can only discourage the supplier from devoting any effort toward out-performance of that standard.

Accordingly, performance payments must form a continuum, payments increasing continuously with quality of performance. There must be no single figure respresenting satisfactory performance which, once achieved, entitles the payee to receive all or even the bulk of the performance compensation.

(2) It is essential that there be a large *difference* between the total payment awarded upon exemplary performance and that receivable when performance is poor. What matters is not so much the level of payment, but the magnitude of its *variation* as quality of performance changes. Ideally, payment for poor performance should be so low that it threatens real financial difficulties for the recipient, while payment for exemplary peformance should offer a very real promise of profitability. This feature of performance incentive programs is comparable to the workings of a competitive market with its high profits for those firms that serve buyers efficiently and effectively, and the losses of firms that fail to do so.

(3) An effective incentive program must provide significant rewards for economy and efficiency. One promising way to go about this is by analogy with the Schumpeterian process of profits to innovation. In the short run, payments should be fixed on the basis of costs in the recent past with, presumably, some adjustment for inflation. Thus, the supplier who manages to cut costs below those of the recent past retains the savings as a reward to himself. However, the schedule of payments to the supplier should be reviewed at intervals (it is probably best for these intervals to be somewhat irregular and unpredictable). At such a review the payments should be modified to reflect any cost reductions which had been achieved in the interim. Thus, from this point on the supplier would no longer benefit from any savings he had achieved during the previous interreview period of (say) three or four years, and he would be forced to look for new sources of economy in order to preserve the flow of profits from this source.

SOME BASIC CHOICES

Even when these three principles are agreed upon, crucial general choices about the structure of the incentive payment program must be made. The basic issue is the choice of objective function—the criterion of good performance upon which performance payments are to be based.

The issue is illustrated by the case of the Amtrak contract, in which, as had been noted, promptness of arrival was the key index of peformance quality. As a matter of fact, it was not the only feature taken into account. In the initial incentive contract less-powerful incentives were provided for several other features of performance, among them, schedule improvement, serviceability of locomotives and cleanliness of cars. The last of these illustrates a basic difficulty. Just how does one measure the cleanliness of a car? In the Amtrak case the problem was dealt with by promulgating elaborate instructions running over many pages, specifying exactly what had to be done during the cleaning process. The lavatory cleaning instructions alone constituted a lengthy piece of reading. Inspectors were then given the power to certify whether or not a particular car had or had not been cleaned acceptably, making it eligible for compensation payment. Railroads were then given the right to appeal the decisions of the inspectors. The shortcomings of this arrangement are too obvious to require discussion.

In the more recent consultations the same issues raised themselves immediately, with at least some members of the government agencies to which we were reporting initally inclined to use a detailed list of performance criteria which, as in the Amtrak case, would serve as the basis for a schedule of payments.

We did indeed consider such a list of performance criteria as one possible organizing principle for the arrangement. But we also examined two other possibilities. One was a payment based on the absolute number of passenger miles the railroads were able to attract in any given year. Our third and last candidate criterion was the percentage *rate of growth* in number of passenger miles. Let me discuss each of these criteria briefly.

A COMPENDIUM OF PERFORMANCE CRITERIA

Both the government agency and the railroads had a number of reasons which, at least initially, predisposed them toward the explicit list of performance criteria. First, under a system of rewards based on increased promptness, better control of interior temperatures, smoother ride, and so forth. Everyone knows just what has to be done. The problems are "technocratic" in character—the natural province of engineers and designers of timetables. By contrast, no one is quite sure what measures, if any, will succeed in attracting more riders.

Another way of looking at the issue is to note that a multivariate list of criteria instantly signals particular trouble spots and suggests what can be done about them.

The problem of constructing direct quantitative measures of attributes such as car cleanliness, smoothness of ride, politeness of personnel and so on, need not be an overwhelming obstacle. The problem can be solved by a continuing survey of passengers carefully designed and carried out. Month to month variations in number of customer complaints or in some other customer rating that is agreed upon can easily serve as the required quantitative measure.

The basic difficulty besetting the multiple-criteria approach, then, is not unworkability. Rather, it is a matter of relevance and relative importance of the criteria selected. Just how much weight should be given to smoothness of ride vis-a-vis cleanliness in the reward system? Is this a matter for arbitrary choice, or is this, too, to be based on relative number of customer complaints?

Moreover, if it turns out that smoother rides and politer personnel make the old customer of the railroads happier, but attract few additional riders, has any improvement in these areas really served its basic purpose?

PAYMENTS BASED ON RIDERSHIP

It would seem that the logical candidate for a univariate payment criterion is number of passenger miles or some other measure of ridership. After all, that is the ultimate objective of the program. However, the complexities of the real world plague even such an obvious choice.

The first source of difficulty is that, for political as well as other reasons, it is the desire of government to prevent abandonment or even substantial deterioration of service quality on some routes that are very sparsely traveled, either in order to prevent the acquisition of monopoly power by other means of transport, or for fear of effective isolation of particular communities where there is always strong pressure for continuation of service. Unless special payment arrangements are set up for such routes, any incentive program based on ridership alone is likely to accelerate the railroad's attempts to remove its resources from these sparse routes.

Second, in a declining industry, any attempt to base rewards on actual sales volume is likely to induce panic among suppliers who are likely to have little confidence in the opportunities for expansion of their market. This may not be the best of psychological circumstances under which to launch an incentive program.

As an alternative, it was therefore proposed that the parties consider a system of payments based not on *number* of passenger miles, but on *changes* in its rate of growth. Specifically, it was proposed that if the decline in number of passenger miles were reduced to, say, 2 percent per annum from a previous rate of fall of, say, 5 percent, this should be considered an achievement that merits an increase in payment. The objective of this approach is a double one: first, to reward improvement from whatever the initial circumstances happen to be, and second, to prevent the recipients from resting on their laurels, since repeated incentive payments would be made conditional upon repeated *improvements*.

There is, however, a danger in this proposal. It may, indeed, make things easier for the supplier at the inception of the program. Starting out with a poor record of performance it may be easy enough to achieve improvements, at first. But if, as is to be hoped, performance grows more and more meritorious, successive improvements may become more and more difficult to achieve. Increasing costs of further improvement may then ultimately emasculate the program.

Obviously, combinations of our three approaches suggest themselves. For example, there may be advantages to starting the program off with payments based on rate of growth and then, after a prespecified period, switching over to an arrangement based on absolute volume of sales.

The objective here is not to conclude that some one approach is preferable to the others. Rather, the goal is to illustrate the issues that complicate any such approach in reality.

CONCLUDING COMMENT

Despite all the complications drawn to the reader's attention in this chapter, it must be emphasized that I remain a confirmed supporter of pricing devices as a means to strengthen the invisible hand. The catalogue of shortcomings of direct controls and other standard instruments of regulation is long and impressive.

But we economists must remember that the ideal pricing mechanisms which populate our theoretical models must undergo modification and encounter new difficulties when they enter into the world of reality. By preparing themselves for the resulting problems economists can become more effective advocates of the pricing approaches. More important, they can make themselves more useful in the demanding task of translation of the theoretical concepts into usable and acceptable measures for practical policy.

NOTE

1. Between 1973 and 1975 on time performance improved, on the average from about 60 to 75 percent for those railroads on Amtrak contracts *without* incentive contracts in both years. For the railroads *with* incentive contracts the average number of arrivals on time rose from 60 to about 90 percent of the total trips.

REFERENCE

SMITH, A. (1937) An Inquiry into the Nature and Causes of the Wealth of Nations, edited by Edwin Cannan. New York: The Modern Library (Reprint of 5th edition dated 1789).

Chapter 6

A STUDY IN CONFLICTING GOALS:
FEDERAL STABILIZATION AND
MORTGAGE MARKET POLICIES

H E R B E R T   M.   K A U F M A N
Arizona State University

I. INTRODUCTION

The disproportionate impact of monetary policy on housing is a well known and thoroughly discussed problem in stabilization policy. The prominence of the housing sector as a focal point of governmental policy is also well documented, encompassing as it does various programs to provide direct assistance to the housing and mortgage market and indirect assistance through programs that support the private institutions that are primarily involved in the mortgage market. The regulatory framework associated directly and indirectly with the mortgage market and mortgage market institutions is also elaborate. In discussing the conflict between one form of governmental regulation, FHA-VA mortgage interest rate ceilings and state usury ceilings, Dwight Jaffee puts the problem succinctly. He says: "It is a classic case in which one form of government intervention—ceilings—invites further intervention—mortgage support —in a lengthening chain of inefficiency" (1976:174).

In this quotation, Jaffee is referring to the further intervention of the federal mortgage market agencies, but it also summarizes very well the problem in a much broader context. For example, the fact that monetary policy disproportionately impacts upon housing, increases the need for agencies that attempt to insulate housing from the effect of tight monetary policy. At the same time, if monetary policy did not impact on housing so significantly, it follows that monetary policy would have to be more severe than is presently required to restrict expansion in the economy. Moreover, these factors are interrelated. The existence of Regulation Q interest rate ceilings is partly responsible for the disproportionate impact

AUTHOR'S NOTE: I shall always be grateful to Will Mason for the intellectual stimulation provided by his teaching, research, and example, and for his encouragement. I would like to thank Michael Greenwood for very helful comments on an earlier draft.

of monetary policy, because of the reduction in traditional mortgage lender liabilities through disintermediation during periods of rising open market interest rates.

James Pierce and Mary Ann Graves are among those concerned with the affect of monetary policy on housing. They agree, however, that monetary policy would have to be more severe if it did not affect housing to the degree it does. To test this proposition the FRB-MIT model is used to simulate a situation in which the housing sector has been successfully insulated from the effects of tight monetary policy. Pierce and Graves conclude that: "With a stabilized housing sector, substantially larger variations in monetary policy would have been required to achieve the control path of nominal GNP" (1972:343). Further they state that "it seems clear that stabilizing housing would substantially increase the burdens placed on general monetary policy and would reduce its reliability" (1972:344).[1]

Related to the Pierce and Graves result, Jaffee raises an important point. "Moreover, a stronger monetary policy would lead to more claims for protection from the unprotected sectors, and leave us either without a monetary tool or right back where it started from. Countering this, however, is the proposition that without the constraint of the housing sector, the Federal Reserve could carry out monetary policy in a more flexible and effective manner" (1976:164).

Therefore, a number of issues need to be addressed in this chapter. Clearly, to the extent that monetary policy, and to a lesser degree government regulatory policy, brings about the need for federal mortgage market agency activity, there is a conflict in governmental policy. What are the chances of the mortgage market agencies succeeding in insulating the housing market? If they do succeed, what does this imply for monetary policy? Further, can monetary policy be conducted in such a way as to minimize the conflict with the housing goals of the economy without risking its position as an effective stabilization device? The conflict between the goals of the regulatory framework that has been established and its effectiveness also needs examination. A new and important issue has been introduced recently into the debate. To what extent should agencies designed to provide assistance to housing in general also attempt to put into place other more specific housing goals of the government, namely aid to urban and moderate income housing? That is, can both types of goals be achieved simultaneously? (See for example, Proxmire and Cranston, 1977.) The discussion of these issues will be the focus of this chapter.

The chapter is organized as follows. Section II provides some background on the federal mortgage market agencies and the mortgage market. Section III contains a discussion of whether agencies actually do insulate the mortgage market, and the conflict with monetary policy is explored in more detail. Section IV is concerned with the regulatory environment as it relates to housing, monetary policy and the agencies. In section V the new discussion of the social responsibility of the agencies in helping particular categories of housing is addressed, and the question of whether the agencies can assist housing in general and specific housing sectors is evaluated. Finally in section VI, conclusions are drawn and recommendations are made.

II. SOME BACKGROUND ON
FEDERAL MORTGAGE AGENCIES
AND THE MORTGAGE MARKET

The primary federally sponsored agencies designed to assist the mortgage market are the Federal Home Loan Bank System (FHLB), the Federal National Mortgage Association (FNMA), and the Federal Home Loan Mortgage Corporation (FHLMC). FNMA and FHLMC are expected to accomplish their assistance function by buying mortgages in the secondary market, with FNMA buying primarily from mortgage bankers[2] and FHLMC buying primarily from savings and loan associations. As of the end of 1976, FNMA's mortgage holdings stood at $32.9 billion while FHLMC, a much newer and smaller agency, had holdings of $4.2 billion.[3] The Federal Home Loan Bank System on the other hand provides its assistance indirectly by making loans, called advances, to savings and loan associations which in turn are expected to use the proceeds of the loans to make mortgage loans.[4]

All the assistance activity provided by these agencies must be financed in the open market. The extent of this financing, therefore, is quite large. For example, by year end 1976 FNMA had debt outstanding of $30.6 billion. In one recent year, before the extraordinary federal budget deficits of the last few years, FNMA and the FHLB raised almost as much as the Treasury in new money (1974—13 billion dollars vs. 17 billion dollars for the Treasury) in the open market. In fact, FNMA has grown so significantly in the past decade that it is now the second largest borrower in the financial markets after the Treasury.[5]

The stabilization function of the federal mortgage market agencies is also rather narrowly defined. Their purpose is to assist housing. In this regard, the conduct of their stabilization function is basically nonsymmetrical. Although they are often thought of as moderating the credit cycle in the mortgage market, they almost never do anything purposefully to counter housing and mortgage market booms,[6] while they become very active during housing and mortgage market downturns.[7]

The common thread that runs through all agency assistance activity is that by affecting credit the agencies will affect housing. The traditional mortgage lending institutions are the beneficiaries of the assistance. Savings and loan associations are the largest of the mortgage lending institutions. They are final mortgage investors. This means that they hold mortgages in their portfolios for long-term investment, and in fact, mortgages constitute by far the largest part of their portfolio. The activity of both the FHLB and the FHLMC are designed to assist these institutions.[8] Commercial banks, mutual savings banks, and to a much lesser extent, life insurance companies are also significant mortgage investors. There is also nondepository source of mortgage financing in the market provided by the mortgage bankers, who act as brokers between mortgage borrowers and final mortgage investors. Since they are not permanent holders of mortgages, they must find sales outlets for the mortgages they originate, and one of the prime outlets, especially during periods of stringency in the market, is FNMA. They are that agency's biggest customers.

The proposition that by influencing mortgage credit housing will be assisted, is based upon considerable amounts of research, both formal and informal, over at least fifty years. However, there is one prominent demurral from this conclusion. Allan Meltzer (1970, Arcelus and Meltzer, 1973) argues that credit conditions do not affect the mortgage market to an important extent and, therefore, one must look at the "real" variables. However, Meltzer's argument has not convinced a large body of researchers in this area[9] and certainly not the policy makers.

In addition, there is a related argument concerning the effectiveness of these agencies. Since the federal agencies influence credit and credit is fungible, it does not mean that credit assistance provided by the agencies will convert into mortgage or housing market assistance. This argument becomes particularly telling when one examines those institutions with portfolio flexibility, such as commercial banks and mutual savings banks. To the extent that credit assistance does not convert into additional mortgages and housing, the objective of the policy is not attained. As with the first argument, certainly the agencies behave as if this were not true. Agency effectiveness will be discussed more formally below.

The housing agencies were created for the express purpose of moderating the cycle that exists in housing. However, to the extent that the implementation of monetary policy serves to exacerbate that cycle, one arm of the federal government is causing part of the problem that another arm is expected to correct. We now turn to a more detailed examination of this issue.

III. MONETARY POLICY, THE FEDERAL AGENCIES, AND THE MORTGAGE MARKET

Warren Smith has stated:

> Under the present system, the largest and fastest impact of monetary policy is on residential construction, and this impact is to a considerable extent attributable to changes in mortgage credit availability. If the availability effects on housing were eliminated, monetary policy would, I am convinced, be significantly weakened. It would take larger monetary policy actions and larger swings in interest rates to produce a given effect, and the lags of response would become longer (1970:101).

This quotation succinctly reflects the prevailing view, though it is not unanimous, on the importance of fluctuations in the mortgage market and housing for the ability of the Federal Reserve to conduct effective countercyclical monetary policy. Yet starting in the 1930s the federal government has played an increasing role in attempting to alleviate the impact of particularly stringent credit on the housing and mortgage market.[10] In the last fifteen years or so this activity has taken the form of the maturing of the federal agencies, as well as the implementation of various subsidized housing programs. Although the latter were not designed to be primarily countercyclical, they have some countercyclical characteristics that arise from the way in which they have been implemented. President Johnson in 1968 even stated a housing goal, which was incorporated into the 1968 Housing and Urban Development Act, of twenty-six million new or significantly rehabilitated housing units for the following ten years.[11] To understand this paradox in policy, it must first be realized that different forces are at work on federal policy.

Monetary policy is conducted with the stabilization of the whole economy in mind. The outlook is broad macroeconomic stabilization without too much attention paid to the channels through which this stabilization function takes place. That the Fed is not, however, unaware of the differential impact of monetary policy on housing is clear from the research that has been undertaken under its auspices in recent years. Some of this research resulted in a large compendium of papers published by the Fed in 1972 entitled *Ways to Moderate Fluctuations in Housing Construction*, which was developed in response to congressional requests for study of the problem.

It is also important to recognize that policy conflicts are not symmetrical over the credit cycle. During periods of relatively easy credit the housing sector and policy do not conflict. Housing is usually relied upon to be one of the main sustaining devices in a recovery. In fact, in the recovery from the 1974-1975 recession, it would not be too much to say that the buoyant housing sector has been the crucial element in the robustness of the recovery. For example, housing starts reached about two million units in 1977. This housing expansion has been credited with taking up the slack from relatively weak recovery in the capital spending sector.

But in periods of credit stringency, it is clear that housing suffers a great deal, and bears a disproportionate burden of the decline in economic activity. The periods that are most prominent in recent years are 1966,[12] 1969-1970, and 1973-1974 when housing went literally into a tail spin when tight money became effective. Figure 6.1 presents housing starts quarterly from first quarter 1966 through second quarter 1977. It is clear that the association is very close between periods of tight money and (with some lag) the decline in the fortunes of the housing industry. It is also clear that particularly since 1968, when the mortgage market agencies were allowed much more latitude in their activities, the existence of vigorous activity on the part of the federal mortgage market agencies has not appeared to cushion very substantially the fall off in housing activity.[13] However, things may have been much worse without them. The question is, therefore, have the agencies been effective in providing the assistance to housing that they were expected to? Further what does it mean for stabilization policy if they are more effective in the future in actually cushioning the impact of monetary policy on housing?

The importance of housing to the American public as well as to powerful special interest groups resulted in pressure being exerted on our legislative and executive branches to insure adequate housing for the population. Federal Housing Administration and later Veteran Administration mortgage guarantees were an early manifestation of this concern. The development of the FHLB and the precursors of the modern FNMA[14] were products of the great depression when massive foreclosures on residential property led to human suffering and the intensification of the economic slump. The conflict between housing assistance legislation and accompanying agency development and monetary policy was only slowly recognized, and did nothing to slow the development of the agencies. In fact, it intensified this development. In the 1960s this concern for housing resulted in the subsidy programs which stemmed from President Johnson's "Great Society" programs of the latter 1960s. It also resulted in releasing the agencies from the confines of the federal budget in 1968 so they would be freer to pursue their stabilization function in the housing market. They had been severely restricted in what they could do in 1966 because their operation added to the federal deficit.

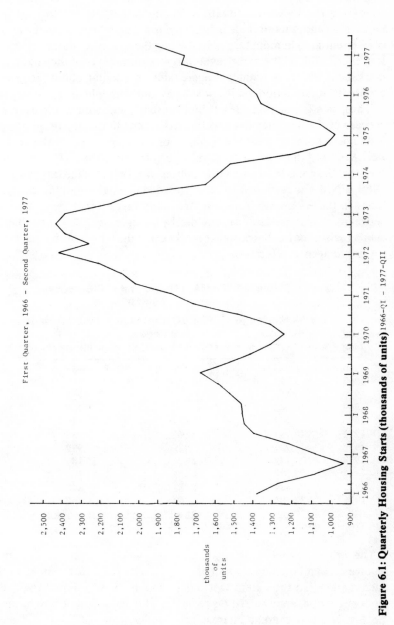

First Quarter, 1966 – Second Quarter, 1977

Figure 6.1: Quarterly Housing Starts (thousands of units) 1966-QI – 1977-QII

135

The conflict that arises, therefore, between the two goals of economic stabilization and the stabilization of housing can be seen clearly by pondering the following situation. Suppose that the housing cycle is moderated and, therefore, is insulated during downturns from the effects of differential tight monetary policy. Then the monetary authority will be less successful, at the same level of restraint, indexed either by money market conditions or monetary aggregates, in bringing about the general economic stabilization goal it wishes to and with which it is charged.

Thus, one factor that the conflict presently turns on is the degree of success of the agencies in providing assistance to the mortgage market. Table 6.1 shows by year the holdings of mortgages by FNMA and the FHLMC, and the level of outstanding advances by the FHLB. It can be seen that the gross levels are fairly impressive. In fact in the last quarter of 1969, FNMA is reckoned to have provided one half of all the mortgage funds in the economy. Yet there are many factors that may intervene between the gross assistance provided by the agencies and the net impact of this assistance on the mortgage market, and thus the table by itself does not prove agency effectiveness.

Table 6.1: FNMA, FHLMC and FHLB Activity
(Annual 1966-1976)

Year	FNMA Mortgage Holdings (millions of dollars)	FHLMC Mortgage Holdings (millions of dollars)	FHLB Advances (millions of dollars)
1966	4,396		6,934
1967	5,522		4,386
1968	7,167		5,259
1969	10,945		9,289
1970	15,492	325*	10,615
1971	17,791	968	7,936
1972	19,791	1,789	7,979
1973	24,175	2,604	15,147
1974	29,578	4,586	21,804
1975	31,824	4,987	17,845
1976	32,904	4,269	15,862

*Note: 1970 was the first year in which FHLMC operated.

The critical problem in evaluating the level of agency assistance revolves around the fact that all agency activity must be financed in the open market. To the extent that this financing raises interest rates, the gross effect of agency activity is reduced. This reduction occurs because the higher open market interest rates induce an outflow of interest sensitive funds from traditional mortgage originating institutions (disintermediation), and to the extent that this outflow occurs the agency assistance merely replaces the funds that have been removed from the mortgage market due to agency activity.

Leo Grebler has pointed out that measuring the induced outflow from traditional mortgage lenders requires rather detailed empirical analysis: "Ideally, an estimate of the diversion of savings deposits to Federal agency issues would be based upon data on cross elasticities of household demand for financial assets, together with some knowledge of the income and wealth effects of additional residential construction financed with mortgage loans made from the proceeds of security issues" (1972:229). Without having the information that he indicates is necessary, Grebler makes various assumptions and certain calculations and concludes that, "the net contribution of FNMA and the FHLB System to the residential mortgage market in the two crucial years 1966 and 1969 was about 80 percent of these two organizations' gross contribution" (1972:186).[15]

Dealing with the FHLB and using computer simulations, Craig Swan (1976:225), has drawn somewhat different conclusions: "The simulation results discussed above suggest that a one-time $1 billion expansionary FHLB action will increase residential construction in the first four quarters by $300 to $600 million."[16] Swan also discusses whether there is any permanent effect on housing from agency activity and states that even if the effect is not permanent, "it may still be that FHLB actions have important short-run timing impacts on the flow of new housing units over time" (1976:224).

Even though the net assistance provided by agencies cannot be determined precisely, the data presented in Figure 6.1 clearly indicates that it has not been sufficient to modify substantially and certainly not to eliminate housing downturns. Thus, the question of what would of necessity happen to Federal Reserve policy if the agencies could counteract the impact of tight monetary policy has been moot. Yet as the discussion in the introduction to this chapter has shown, the concensus is that monetary policy would have to be more severe if the housing sector is truly insulated from the effects of credit restraint. As Jaffee (1976) has pointed out, this would no doubt mean differential impacts of more severe magnitudes on other sectors of the economy. Perhaps if these sectors are viewed as important enough, the cries for special help would no doubt materialize for these other impacted areas. Thus, a new conflict would develop in governmental policy. And as Kane (1977) has discussed, the intervention in the market by government is costly to society.

Moreover, it has often been argued that since housing is a postponable consumer durable, differentially impacting upon housing is more desirable than severely affecting other sectors instead. This argument has clearly not been reflected in the view that has had prominence in the federal government programs and has led to the rise of the agencies.

In addition, certain regulations like Regulation Q and usury ceilings which have impinged on housing, sometimes in a way contrary to that intended, lead to additional conflicts in goals. We now turn to an examination of regulatory conflict.[17]

IV. REGULATORY CONFLICT

The major regulations that have been designed and implemented over time to help the mortgage market (by aiding the institutions and consumers that compose it) are Regulation Q ceilings on time and savings deposits, FHA-VA mortgage interest rate ceilings, and state usury ceilings on mortgage interest rates. The question that we take up in this section is how effective have these regulations been in accomplishing what they were designed to do. Examples can be used to illustrate that they may have been counterproductive. State usury ceilings may not help the consumer if mortgage rates are kept artificially low, making it very difficult (or impossible) for the consumer to get a mortgage loan. Regulation Q ceilings may prevent thrift institutions from raising time deposit rates sufficiently to attract or keep funds necessary to make additional mortgage loans in periods of high open market interest rates, despite a rate advantage over commercial banks. The effectiveness and the conflicts with other goals of these regulations will be discussed in this section.

The original rationale behind Regulation Q ceilings (which are under the control of the Fed) was to prevent undue competition between commercial banks for time deposits. It was feared that such competition would result in unsound lending practices. There was also something of a populist notion inherent in this, i.e., if you hold down the cost of the inputs, you can hold down the cost of the output and so have lower interest rates. The extension of these ceilings to the savings and loan and mutual savings bank industries in 1966, through agreement with the various governing bodies,[18] provided at the same time a differential in the ceilings between these institutions and commercial banks. This was done to ensure that commercial banks, with their substantial advantage in asset flexibility, could not simply outbid thrift institutions for deposits. When the advantage of commercial banks in asset flexibility was combined with the advantage of banks as "full service" institutions, the reasoning behind the differential was believed to be compelling.

Most economists do not find the notion of deposit ceilings attractive or useful. The Hunt commission report (Report of the President's Commission on Financial Structure and Regulation, 1971), a comprehensive study of our financial institutions, recommended the abolition of these ceilings over time, although coupling this recommendation with increased asset flexibility for the thrifts. Other federally sponsored studies have reached similar conclusions. Despite these recommendations, however, the removal of these ceilings has not taken place because of the opposition of special interest groups.

Dwight Jaffee has succintly brought into focus the notion of this kind of regulatory interference on the part of government and its connection with mortgage agency activity. He states that, "Deposit rate ceilings . . . create disequilibrium, and this provides grounds for government support of affected markets. But, the conclusion on usury ceilings holds equally for deposit ceilings—government support of deposit markets is a 'second best' solution compared to simply removing the ceiling" (1976:182). While most economists would probably agree with this assessment, the industry clearly does not. They have thus far lobbied successfully in Congress to prevent the removal of these ceilings, even if coupled with increases in asset flexibility.

Kenneth Thygerson perhaps states the industry case most clearly when he argues, "this analysis suggests that if the institutions were given this increased freedom (more portfolio flexibility) . . . at the same time they lose their Regulation Q advantage they would still be at a competitive disadvantage" (1973:115, parenthesis added). However, there is little evidence of what the competitive position of these institutions would be in such a new environment. Even the evidence of the impact of Regulation Q ceilings on the competitive position of these institutions in the current environment is sketchy. Therefore, it is not clear that the existence of Regulation Q ceilings as a whole enhance the competitive ability of thrift institutions to attract funds in periods of credit stringency. Thygerson is arguing against removing the differential ceilings on savings deposits at thrifts and at commercial banks. However, if ceilings were removed entirely there is no evidence to suggest that thrift institutions and hence the mortgage market, will be worse off, especially with additional asset and liability flexibility for thrifts to counter the "full service" advantage of banks.

Although not made as part of the industry case, it seems likely that the S&Ls also do not want the ceilings removed because many of the depositors at these institutions are small savers unable to take advantage of the higher open market rates in periods of tightness. In this regard, both Edward Kane (1976) and Robert Lindsay (1970) among others, have pointed out that the imposition of ceilings conflicts with what at least ought to be a goal of public policy. This is the consideration of equity. The small saver who cannot take advantage of the higher rates that exist in the open market during periods when disintermediation becomes a problem is discriminated against. Because of the large denominations of most open market securities, transactions costs, and the lack of information, the small saver accepts the lower rate on thrift deposits. This is hard to justify when the evidence is unclear on the harm that would befall the mortgage market if ceilings were removed. In addition, it has led to the development of such resource using innovations as money market mutual funds to attempt to circumvent the effect of this regulation.

There are other important regulations that affect the mortgage market as well. These are usury ceilings imposed by states, and FHA-VA interest and loan amount ceilings. These regulations are clearly in conflict with the desire to help the mortgage market and housing. They are even in conflict with the intent of the laws that put them into place, i.e., the desire to aid the housing consumer.

Usury ceilings were designed so that borrowers would not be "over charged" on their mortgage borrowing. Of course this means that during periods of high open market rates, those financial institutions with portfolio flexibility, commercial banks and mutual savings banks, leave the mortgage market, thus exacerbating the problem arising from disintermediation.[19] For some potential mortgage borrowers willing to pay higher mortgage rates if they could obtain the mortgage, the funds are simply not available.

In a recent study of the effect of usury ceilings on the mortgage market, James Ostes concludes:

> Legal restrictions on contract interest rates resulted in noninterest rationing of borrowers through (1) the requiring of higher loan fees, (2) the requiring of higher downpayments, and (3) the requiring of shorter loan maturities. Moreover, it was concluded that contract interest rate restrictions reduced the incentive of lenders to make mortgage loans, with loan volume being reduced and new construction concommitantly curtailed.

> Policy recommendations follow easily from the study's conclusions. One obvious policy solution to the problems arising from rate regulations is simply to rescind the rate regulations (1976:831).

The ceilings on FHA-VA mortgages are another intrusion into the workings of the mortgage market. By keeping these ceilings artificially below the actual market rate, the private sector is forced to make adjustments that are not necessarily in the long-run interest of the mortgage market. Additional mortgage charges (points) are a common way for institutions to compensate for a ceiling rate that is out of line. For a whole host of reasons, not just the ceilings, the largest mortgage lenders, savings and loan associations, have traditionally shied away from making government insured loans. Furthermore, the interest rate ceilings are coupled with a maximum on mortgage size. This has further stifled some home mortgage lending and the associated home building that would have taken place. In fact, with the recent existence of private mortgage insurance which imposes no such ceilings, conventional mortgage lending, as opposed to government insured mortgage lending, has become more and more dominant in the market. When the history behind the establishment of the FHA is taken into account and its goal of helping people get and keep homes is recognized, the imposition of these types of constraints appears thoroughly counterproductive. Further, any short-fall in mortgage lending that results calls for additional government action through agency activity.

All of these policies taken together have appeared to interfere with the efficiency of the mortgage market, and have clearly contributed to an intensification of the housing-mortgage credit cycle. Thus, their existence has necessitated the creation of additional governmental intercession in the market in the form of the increased mortgage market agency activity. Once again, we find a case of government policies in conflict.

V. HOUSING POLICY CONFLICTS

Certain events dramatically illustrating the conflicting goals of federal policy related to mortgage market agencies have recently taken place. On April 27, 1977, Senator William Proxmire, Chairman of the Senate Committee on Banking, Housing and Urban Affairs, introduced a bill for himself and Senator Cranston designed to amend the Federal National Mortgage Association Charter (Proxmire and Cranston, 1977). The impetus for the bill came from the Senators' belief that FNMA has not fulfilled or been sensitive to the needs of the urban housing market. Rather, it has been too concerned with its own profitability in its purchase of mortgage loans. Patricia Harris, Secretary of HUD, appears to feel much the same way. On February 24, 1978, the Wall Street Journal reported that HUD has promulgated new regulations which it plans to put into place to ensure that at least 30 percent of FNMAs mortgage purchases be made in central city areas, and at least 30 percent of its purchases be for low and moderate income-family housing.[20]

While the status of the Proxmire-Cranston bill is still uncertain, extensive hearings on the proposal before the Senate Committee on

Banking, Housing, and Urban Affairs under the Chairmanship of William Proxmire were held on July 7 and 8, 1977. Further, the HUD proposals are being put forward for public response and have not yet been implemented at this writing. However, it is clear from this activity that another important element has entered into federal housing policy as it relates to the agencies, in this case specifically FNMA, but also the FHLMC.

The freeing of the agencies from the federal budget in 1968 and the removal of the special assistance function from FNMA, and its transference to the newly created Government National Mortgage Association (GNMA) was done so that FNMA could, unencumbered by the size of the federal deficit, more fully concentrate on the stabilization of the mortgage market by further development of its secondary market facility. The introduction of a special assistance function for FNMA will alter its operations.

However, it is not at all clear that FNMA has been remiss, within the context of its operation, in specifically carrying out socially motivated activity. Warren Farb and Douglas Bendt (1976), in a background paper prepared for the Proxmire committee, have pointed out the important role that FNMA has played in providing a secondary market for HUD subsidized programs in the past. These included HUD programs 235, 236 and 221 (d)(3).[21] Farb and Bendt have shown that FNMA has accounted for as much as two-thirds of these mortgages since the inception of the programs. By doing so they say "FNMA has helped establish a high degree of acceptability for these mortgages in the secondary market by its willingness to buy a large proportion of these mortgages" (1976:55). Thus, the debate really comes down to whether FNMA should go further than it has.

It is clear that Senate Proxmire and Secretary Harris believe that it should go further, and in late 1977 and early 1978 there was a running battle with FNMA management over this issue. The battle is still being waged as this chapter is being written, although it is in a quiescent state, with the outcome uncertain. It is clear, however, that the more explicit directive to FNMA to support moderate and low income housing, will give FNMA less flexibility in conducting its secondary market facility. The question reduces to one between the narrow stabilization function FNMA has and the even more explicit allocation of credit which permeates many governmental programs.

There are, however, other factors that have also served to provoke the current controversy and that have figured in the debate in an important way. These are perhaps even more fundamental to FNMA's original purpose. One such factor concerns the way in which FNMA has interpreted its stabilization function. FNMA has been loath to sell mortgages during periods of credit ease, concentrating only on supplying funds to the mortgage market. That is, it has not sufficiently recognized the fact that the mortgage cycle has some symmetry and that perhaps by selling more aggressively during periods of ease, it could remove some of the speculative excesses that inevitably lead to further problems when the market tightens. This charge is clearly supportable, although Farb and Bendt attempt to argue against it. They believe that FNMA has tried to offset the speculative excesses in the mortgage credit cycle. However, the evidence they cite is unconvincing: "Even though FNMA sales mortgages have never exceeded $775 million annually since 1961, and are often at or near zero, they are greatest during periods of relative credit ease" (Farb and Bendt, 1976:43). Yet their own figures show that FNMA sales have amounted to only $643 million since the association became a private corporation in 1968. This compares to a portfolio of mortgages that is currently around $38 billion. Clearly, FNMA has not been aggressive in its sales program.[22]

Henry Schecter, a housing economist with the AFL-CIO, in testifying at the Proxmire hearings, made an additional point concerning FNMA's aggressiveness even during periods of credit stringency. He argued that:

> If FNMA had at various times pursued a more aggressive policy to nudge mortgage interest rates down faster, it would have given greater support to the moderate priced segment of the housing market. It would have helped more than it did to achieve the national housing goals. They could have followed such a policy in 1976, when private mortgage lenders had an excess of mortgage funds, but were slow in lowering mortgage rates. If FNMA had done so, probably they wouldn't have achieved as high a rate of return.

> FNMA still constitutes a public-private partnership. There is a question of how the benefits are to be divided between stockholders' interests and the public interest, in light of the charter act and accompanying privileges that were bestowed on the private stockholders by the Congress (Committee on Banking, Housing and Urban Affairs, 1977:72).

Thus, Schecter appears to be arguing for an even more aggressive purchase program during periods of credit ease in order to achieve the social goal of more moderate income housing. The difficulty in which FNMA finds itself in is clear.[23]

Moreover, in all fairness to FNMA, research has not demonstrated that profit has been the overriding consideration in FNMA's activity, although FNMA has clearly been profitable. Kenneth Rosen (1977) has argued that in modeling FNMA policy reaction functions, the inclusion in the policy reaction functions of well established goals for FNMA, like housing starts, add considerably to profitability as an explanation of FNMA behavior. In my own work (Kaufman, 1977), it is clear that FNMA does respond to the needs of the mortgage market, and does not emphasize profit.

Therefore, the arguments over FNMA's role and its implementation of its charge highlights once again the difficulties inherent in conflicting goals in policy formulation, in this case between helping housing in general and aiding specific sectors of the housing market. Where this particular conflict will be resolved is still to be determined.

VI. CONCLUSIONS AND RECOMMENDATIONS

The discussion in this chapter has focused on the inherent conflicts between federal government policies designed to assist the housing market in general and overall economic policy, regulation, and special assistance. It is clear by now that in many cases the existence of one policy to fulfill one goal brings about the need for other policies to fulfill other goals. It is of course not a situation that can be simplistically remedied by doing away with all government policy, although at times this appears to be the most attractive alternative.

Rather what appears to be called for is the cessation of needless intervention via regulation, and perhaps the realization that all goals are simply not obtainable simultaneously. There appears among most economists a consensus that such requirements as Regulation Q ceilings, usury ceilings, as well as the ceilings on FHA-VA mortgages, have outlived whatever usefulness they may have once had. Just eliminating these should restore some efficiency to the credit markets in general and to the mortgage market in particular.

The likelihood that monetary policy can be designed so as to mitigate its heavy impact on the mortgage market appears doubtful.[24] Some would argue, as the Smith quote above shows, that if monetary policy did not differentially affect housing, it would need to be even more stringent. Allan Meltzer has even gone further arguing that it is quite appropriate that housing be affected differentially so that other sectors need not be. He argues:

> The housing industry is relatively labor-intensive and has a relatively low rate of productivity increase. Given the very large adjustments that *mistaken* public policies—fiscal and monetary—force on the private sector from time to time, it is hard to think of another industry that can release so many skilled workers at such low social costs (1970:51, emphasis added).

He is arguing that in an expansion, housing should bear the burden of restrictive policies. It has also been argued that housing is an easily postponable consumer expenditure, and thus the adjustment to restriction in housing is not a large threat to consumer welfare.

If the above arguments are accepted, where does this leave the federal agencies? It is clear from the discussion in this chapter that they have not been able to insulate the mortgage and housing sector. The most recent dramatic example of that came in 1975 when housing starts were less than a million units in some months in a period of significant agency activity. The most that the agencies appear to have been able to do is moderate the decline in the housing and mortgage market, and provide liquidity in a market that is notoriously illiquid.

In conclusion, perhaps analysts have expected too much of the agencies. Policy makers clearly have and are continuing to do so—witness the recent conflicts discussed in section V. This may lead to yet another structure of conflicting goals and requirements. If any lesson is to be drawn from previous experience, it is that such activity is not always desirable and has been in many cases, counterproductive.

NOTES

1. Jaffee agrees stating, "If the housing sector is protected, then monetary policy would have to be even stronger to carry out a given macroeconomic goal" (1976:164). Smith (1970) also believes this to be true. However, for a recent disssenting view see Cooley and Corrado (1978).

2. Mortgage bankers are nondepository institutions which essentially perform a brokerage function between borrowers and ultimate mortgage holders.

3. For a more detailed discussion of FNMA see Kaufman (1975, 1977); Rosen (1977).

4. For further discussion of the FHLB see Jaffee (1976). Jaffee points out that there may be a slip between the provision of assistance to the mortgage market and the presumed transfer to housing (1976:165), that is, such transference is not automatic. There is, in addition, another federal agency which differs from those mentioned above in that its activities are part of the federal budget. The Government National Mortgage Association (GNMA) assumed the assistance function of the old FNMA when the latter was made a private corporation in 1968. More will be said about this agency below since it provides subsidized housing support.

5. Perhaps, the best way of explaining the manner in which the agencies operate in implementing their stabilization function is to contrast their operation to that of the Federal Reserve System. For example the Federal Reserve does not go to the open market to finance its activities. When it purchases securities it does so simply by crediting reserves to member bank accounts. This is an important difference.

6. There is nonetheless some reduction of FHLB assistance during housing booms. The FHLB responds endogenously to the initiative of the S&Ls, (e.g., see Silber, 1973), in generating its advances. These are pared down as S&Ls repay during periods of large saving inflows, thereby reducing FHLB assistance.

There are those that argue, Smith (1970), that this asymmetrical behavior on the part of agencies is as it should be. However, others including the author (1975) would disagree (see, for example, Farb and Bendt, 1976, and Committee on Banking, Housing and Urban Afairs, 1977).

7. This contrasts with the Fed's much broader and symmetrical stabilization function. The Fed is presumably equally concerned with expansionary excesses as it is with cyclical downturns. Further, the activity of the Fed is directed at impacting upon the general economy while that of the agencies is directed at impacting on the mortgage market and hopefully the housing market.

8. The FHLB does this by providing funds through its advances program which presumably allows these institutions to make additional mortgage loans above those permitted by their own funds inflow. The FHLMC by buying mortgages from S&Ls and then packaging them for resale permits additional mortgages to be made.

9. For example Swan (1973) strongly criticizes the methodology utilized by Arcelus and Meltzer (1973) and, hence, their findings.

10. Edward Kane in talking about controls as credit allocation devices and controllers as credit allocators has said: "Markets settle differences in priorities by tallying dollar weighted 'votes.' Credit allocators seek to rerun disputed elections with 'individuals' preferences weighted instead by politically determined indices of social worth" (1977:57). What Kane is really getting at in the article from which the quotation is drawn is perhaps the fundamental misunderstanding of the credit process inherent in the federal government view of that process. It is no doubt true, as will be discussed later, that one of the main reasons for the disproportionate impact of monetary policy on the mortgage and housing markets, is the existence of other governmental regulaticns, such as Regulation Q.

11. This goal has not been reached and perhaps was totally unrealistic even without the difficulties that the housing market experienced in 1969-1970 and 1974-1975.

12. In 1966, Regulation Q ceilings which had first been imposed on commercial banks in the 1930s were first effective. In the same year they were extended to thrift institutions.

13. In the Housing Act of 1968, the mortgage market agencies were freed from the federal budget and no longer were impeded by the impact of their activities on the federal deficit. This is discussed further below.

14. See Kaufman and Schwartz (1973) for a discussion of FNMA's development.

15. Grebler was writing prior to the most recent difficult period for housing, 1974-1975. In an updated version of this study, but one which uses similar methodology, he finds that disintermediation induced by agency activity reduced the net effectiveness in this latter period to 50 percent of gross assistance (1975:82).

16. It should be noted that for Swan the reduction in gross assistance is due to more than the induced disintermediation effect discussed above. It includes the reallocation of the resources of those institutions with portfolio flexibility (MSBs and CBs) out of the mortgage market to take advantage of higher rates available on other kinds of securities.

17. Before taking up regulatory policy, however, there are two related problems that require some mention. The most important of these problems at least until now, relates to the fact that agencies must receive permission from the U.S. Treasury to come to market to finance their activities. The Treasury is naturally interested in minimizing the cost of its own borrowing. Since the Treasury has been in deficit over virtually the whole postwar period, and in large deficit over the past ten years when the agencies have been particularly active, the Treasury is always financing when the agencies are. Since agencies come to market most heavily during periods of credit restraint when interest rates are already high, the Treasury has not been loath to force the agencies to change some of the timing and terms of their security issuance. While this has not been a serious problem, it is useful to keep in mind particularly with the extraordinary financing needs of the Treasury in recent years.

The second point is that the Secretary of the Department of Housing and Urban Development (HUD) must also approve the FNMA's financing requests. This has generally not been a problem. In late 1977 and early 1978, however, this has presented difficulties. The secretary of HUD, Mrs. Patricia Harris, is not pleased with the way FNMA has responded to what she regards as legitimate urban housing needs, and in order to put pressure on FNMA, the Secretary has only authorized stop-gap financing for FNMA. The whole question of control, what agencies should be doing, and the implications that these issues raise will be discussed more fully below.

18. The ceilings are now set by an interagency coordinating committee.

19. Of course, the reallocation of portfolios by these institutions cannot be blamed entirely on usury ceilings. For example, it is well known that mortgage rates lag open market rates in adjustment.

20. Notice the analogy of this discussion with the discussions concerning "redlining" by private mortgage market institutions which have been accused of placing whole neighborhoods into categories for which no mortgage loans would be made.

21. HUD programs 235 and 236 provide interest rate subsidies. Section 221 (d) (3) is a rent subsidy program. In general, the provision of a secondary market by FNMA should not be ignored. The increased liquidity of the mortgage instrument has been a major change in the last decade.

22. I do not want to leave the impression that Farb and Bendt believe that FNMA has been at all aggressive in its sales program. They do point out the "paucity" of mortgage sales in the 1970s (1976:43).

23. The analysis of FNMA by Farb and Bendt, and Schecter assume that FNMA is quite important in the mortgage market. The question of just how important FNMA has been in the mortgage market is still being addressed, as discussed above.

24. The removal of Regulation Q should, however, help in this regard.

REFERENCES

ARCELUS, F. and MELTZER, A.H. (1973) "The Markets for Housing and Housing Services." Journal of Money, Credit and Banking (February):78-99.

Committee on Banking, Housing and Urban Affairs [senate] (1977) Hearing on the Federal National Mortgage Association Charter Act, (June 7 and 8).

COOLEY, T. and CORRADO, C. (1978) "Competing Goals of Stabilization Policy: A Reassessment of Policies Towards Housing." (January):mimeo.

FARB, W.E. and BENDT, D.L. (1976) "The Role of the Federal National Mortgage Association in the Secondary Mortgage Market." The Library of Congress, Congressional Research Service, (December 3).

GREBLER, L. (1972) "Broadening the Sources of Funds For Residential Mortgages." Pp. 177-252 in Ways to Moderate Fluctuations in Housing Construction, Board of Governors of the Federal Reserve System.

_____(1975) "The Role of the Public Sector in Residential Financing." Pp. 67-116 in Resources for Housing, Federal Home Loan Bank of San Franciso (December).

JAFFEE, D.M. (1976) "The Federal Home Loan Bank System Since 1965." Journal of Monetary Economics, Supplement Vol. 4: 161-203.

KANE, E.J. (1976) "Federal Home Loan Bank Board Policy and the Plight of Savings and Loan Associations: A Comment on the Jaffee and Swan Papers." Journal of Monetary Economics, Supplement Vol. 4: 237-245.

_____(1977) "Good Intentions and Unintended Evil: The Case Against Selective Credit Allocation." Journal of Money, Credit and Banking (February): 55-69.

KAUFMAN, H.M. (1975) "The Role of FNMA in the Mortgage Market," Paper presented at the Western Economic Association Annual Meetings (June).

_____(1977) "An Analysis of Federal Mortgage Market Agency Behavior." Journal of Money, Credit and Banking (May): 349-355.

_____and SCHWARTZ, H.S. (1973) FNMA Background and History, Washington, D.C.: Federal National Mortgage Association (December).

LINDSAY, R. (1970) "Regulation Q: The Money Markets and Housing—II." Pp. 52-67 in Housing and Monetary Policy. Conference Series No. 4, The Federal Reserve Bank of Boston (October).

MELTZER, A.H. (1970) "Regulation Q: The Money Markets and Housing—I." Pp. 41-51 in Housing and Monetary Policy. Conference Series No. 4, Federal Reserve Bank of Boston (October).

OSTES, J.R. (1976) "Effects of Usury Ceilings on the Mortgage Market." Journal of Finance (June): 821-834.

PIERCE, J.L. And GRAVES, M.A. (1972) "Insulating Housing: Effects Upon Economic Stabilization." Pp. 337-344 in Ways to Moderate Fluctuations in Housing Construction, Board of Governors of the Federal Reserve System (December).

PROXMIRE, W. and CRANSTON, A. (1977) "A Bill to Amend the Federal National Mortgage Association Charter Act." Congressional Record (April 27): 56483-56485.

Report on the President's Commission on Financial Structure and Regulation. (1971) Washington, D.C.: Government Printing Office (December).

ROSEN, K.T. (1977) "The Federal National Mortgage Association, Residential Construction, and Mortgage Lending." Paper presented at the American Real Estate and Urban Economics Association (December).

SILBER, W.L. (1973) "A Model of Federal Home Loan Bank System and Federal National Mortgage Association Behavior." The Review of Economics and Statistics (August): 308-320.

SMITH, W.L. (1970) "The Role of Government Intermediaries." Pp. 86-101 in Housing and Monetary Policy. Conference Series No.4, The Federal Reserve Bank of Boston (October).

SWAN, C. (1973) "The Markets for Housing and Housing Services." Journal of Money, Credit and Banking (November): 960-972.

_____(1976) "The Impact of Residential Construction of Federal Home Loan Bank Policy." Journal of Monetary Economics Supplement Vol. 4: 205-229.

THYGERSON, K.J. (1973) "The Effects of Government Housing and Mortgage Credit Programs on Savings and Loan Associations." Occasional paper No. 6, U.S. Savings and Loan League.

Chapter 7

THE THREE FACES OF COMMERCIAL BANK LIABILITY MANAGEMENT

E D W A R D   J.   K A N E
Ohio State University

INTRODUCTION

Whether we focus on buildings or balance sheets, the nation's largest banks hardly look like banks any more. Increasingly, these banks inhabit colorful glass-covered towers and boxes, whose contours, materials, and hues contrast vividly with the austere pagan temple structures that until about 1960 served as the industry norm. Perhaps because form does follow function, during the era when banks restricted themselves to classical buildings, their balance sheets respected classical proportions, too. Bank liabilities were called simply deposits and came in relatively few unchanging varieties. However, as banks adopted modern architecture, categories of bank liabilities mutated with disarming speed.

This chapter seeks to document these mutations and to explain why their rate of occurrence surged in the 1960s and 1970s. Our explanation is rooted in the profit motive and concentrates on three relatively unchanging aspects of the U.S. commercial-banking business:

(1) banks' desire to minimize deposit interest costs by varying applicable deposit rates with the interest sensitivity of specific pools of customer funds;
(2) banks' written and unwritten commitment to meeting spurts in loan demands even when the Federal Reserve seeks in monetarist fashion to restrain aggregate deposit growth;

AUTHOR'S NOTE: The author wishes to thank Edward Fry and Thomas D. Simpson of the Federal Reserve Board staff for assembling previously unpublished data and to acknowledge valuable comments received on an earlier draft of this paper during a seminar at Bocconi University.

(3) banks' desire to offset regulatory burdens imposed on them by reserve requirements, deposit-rate ceilings, and deposit-insurance fees.

In the fundamentals of turning a long-run profit, U.S. banks have changed hardly at all. As before, banks act essentially as *arbitrageurs*. They borrow in cheap markets to lend simultaneously in dearer ones. As before (though to a lesser extent), U.S. banks' dominant activity is the business loan. Business loans are dominant not only because of the high net rate of interest they earn, but more importantly because of the broad-based relationship they establish with the borrower.[1] Loans bring valuable deposit and ancillary fee-for-service business in their wake.

Over the last thirty years, rising rates of interest on marketable securities have raised the opportunity costs to banks of depositor interest sensitivity, loan commitments, and banking regulations. In turn, these increasing opportunity costs have reshaped bank competition for loanable funds, producing a banking system that is dangerously vulnerable to financial panic.

WHAT IS LIABILITY MANAGEMENT?

Banks traditionally borrow in *deposit* markets, but regulation-induced innovations in the contractual form of U.S. bank liabilities are transforming the liability side of the banking business. To raise funds to meet loan demands profitably, U.S. banks have developed new instruments whose interest, maturity, and service elements differ in important ways from conventional deposits.

Banks' efforts to develop nontraditional borrowing arrangements and to use them profitably (especially to meet loan demand) are called *liability management*. However, the term covers two distinct phenomena. For convenience, we label the concept of supplementing asset management only with very-short borrowing as money-desk or reserve-position liability management (LM-1), and the concept of closely managing all liabilities whatever their maturity as generalized or loan-position liability management (LM-2).

Asset management describes the process of allocating a given quantity of funds across a series of alternative investment opportunities. Asset managers focus on finding the optimal *composition* for a portfolio whose size is determined exogenously. Customer requests to exercise claims against this portfolio must be accommodated either by drawing down cash balances or by selling off earning assets. Asset managers seek an allocation that balances such conflicting objectives as yield, liquidity, safety, and the desire to comply with various government-imposed restraints.

Liability managers seek to maintain or increase portfolio size by "purchasing" funds. LM-1 and LM-2 comprise methods for profitably expanding the total amount of a bank's investable funds. The two varieties of LM differ primarily in time frame. Reserve-position liability management is a policy of systematically relying on a bank's ability to issue new liabilities as a source of short-term liquidity. The strategy is to *purchase* liquidity as needed to supplement liquidity *stored* in cash and readily marketable assets.[2] In LM-1, the principal portfolio benefit is *compositional*. It allows a bank to hold a higher average ratio of illiquid high-yield assets than it could sustain if it were to plan to meet temporary cash stringencies solely from stored liquidity. In the United States, a large bank's purchase of one-day federal funds constitutes a prime example of LM-1. Typically, such a bank bids for one-day federal funds when it temporarily loses reserves due to deposit outflows or net acquisitions of earning assets, while it offers these funds when it gains reserves temporarily.

Generalized liability management covers efforts to expand permanently the amount of investable funds at a bank's disposal. The strategy seeks primarily to enlarge the bank's earning-asset capacity by discriminatory interest-rate competition focused on nontraditional liabilities, and *perhaps* also to reduce deposit volatility by extending the average maturity of its liabilities. The development of LM-2 can be interpreted as a series of regulation-induced innovations. LM-2 has developed as a way to evade Fed limitations on aggregate deposit growth and to reconcile inflation (and the higher interest rates and growing competition from less closely regulated institutions and markets that it brings about) with regulatory restraints. In the absence of regulatory restrictions, market discipline would have forced bank interest-rate competition to develop more straightforwardly. The crazy-quilt pattern of LM-2 activities we observe is best explained as an effort to discriminate in favor of interest-sensitive customers, and as a dialectical response to burdensome governmental restrictions on banks' ability to compete for traditional deposit funds. Chief among these restrictions are high reserve requirements on traditional deposits and low ceilings on deposit interest rates. But deposit-based fees for FDIC insurance play a role, too. U.S. banks' use of negotiable certificates of deposits (CDs) provide a good example of LM-2.

Both types of liability management presume an active rather than passive attitude toward the solicitation of customer funds. Liability managers do not simply post a schedule of customer services and deposit rates and let events determine their bank's size. They persistently strive to develop new initiatives. They remain continually alert for profitable new ways to package (or price) their liabilities that—without disturbing the cost of interest-*in*sensitive funds—promise to attract additional funds and/or to retain deposits that might otherwise be drawn away from the bank by interest-rate and service competition from bank and nonbank institutions.

LM-1 increases the efficiency of commercial-bank intermediation between savers and deficit spending units and, reinforced by deposit insurance and central-bank willingness to act as lender of last resort, probably enhances the stability of the banking system to downward shocks. On the other hand, while LM-2 also increases the cum-regulation efficiency of bank intermediation, its emphasis on nonprice competition produces a banking system that discriminates against small account-holders and appears more vulnerable to epidemic runs and financial panic.

LM-1: BANK LIABILITIES HAVE TRADITIONALLY SERVED AS A SOURCE OF LIQUIDITY

Unlike LM-2, there is in principle nothing new about LM-1. U.S. banks have, since their inception, regularly borrowed funds (i.e., purchased liquidity) from each other. Establishing the Federal Reserve System undoubtedly increased the pace of this borrowing. The Fed helped to perfect the market for interbank borrowing in three ways: by reducing the marginal cost of interregional clearing, by introducing an additional source of short-term credit, and by creating a new reason for borrowing (specifically, to meet Fed reserve requirements).

As a longer-lending short borrower, a bank must anticipate occasional cash emergencies. To what extent temporary cash emergencies are resolved by selling liquid assets or by borrowing depends at any time on the relative costs of each avenue of adjustment.[3] In general, a bank should seek the combination of asset sales and borrowing that minimizes the transactions and interest costs of financing its cash shortfall.

Interbank loans are advantageous for lenders and borrowers alike. They allow temporary excess inflows of bank cash to be invested profitably even as they allow banks pressed for cash to adjust their balance sheets gracefully. Since individual banks' temporary surpluses and deficits tend to a large extent to cancel out at any point in time and in many cases tend further to reverse themselves in a few days, it is inevitable that banks would bid and offer these funds.

In the modern United States, these bids and offers clear institutionally through the federal-funds market, and travel to and from balances at the Fed or at correspondent banks. Technically, federal funds may also be purchased from nonbank customers "off the books" of the borrowing bank. This type of borrowing is more in the nature of LM-2 and often has a longer term-to-maturity than customary one-day interbank transactions. Even though a 1970 restriction now limits the opportunity to lend federal funds to a narrow class of institutions, differences between the gross amounts of federal funds purchased and sold by commercial banks are sometimes substantial. While federal-funds transactions are combined with repurchase agreements in regularly published Federal Reserve statistics, Table 7.1 reports separate values for federal-funds borrowings and repurchase agreements observed in a special one-week survey of forty-five large commercial banks. During the sample week in 1974, interbank loans averaged 70 percent of all one-day borrowings, and 77 percent of survey banks' federal-funds purchases. As panels I through III of Table 7.2 show, these proportions were between 10 and 20 percentage points lower at year-end 1976, with roughly half of the interbank loans flowing from ordinary banks to a few hundred of the nation's very largest ones. These largest banks account for the lion's share of all purchases of LM-1 funds.

Member-bank borrowing from the Federal Reserve System tends to vary over the business cycle both with banks' aggregate need for reserves and with the differential between bank earnings rates (especially, the federal-funds rate), and the Fed's discount rate. Since the discount rate tends to fluctuate over a much narrower cycle than market interest rates, the Fed finds that it has to police member-bank borrowing during interest-rate upswings.

Although this chapter focuses predominantly on LM-2, the same themes could be sounded to explain the rapid growth of LM-1 activity in the 1960s and 1970s. In particular, episodes of tight money and relaxations and tightenings of various regulatory restrictions on participation in the federal-funds market have had a great deal to do with the market's uneven pattern of development.

LM-2: TWO PRELIMINARY DISTINCTIONS

To understand the evolution of LM-2 in the United States, it is important to grasp two preliminary distinctions:

Table 7.1: Gross Borrowings of Immediately Available Funds
Daily Average for Week Ending April 24, 1974
(Amounts in Billions of Dollars)
45 Large Banks

BORROWED FROM	Regular Federal Funds[1] (1)	Repurchase Agreements Secured By U.S. Gov't and Agency Securities (2)	Total (3)	Amount Maturing in One Day[2] (4)
I. LENDERS FROM WHOM MEMBER BANKS MAY BORROW "REGULAR" FEDERAL FUNDS				
1. Member commercial banks	13.1	1.0	14.1	12.8
2. Nonmember commercial banks	3.9	0.5	4.4	4.2
3. Domestic offices of foreign banks	3.2	*	3.2	2.4
4. Edge Act and Agreement Corp.	0.1	*	0.1	0.1
Commercial Bank Subtotal	20.3	1.5	21.8	19.5
5. Savings and loan associations and cooperative banks	2.9	*	2.9	2.3
6. Savings banks	1.6	*	1.6	1.6
7. Federal Home Loan Banks and Board	1.2	*	1.2	0.7
8. All other agencies of the U.S.	0.5	0.2	0.7	0.4
9. Securities Dealers	*	0.9	1.0	0.2
TOTAL	26.5	2.6	29.2	24.7

Table 7.1: Gross Borrowings of Immediately Available Funds
Daily Average for Week Ending April 24, 1974
(Amounts in Billions of Dollars)
45 Large Banks Cont'd.

BORROWED FROM	Regular Federal Funds[1]	Repurchase Agreements Secured By U.S. Gov't and Agency Securities	Total	Amount Maturing in One Day[2]
II. LENDERS FROM WHOM MEMBERS BANKS MAY NOT BORROW "REGULAR" FEDERAL FUNDS				
1. Business corporations	—	2.1	2.1	1.2
2. State and local governments	—	3.0	3.0	1.4
3. Foreign banks and foreign official institutions	—	0.6	0.6	0.5
4. All other	—	0.2	0.2	0.1
TOTAL	—	5.9	5.9	3.2
GRAND TOTAL	26.5	8.7	35.3	27.9
MEMO: Noncommercial Bank Subtotal	6.2	7.2	13.5	8.4

1. May be secured or unsecured.
2. Includes continuing contracts which have no maturity but can be terminated without advance notice by the lender or the borrower.
* Less than $500 million.
NOTE: Total may not add due to rounding.
Source: Special Federal Reserve Survey.

155

Table 7.2: Nondeposit Funds at Commercial Banks
December 31, 1976
(billions of dollars)

	Total	Commercial Banks		Large Bank Share(%)
		Large Banks[1]	Other	
I. Fed funds purchased & security RPs[2]	72.8	62.6	10.2	86
a. from commercial banks[3]	42.8	36.6	6.2	86
b. from brokers & dealers[3]	5.6	5.3	.3	95
c. from others[3]	24.4	20.8	3.6	85
II. Other liabilities for borrowed money[2]	7.3	4.6	2.7	63
a. from commercial banks (est)	4.5[4]	n.a.	n.a.	n.a
b. from others (est)	2.8[4]	n.a.	n.a.	
III. Interbank loans[2]	44.7	21.2	23.8	47
a. Fed funds sold and securities resales[2]	40.2	19.0	21.2	47
b. other[2]	4.5	2.2	2.3	49
IV. Total Fed funds, security RPs, and other liabilities for borrowed money from nonbank public (I + II − III)	32.8	28.4	4.3	87
V. Other nondeposit funds[2]	9.0	9.0	--	100
a. liabilities to own foreign branches[2]	5.2	5.2	--	100
b. loans sold to affiliates[2]	3.8	3.8	--	100
VI. Total nondeposit funds (I + II + V)	89.1	76.2	12.9	86
VII. Total nondeposit funds from nonbank public (VI − III)	41.8	37.4	4.3	89

n.a.—Not available
1. Includes about 320 large banks that report weekly condition statements
2. Reported or estimated weekly
3. Available on quarterly calls beginning March 1976
4. Derived from IIIb
Source: Unpublished estimates compiled by the staff of the Banking Section of The Federal Reserve Board.

(1) between anticipated and unanticipated inflation;

(2) between explicit and implicit interest payments.

ANTICIPATED AND UNANTICIPATED INFLATION

At any time and in any country, past experience and developing economic data give rise to "rational" or consensus forecasts of future inflation.[4] For each future period, the consensus forecast represents the best estimate of inflation that can be formulated, given the state of current economic theory and available empirical information. These forecasts are "best" in the sense that any borrower or lender that acts as if future inflation rates will be higher or lower runs what to the market as a whole appears to be an undue risk.

Of course, every forecast is, in the end, only a guess. Except for the prophets (who were fiendishly difficult to interpret *ex ante*), even the best forecasters are far from perfectly accurate. Nevertheless, in any forecast, the *anticipated* forecast error is zero by definition. Hence, after the fact, observed rates of inflation can be decomposed into an anticipated and an unanticipated component.

Anticipated inflation clearly affects the terms of loan contracts. Lenders want to exact a nominal rate of interest that exceeds the anticipated rate of inflation by what appears to be the "real" opportunity cost of their funds. In turn, borrowers can afford to pay nominal rates of interest that exceed the anticipated rate of inflation by the amount of the funds' perceived "real" productivity in the use to which they are going to be put. Hence, market interest rates tend to rise and fall with the level of anticipated inflation (Fisher, 1930).

EXPLICIT *VERSUS* IMPLICIT INTEREST

As any other borrower, banks pay explicit interest in the coin of the realm: dollars in the United States, lira in Italy. U.S. laws forbidding banks to pay explicit interest on demand deposits do not stop them from competing for profitable accounts. These laws merely change the thrust of the competition from explicit to implicit payments.[5] Implicit interest takes the form of merchandise premiums, free checks, longer banking hours, and superfluous branch offices as well as discriminatory price and service concessions to valued customers. In what amounts to a tied-sale agreement, U.S. banks stand ready to perform an array of accounting and financial services for *selected* customers at charges well below marginal costs. In particular, a U.S. bank is expected to grant loans to good customers at favorable interest rates, and to commit itself to furnish them needed loan funds almost irrespective of the tightness of its own reserve position.

Implicit interest is fundamentally less efficient than the explicit variety. It moves the economy back toward barter. When services are underpriced or given away, customers lack the incentive to see that society's resources are used economically. Costs to banks of providing the bartered services inevitably exceed the value of these services to the customers who receive them. In competitive markets, when interest is paid in the coin of the realm, costs and user benefits are properly equated.

Of course, even without deposit-rate regulation, implicit interest is attractive to customers as a form of tax-exempt income, and to banks as a hard-to-police way to engage in price discrimination. It allows banks to offer different interest rates to different depositors without showing obvious bias. Some of the specific services a bank chooses to subsidize may be tailored to the needs of particular customers. Also, a bank can vary as it wishes the portion of any individual customer's loan needs that it offers to finance at advantageous terms. From the point of view of society, deposit-rate regulation is defective in that it promotes tax avoidance and makes discrimination more respectable and less likely to alienate disfavored customers. This subtle and systematic discrimination against owners of interest-*in*sensitive funds (predominantly the old and the poor) is the ugliest face of liability management.

UNANTICIPATED INFLATION AND REGULATORY RESTRAINTS AS CAUSES OF LM-2

Inflation reduces the real value of fixed-income securities. Although the effects of *anticipated* inflation tend to be offset by correspondingly higher nominal interest rates, unanticipated inflation transfers real wealth from creditors to debtors. In unfettered competition, unanticipated inflation would hurt banks not just because they are net creditors. It would hurt them further because, due to differences in average maturity, the yields on their liabilities would be renegotiated more frequently than those on their assets. This would cause their borrowing costs to respond more quickly to changes in expected future inflation than the interest rates they earn on their investments.

DEPOSIT-RATE CEILINGS

Ceilings on explicit deposit rates destroy industry patterns of cyclical price leadership and generally slow down needed adjustments in bank-liability yields. In an era of secularly rising interest rates, by outlawing higher levels of explicit interest, rate ceilings force banks to invest time dreaming up and testing attractive ways of offering additional implicit interest. Typically, raising implicit interest rates involves expanding the range of customer services and/or the extent to which any service is offered below the bank's cost of performing it.

When interest rates on open-market securities rise above deposit-rate ceilings, bank deposits become relatively less attractive unless and until banks offer implicit interest. The greater the differential between market rates and deposit rates and the longer an attractive differential persists, the more depositors become aware of the advantages of placing at least some of their funds elsewhere. Under such circumstances, depositors shift more and more balances out of depository institutions into both marketable securities and nontraditional intermediaries whose payout rates are unregulated. This shift from lending through intermediaries to direct lending and other less-traditional patterns of transferring funds from savers to would-be deficit-spending units is called *disintermediation*.

Banks' need to accommodate the loan demands of their important demand-deposit customers leads them to experiment with new types of borrowing arrangements when monetary policy becomes tight. Moreover, innovative nondeposit liabilities can be designed, such as repurchase agreements, both to escape deposit-insurance fees and burdensome reserve requirements (requirements which of course become more onerous as market interest rates rise), and to appeal specifically to owners of interest-sensitive funds.

In the short run, innovative borrowing arrangements and other schemes for paying implicit interest are less flexible—both upward and downward—than explicit interest on deposits. With market interest rates during the last fifteen years showing an upward trend and only mild downward fluctuations, implicit interest rates paid by U.S. banks have risen during booms without falling back noticeably in recessions.

RESERVE REQUIREMENTS

Reserve requirements are a tax. Reserves in excess of what a bank would voluntarily hold may be interpreted as a 100 percent tax levied on the income the bank would otherwise have earned on the funds put aside to meet the requirement.[6] Membership in the Federal Reserve System is optional for state-chartered banks, who may accept instead less-restrictive requirements imposed by their home state. Burdensome Federal Reserve reserve requirements create an incentive for commercial banks to quit or to refrain from joining the Federal Reserve System. This incentive is especially strong for small banks for whom the value-of-service benefits of System membership have traditionally been small. This exit incentive varies with the net onerousness of reserve requirements applicable to comparable nonmember banks in the same home state, with the level of interest rates on earning assets, and inversely with correspondent-bank fees for clearing checks through them. Increases in interest rates decrease the proportion of cash assets a bank would voluntarily hold and increase the amount of income forgone per dollar of involuntary reserves. Hence, the cost advantages enjoyed by nonmember banks and by nonbank institutions increase with market interest rates. Although Fed officials want to stabilize this incentive by setting a variable rate of interest on member-bank reserves, congressional authorization has not been forthcoming. Moreover, differences in the level of reserve requirements on different types of liabilities (including zero requirements on innovative liabilities) lead member banks to promote the expansion of their less heavily taxed sources of funds. Because liability innovations reduce deposit-insurance fees and effective reserve requirements, it pays banks to innovate beyond the point where marginal after-tax benefits to users equal marginal cost to the banks.

STRUCTURE OF FEDERAL DEPOSIT INSURANCE

Just as we need to recognize the relevance of both implicit and explicit interest, so must we acknowledge the existence of implicit and explicit elements of FDIC deposit insurance coverage and fees. Explicitly, the FDIC insures a bank's deposits up to $40,000 per account (up to $100,000 in the case of state and local government accounts) for a partially rebatable fee of 1/12 of 1 percent of the bank's total domestic deposits (insured and uninsured). Implicitly, the FDIC insures virtually all accounts in full by its efforts to manage bank failures in ways that maintain confidence in the banking system by avoiding as far as possible any losses to depositors (Barnett, Horvitz, and Silverberg, 1977).

Because the explicit fees for FDIC insurance are unrelated both to a bank's asset structure and to the amount of its uninsured liabilities, banks face incentives to improve their bargain with the FDIC by taking on additional asset risk and reclassifying large deposits as nondeposit liabilities. With the marginal explicit insurance cost of asset risk equal to zero, the FDIC is forced to restrain bank efforts to assume high levels of asset risk by imposing implicit insurance premiums via the examination and regulatory process. FDIC examiners (fully 2/3 of FDIC employees) are continually on the alert for sharp practices, and FDIC lawyers continually formulate and reformulate regulations to control so-called "unsafe and unsound" bank behavior.

LM-2 AS A MANIFESTATION OF THE REGULATORY DIALECTIC

Episodes of tight money push banks to invent new ways to meet their loan commitments. But besides encouraging banks to devise socially wasteful ways of offering implicit interest, deposit-rate ceilings, and deposit-based reserve requirements and FDIC insurance fees encourage higher-cost firms in less closely regulated financial sectors to develop deposit substitutes (e.g., payable-through drafts on mutual funds or brokerage accounts). As part of a "regulatory dialectic," regulatees' inventive schemes for paying implicit interest and unregulated firms' development of deposit substitutes interact with regulator efforts to expand and adjust the network of restraints to make them either more effective or more livable. In this way, regulation becomes an ongoing force for institutional change. In any regulated industry, institutional arrangements are shaped and reshaped by dialectical collisions between economic and political forces. Economic forces express themselves in changes in the profitably or desirability of different goods and services. Political forces express themselves mainly in adjustments in applicable regulatory restraints and in the structure of pertinent taxes. Whether initiated by demand shifts, innovation, or regulatory action, market adaptation and regulatory reaction interact in Hegelian fashion. Regulatees strive consistently to rearrange their activities to cushion the reduction in profits that regulation would otherwise impose on them. Simultaneously, unregulated firms try to devise ways of invading the regulatees' now more-vulnerable markets. These efforts cause politicians and regulators to reconsider, redesign, and perhaps even to abandon the restrictions. Each step in the process triggers another round of market adaptation and regulatory readjustment. Just as a chunk of clay might be shaped and reshaped by the hands of a finicky artisan, financial institutions are continually refashioned by the "invisible hand" of market incentives and the all-too-*visible* hand of political pressures.

LM-2 AND THE PROHIBITION OF DEMAND-DEPOSIT INTEREST

The U.S. prohibition of explicit interest on demand deposits was introduced in the 1930s as a way of preventing banks from competing "excessively" for demand-deposit business. As long as market interest rates remained relatively low, this interest prohibition merely promoted nonprice competition for these funds by banks. Banks paid implicit interest by performing services for accountholders at charges below the cost to the banks of providing them. However, in the 1960s as market interest rates rose under the impact of accelerating inflation, the interest prohibition led nonbank institutions, subject to lower (often zero) reserve requirements, to invade these markets by designing interest-bearing instruments of their own that function in one or more ways like checking accounts. Today, thanks to bank and nonbank LM-2 activity, the litany of checking-account substitutes runs from NOW accounts and drafts payable against money-market mutual funds and brokerage accounts, through written and telephonic thrift-institution payment orders, to electronic access to savings accounts at off-premises terminals.

Although the interest prohibition was intended to preclude "destructive" competition for demand deposits among banks, it merely transferred the competitive thrust to nonprice terms and eventually to nonbank institutions. For example, some of the push for electronic funds transfer (EFT) among U.S. savings and loan associations (S&Ls) comes from the perception that forward-looking managers can use EFT to gain an unshakeable foothold in local markets for payment services[7] that would help their institutions to become "full-service financial centers for households." Similarly, many money-market mutual funds have made their accounts into substitutes for demand deposits by allowing customers to draw bank drafts against holdings in the fund. Through automated repurchase agreements and automatic transfers between time and demand accounts, many commercial banks are already paying substantial interest rates on what are essentially demand funds.

However, these schemes are socially less efficient than paying explicit interest on checking accounts. LM-2 arrangements lead banks and customers to expend time and effort that could be saved if checking-account interest could be paid. Ending the prohibition of demand-deposit interest would help to rationalize the pricing of funds-transfer services and to prevent commercial banks and U.S. society at large from bearing the long-run burden of higher-cost competitors' invasions of retail deposit markets.

LM-2 AND CEILINGS ON OTHER DEPOSIT RATES

During the years 1936-1961, longstanding commercial-bank disinterest and regulatory restrictions cartelized the U.S. market for household savings along institutional lines. Households' accumulations of small amounts of long-term funds went primarily into U.S. Savings Bonds and only three types of deposits were important: demand, time, and passbook savings accounts. Checking accounts and corporate time deposits remained the exclusive preserve of commercial banks. While the market for household savings was shared by commercial banks, mutual savings banks (MSBs), S&Ls, and some small credit unions, commercial banks were less free to compete explicitly for interest-sensitive funds. These funds were pursued aggressively by only a small portion of the S&L industry, principally by major S&Ls in the fast-growing Western sunbelt states of California and Arizona. These firms paid substantially higher interest rates than Eastern and Midwestern institutions, and advertised their high-interest savings-by-mail plans in national publications. Commercial banks were free to operate in all three deposit markets, but federally insured banks were prohibited from paying explicit interest on demand deposits and subjected to a low 2-1/2 percent Regulation Q ceiling interest rate (raised to 3 percent in 1957) on time and savings accounts. Even into the 1960s, much lower ceilings applied to interest rates on time deposits (including CDs) whose maturity was six months or less.

In the early 1960s, banks' growing need to raise funds to meet the loan demands of valued demand-deposit customers (a need that the prohibition of demand-deposit interest made all the more pressing) produced permanent cracks in the longstanding regulator-enforced cartel and the beginnings of LM-2 deposit interest competition by banks.[8] From January 1962 to December 1965, Regulation Q ceilings were raised in various steps to 4 percent on savings accounts and 5-1/2 percent on certificates of deposit (CDs). Table 7.3 shows that during this period CDs first became an important source of funds for commercial banks. In 1966, rising market interest rates on short-term instruments slowed deposit growth at all institutions, but especially at S&Ls. To boost S&Ls' position, Regulation Q ceilings were rolled back half-a-point for banks on multiple-maturity CDs in July 1966, and on small-denomination CDs in September.

Higher market rates of interest sharply reduced the market value of S&Ls' relatively long-term assets and threatened their solvency. To protect weaker S&Ls from intraindustry competition, in fall 1966 the umbrella of deposit-rate ceilings was finally spread over S&Ls and MSBs. But to shelter these mortgage-lending specialists from the full impact of bank competition and to keep credit flowing to the homebuilding industry, thrift-institution ceilings were set at differentially higher levels. Along with the subsequent decison to abandon deposit-rate ceilings on large CDs,[9] this "differential" ceiling has become the centerpiece of thrift and bank marketing and lobbying strategies.

Since this differential gives S&Ls advantaged access to small savings, commercial bank LM-2 has focused predominantly on exempted pools of funds amounting to $100,000 or more. With traditional instruments offering households relatively low yields, institutions and instruments

TABLE 7.3: Outstanding Negotiable Certificates of Deposit Issued in Denominations of $100,000 or More at Large U.S. Weekly Reporting Banks and Short-Term Interest Rates, 1961-1976

Year	Large CDs At Yearend (in billions of dollars, seasonally adjusted)	Average 4-to-6 Months Prime Commer-cial-Paper Rate (in percent)	Average Federal-Funds Rate (in percent)
1961	2.8	2.97	1.96
1962	5.7	3.26	2.68
1963	9.6	3.55	3.18
1964	12.8	3.97	3.50
1965	16.2	4.38	4.07
1966	15.4	5.55	5.11
1967	20.5	5.10	4.22
1968	23.5	5.90	5.66
1969	11.0	7.83	8.21
1970	25.4	7.72	7.17
1971	33.5	5.11	4.67
1972	43.9	4.69	4.44
1973	63.0	8.15	8.74
1974	89.0	9.87	10.51
1975	82.1	6.33	5.82
1976	63.3	5.35	5.05

SOURCES: *Annual Report of the Council of Economic Advisers,* January 1976, and *Federal Reserve Bulletin,* August 1977.

exempt from Regulation Q ceilings have pursued household deposits with great vigor. Among these institutions are credit unions, money-market mutual funds, and real-estate investment trusts (REITs). Among the substitute instruments are share drafts, check-redemption privileges at money-market mutual funds, negotiable-order-of-withdrawal or NOW accounts, repurchase agreements, floating-rate notes, brokerage cash-management accounts, and interest on public-utility and (potentially at least) retailer credit balances. This regulation-induced innovation tends in the long run to shift business away from the institutions that deposit-rate ceilings are intended to protect.

A QUICK LOOK AT TRENDS IN LM-2

For a regularly reporting sample of large banks, Table 7.3 shows how rapidly certificates of deposit grew as applicable Regulation Q ceilings were raised during the early 1960s, and how this growth suffered when open-market rates shot through the applicable ceilings in 1966 and again in 1969. Since the large CD ceilings were suspended (partially in 1970 and completely in 1973), CD growth has conformed positively with changes in open-market interest rates. At the June 1977 call date, U.S. commercial banks had $115.6 billion of large CDs outstanding.

Monthly or quarterly data show an association also between CDs and cyclical movements in loan demand. Comprehensive data shown in Table 7.4 are available only since 1969. Between July 1969 and October 1977, the sum of nondeposit liabilities and large time deposits quadrupled. In October 1977, these innovative liabilities exceeded $250 billion. This amount is: (1) over three times the reported level of equity capital, (2) over 25 percent of total assets, and (3) 20 percent more than passbook savings deposits.

LM-2 AND THE POTENTIAL FOR FINANCIAL PANIC

Large U.S. banks' LM-2 activity has focused on relatively inflexible and cost-increasing schemes for paying implicit interest and on attracting pools of "hot" money. On balance, this strategy increases the volatility of large-bank liabilities. Contingent liabilities have become more extensive and to some extent more risky, too. As a way to earn additional fee income and to reduce the burden of commitments to finance valued demand-deposit customers when money is tight, most large banks offer to guarantee their customers' commercial-paper issues. Partly in consequence, the volume of outstanding commercial paper now exceeds the asset size of the nations largest commercial bank, with large banks guaranteeing a substantial volume of commercial paper from firms whose credit ratings would not otherwise have qualified them to borrow in this market at favorable interest rates. If financial stringency should ever prevent these corporations from paying off guaranteed paper at maturity, banks' standby letters of credit (which stood at $14.5 billion in June 1977) would convert these customers' debts into immediate claims on the assets of the guaranteeing bank. Because arrangements for paying implicit interest are hard to dismantle on short notice, bank profits could be hurt even by a sharp decline in interest rates.

Accompanying their use of liability management, large U.S. banks have tended to accept greater default risk in the asset side of their balance sheets: low-rated municipal securities, loans to REITs, and credits to foreign countries whose balance of payments show persistent deficits and whose governments may be unstable. Even while increasing all these risks, U.S. banks have—in an effort to raise the rate of return on bank capital—allowed their average ratio of capital to risk assets to fall

TABLE 7.4: Nondeposit Sources of Funds and Large Time Deposit at
All Commercial Banks, July 1969 to October 1977
(in billions of dollars)

	Total Nondeposit Funds (Including Interbank Borrowing) (2)+(5)	Federal Funds Purchased, Security RPs, Other Liabilities for Borrowed Money			Eurodollar Borrowings, Loan Sales, Other Misc.	Nondeposit Funds From Nonbanks (4)+(5)	Large Time Deposits, (Including Large Negotiable CDs)
		Total	Interbank	Nonbank			
	(1)	(2)	(3)	(4)	(5)	(6)	(7)
1969-JUL	37.4	19.4	10.6	8.8	18.0	26.8	26.3
-AUG	39.7	20.9	10.8	10.1	18.7	28.9	22.8
-SEP	40.1	21.3	11.4	9.9	18.8	28.7	20.9
-OCT	40.9	21.7	12.2	9.5	19.1	28.6	19.6
-NOV	41.0	21.5	11.7	9.7	19.6	29.3	19.4
-DEC	41.4	22.1	11.4	10.6	19.3	29.9	19.6
1970-JAN	42.2	22.6	11.6	11.0	19.6	30.6	18.8
-FEB	43.2	23.1	11.6	11.5	20.1	31.6	19.2
-MAR	42.6	23.1	12.4	10.7	19.6	30.3	21.1
-APR	42.9	23.6	13.3	10.3	19.3	29.6	24.2
-MAY	44.5	24.2	14.2	10.1	20.3	30.4	25.0
-JUN	44.6	23.8	13.7	10.1	20.8	30.9	25.6
-JUL	43.0	22.9	14.4	8.5	20.1	28.6	30.5
-AUG	41.2	22.2	15.3	6.9	19.0	25.9	34.3
-SEP	37.6	20.9	14.6	6.3	16.6	23.0	37.7
-OCT	35.9	21.4	15.0	6.5	14.5	20.9	40.2
-NOV	35.4	22.3	15.0	7.3	13.1	20.4	42.7
-DEC	35.3	23.2	16.9	6.3	12.1	18.3	45.4

TABLE 7.4: Nondeposit Sources of Funds and Large Time Deposit at
All Commercial Banks, July 1969 to October 1977
(in billions of dollars) cont'd

	Total Nondeposit Funds (Including Interbank Borrowing) (2)+(5)	Federal Funds Purchased, Security RPs, Other Liabilities for Borrowed Money			Eurodollar Borrowings, Loan Sales, Other Misc.	Nondeposit Funds From Nonbanks (4)+(5)	Large Time Deposits, (Including Large Negotiable CDs)
		Total	Interbank	Nonbank			
	(1)	(2)	(3)	(4)	(5)	(6)	(7)
1971-JAN	33.2	22.2	15.9	6.4	11.0	17.3	48.1
-FEB	32.0	22.4	16.1	6.3	9.7	16.0	50.1
-MAR	30.6	22.4	15.6	6.8	8.1	15.0	51.5
-APR	31.6	25.5	18.2	7.3	6.1	13.4	50.9
-MAY	31.0	25.8	18.2	7.6	5.2	12.8	51.6
-JUN	30.9	25.3	17.4	7.9	5.7	13.6	53..9
-JUL	30.7	25.4	17.0	8.4	5.3	13.7	54.9
-AUG	30.9	26.0	17.7	8.2	4.9	13.1	55.2
-SEP	32.9	27.7	19.0	8.7	5.2	13.9	56.1
-OCT	33.7	27.9	18.5	9.4	5.8	15.2	58.9
-NOV	35.6	29.3	18.8	10.5	6.3	16.7	59.3
-DEC	33.6	28.7	19.5	9.2	4.9	14.1	60.0
1972-JAN	33.3	28.5	19.6	8.9	4.8	13.7	60.6
-FEB	33.1	28.6	19.3	9.4	4.5	13.9	62.0
-MAR	35.0	30.6	20.1	10.5	4.4	14.9	61.6
-APR	36.3	32.1	20.3	11.8	4.2	16.0	63.1
-MAY	36.3	32.1	20.3	11.8	4.1	15.9	64.8
-JUN	38.8	34.7	21.0	13.7	4.2	17.8	67.4

Table 7.4: Nondeposit Sources of Funds and Large Time Deposit at
All Commercial Banks, July 1969 to October 1977
(in billions of dollars) cont'd.

| | Total Nondeposit Funds (Including Interbank Borrowing) (2)+(5) | Federal Funds Purchased, Security RPs, Other Liabilities for Borrowed Money | | | Eurodollar Borrowings, Loan Sales, Other Misc. | Nondeposit Funds From Nonbanks (4)+(5) | Large Time Deposits, (Including Large Negotiable CDs) |
| | | Total | Interbank | Nonbank | | | |
	(1)	(2)	(3)	(4)	(5)	(6)	(7)
-JUL	39.6	35.5	23.9	11.6	4.1	15.7	68.6
-AUG	41.5	37.2	24.1	13.1	4.3	17.4	70.7
-SEP	40.4	36.3	24.5	11.8	4.1	15.9	72.1
-OCT	43.3	39.1	24.7	14.4	4.1	18.5	73.7
-NOV	41.6	37.5	23.7	13.8	4.2	17.9	76.9
-DEC	44.7	40.3	26.0	14.3	4.3	18.7	78.9
1973-JAN	47.4	42.9	26.1	16.8	4.5	21.3	81.3
-FEB	49.3	44.9	28.5	16.4	4.5	20.9	89.0
-MAR	50.2	45.4	28.2	17.2	4.8	22.0	98.6
-APR	50.0	44.9	28.5	16.4	5.0	21.4	103.9
-MAY	52.1	46.9	29.3	17.6	5.2	22.8	107.2
-JUN	54.4	49.4	29.4	20.1	5.0	25.1	108.6
-JUL	60.0	54.1	31.2	22.9	5.9	28.7	112.7
-AUG	60.8	54.0	30.7	23.3	5.9	30.1	121.5
-SEP	63.8	57.2	31.1	26.1	6.7	32.7	125.8
-OCT	65.4	58.9	32.2	26.7	6.6	33.2	124.7
-NOV	68.3	61.9	31.4	30.4	6.5	36.9	124.3
-DEC	70.1	63.6	33.4	30.2	6.4	36.7	124.9

TABLE 7.4: Nondeposit Sources of Funds and Large Time Deposit at All Commercial Banks, July 1969 to October 1977 (in billions of dollars) cont'd.

	Total Nondeposit Funds (Including Interbank Borrowing) (2)+(5)	Federal Funds Purchased, Security RPs, Other Liabilities for Borrowed Money			Eurodollar Borrowings, Loan Sales, Other Misc.	Nondeposit Funds From Nonbanks (4)+(5)	Large Time Deposits, (Including Large Negotiable CDs)
		Total	Interbank	Nonbank			
	(1)	(2)	(3)	(4)	(5)	(6)	(7)
1974-JAN	72.4	65.9	35.4	30.5	6.5	37.0	130.0
-FEB	74.9	68.0	37.5	30.5	6.9	37.4	134.1
-MAR	78.0	70.5	37.3	33.2	7.5	40.7	134.1
-APR	76.5	68.5	38.2	30.3	8.1	38.4	142.6
-MAY	76.4	67.6	37.7	29.9	8.8	38.7	149.9
-JUN	77.9	69.5	38.0	31.5	8.4	39.8	153.8
-JUL	80.7	71.5	38.3	33.2	9.2	42.4	158.5
-AUG	79.4	70.3	37.9	32.5	9.0	41.5	161.4
-SEP	79.3	70.7	36.9	33.9	8.6	42.4	162.2
-OCT	77.9	70.1	38.1	32.0	7.9	39.9	164.0
-NOV	76.8	69.2	37.9	31.3	7.6	38.9	164.5
-DEC	77.4	69.1	39.8	29.2	8.4	37.6	168.2
1975-JAN	70.6	63.1	36.5	26.6	7.6	34.2	172.2
-FEB	72.3	65.8	39.7	26.1	6.5	32.6	172.6
-MAR	70.5	64.0	40.9	23.2	6.5	29.7	168.8

TABLE 7.4. Nondeposit Sources of Funds and Large Time Deposit at All Commercial Banks, July 1969 to October 1977 (in billions of dollars) cont'd

| | Total Nondeposit Funds (Including Interbank Borrowing) (2)+(5) | Federal Funds Purchased, Security RPs, Other Liabilities for Borrowed Money | | | Eurodollar Borrowings, Loan Sales, Other Misc. | Nondeposit Funds From Nonbanks (4)+(5) | Large Time Deposits, (Including Large Negotiable CDs) |
| | | Total | Interbank | Nonbank | | | |
	(1)	(2)	(3)	(4)	(5)	(6)	(7)
-APR	69.3	62.5	38.9	23.6	6.7	30.4	165.1
-MAY	69.4	61.9	38.2	23.8	7.4	31.2	162.3
-JUN	70.3	63.3	40.4	22.9	7.0	29.9	159.7
-JUL	71.7	64.9	40.2	24.7	6.8	31.5	156.9
-AUG	69.1	62.1	38.6	23.6	7.0	30.6	153.5
-SEP	69.7	62.7	38.0	24.7	7.0	31.8	153.3
-OCT	70.1	62.2	37.7	24.6	7.9	32.4	155.3
-NOV	70.7	62.5	37.9	24.5	8.2	32.7	157.6
-DEC	71.3	62.9	37.6	25.3	8.4	33.7	156.8
1976-JAN	73.5	65.6	37.3	28.3	7.9	36.2	154.1
-FEB	75.1	67.1	38.9	28.3	8.0	36.2	151.5
-MAR	73.2	65.0	39.3	25.7	8.2	33.9	150.1
-APR	76.2	68.7	39.0	29.7	7.5	37.1	148.5
-MAY	77.4	69.8	38.8	31.0	7.6	38.5	143.5
-JUN	75.7	67.3	38.0	29.3	8.4	37.7	146.8
-JUL	78.3	69.5	40.1	29.4	8.8	38.1	147.6
-AUG	83.5	74.5	41.6	33.0	8.9	41.9	141.1
-SEP	86.0	77.8	44.0	33.8	8.2	42.0	137.5
-OCT	88.8	79.8	44.9	34.8	9.0	43.8	135.5

**TABLE 7.4: Nondeposit Sources of Funds and Large Time Deposit at
All Commercial Banks, July 1969 to October 1977
(in billions of dollars) cont'd**

	Total Nondeposit Funds (Including Interbank Borrowing) (2)+(5)	Federal Funds Purchased, Security RPs, Other Liabilities for Borrowed Money			Eurodollar Borrowings, Loan Sales, Other Misc.	Nondeposit Funds From Nonbanks (4)+(5)	Large Time Deposits, (Including Large Negotiable CDs)
		Total	Interbank	Nonbank			
	(1)	(2)	(3)	(4)	(5)	(6)	(7)
-NOV	90.0	81.0	41.9	39.1	9.1	48.2	136.5
-DEC	96.0	86.8	44.6	42.2	9.2	51.4	137.4
1977-JAN	92.1	83.8	41.8	42.0	8.3	50.3	136.3
-FEB	89.9	82.4	39.2	43.2	7.5	50.7	137.4
-MAR	91.7	84.0	39.0	45.0	7.7	52.7	135.2
-APR	94.0	86.2	41.2	45.0	7.7	52.7	133.4
-MAY	98.8	91.0	42.6	48.4	7.8	56.2	133.6
-JUN	97.5	89.1	41.6	47.4	8.4	55.9	137.9
-JUL	101.3	92.8	45.4	47.4	8.5	55.9	140.8
-AUG	102.0	93.4	44.1	49.3	8.6	57.9	141.0
-SEP	105.9	96.8	45.2	51.6	9.1	60.6	142.1
-OCT	107.7	97.7	46.5	51.2	10.0	61.1	147.7

SOURCE: Unpublished estimates prepared by the staff of the Banking Section of the Federal Reserve Board.

subsequently. These increases in asset risk and in leverage have been encouraged by the structure of FDIC insurance premiums, which makes no explicit charge for variations in the riskiness of a bank's assets (or for nondeposit liabilities either).

Banks that adopt these "modern" portfolio policies increase their exposure to liquidity crises, and necessarily become more dependent on the Fed and FDIC to bail them out in the event of adverse market developments. Conversely, federal regulators find themselves worrying about a problem that many observers supposed had been eliminated by federal deposit insurance: the possibility that a chain of bank failures could trigger a nationwide financial panic. Since the spectacular CD and federal-funds runoffs experienced by the Franklin National Bank in 1974, the threat of bank failures has plagued federal regulators.[10]

Large banks' aggressive acceptance of greater interest-rate and default risks imposes potential burdens on the deposit-insurance fund, and underscores the potential conflict between the Fed's duty to fight inflation and its responsibility to maintain confidence in the liquidity and integrity of private financial institutions. One reason for conducting the special survey summarized in Table 7.1 was that in early 1974 the Fed surprised many bankers by continuing to push up interest rates to fight inflation rather than lowering them to boost employment. To pursue speculative profits, many large banks intensified their policy of borrowing billions of dollars in one-day and other very-short funds to lend at longer maturities, leaving them in a poor condition to confront interest-rate increases. Many of these institutions suffered substantial losses and Fed officials wanted to assess the potential for damage if a panicky "run" on the banking system took the form of widespread nonrenewals of large banks' very-short borrowings.

To maintain confidence in the financial system, Fed officials then felt constrained to confirm their intention to lend to troubled banks on an individual-needs basis. To prevent such loans from undermining their fight against inflation, Fed officials insisted that reserves injected in this way would be offset by sales from the Fed's securities portfolio. With LM-1 and LM-2 continuing to grow in the meantime, these promises make ongoing Fed efforts to stop inflation ever more difficult and dangerous.

SUMMARY COMMENT

It is ironic that this gathering long-run crisis traces primarily to authorities' unwillingness to risk a relatively few depository-institution bankruptcies and reorganizations in 1966 and 1967. Enormous long-run costs have been accepted in exchange for short-run benefits that could (in a discounted present-value sense) have been achieved more cheaply in other ways. Whatever degree of financial stringency might have ensued in 1966 is dwarfed by the panic potential built up in the interim by regulation-induced innovations promoted by U.S. authorities' subsequent efforts to hold together an unfair and leak-prone system of comprehensive ceilings on deposit interest. Our analysis finds an instructive parallel in TV commercials that encourage consumers to change automobile oil filters regularly. The commercials pose the issue as one of paying a few dollars for an oil filter several times a year or paying hundreds of dollars for an engine overhaul in a few years time. Sooner or later, pressures generated by regulatory efforts to plaster over depository institutions' festering solvency problems are going to find release. We can only pray that the valves and rods of our national economic engine are not damaged in the process.

NOTES

1. Hodgman (1963) and Kane and Malkiel (1965) emphasize the role that the customer relationship plays in modern loan decisions. Budzeika (1976) shows that the need to meet customer loan demands has dominated the liability-management activity of New York City banks.

2. McKinney (1967) provides the clearest early analysis of the strategy.

3. The interaction of need and profit motives for bank borrowing is central to the theory of how member banks use the discount window. See Polakoff (1960) and Goldfeld and Kane (1966).

4. A "rational" forecast represents the conditional expectation of the variable whose value is being predicted, using all information known to be relevant and available. See Muth (1961) or Rutledge (1974)

5. This refocusing of regulatee activity plays a critical part in what I call the "regulatory dialectic." See Kane (1977).

6. Alternately, one can view reserve requirements as a vector of excise taxes on different types of deposits.

7. Payments services include: deposits, withdrawals, preauthorized drafts, telephone transfers, bill payments, check authorizations, credit authorizations, credit cards, debit cards, federal-government recurring payment, automated teller machines, point-of-sale terminals, cash dispensers, wire transfers, money orders, NOW drafts, NINOW drafts, and checks.

8. Through the 1950s, U.S. banks met surges in loan demand by drawing down holdings of U.S. government securities acquired in great volume during World War II.

9. This abandonment occurred in two stages: in 1970 for short maturities only and on maturities over 90 days in 1973.

10. Crane (1975) provides an interesting analysis of 1974 developments in the market for large CDs.

REFERENCES

BARNETT, R.E. HORVITZ, P.M., and SILVERBERG, S.C. (1977) "Deposit Insurance: The Present System and Some Alternatives." The Banking Law Journal: 304-332.

BUDZEIKA, G. (1976) "A Study of Liability Management by New York City Banks." Federal Bank of New York Research Paper.

CRANE, D.B. (1975) "Lessons From the 1974 CD Market." Harvard Business Review (November-December): 73-79.

FISHER, I. (1930) The Theory of Interest. New York: Macmillan.

GOLDFELD, S.M. and KANE, E.J. (1966) "The Determinants of Member-Bank Borrowing." Journal of Finance (September): 499-514.

HEEBNER, A.G. (1969) "Negotiable Certificates of Deposit: The Development of a Money Market Instrument." New York University Institute of Finance, Bulletin (February).

HODGMAN, D.R. (1963) Commercial Bank Loan and Investment Policy. Champaign: University of Illinois Press.

KANE, E.J. (1977) "Good Intentions and Unintended Evil: The Case Against Selective Credit Allocation." Journal of Money, Credit, and Banking (February): 55-69.

_____and MALKIEL, B.G. (1965) "Deposit Variability, Bank-Portfolio Allocation, and the Availability Doctrine." Quarterly Journal of Economics (February): 113-134.

McKINNEY, G. (1967) "New Sources of Bank Funds: Certificates of Deposit and Debt Securities." Law and Contemporary Problems (Winter): 71-99.

MUTH, J.F. (1961) "Rational Expectations and the Theory of Price Movements." Econometrica (July): 315-335.

POLAKOFF, M. (1960) "Reluctance Elasticity, Least Cost, and Member-Bank Borrowing: A Suggested Interpretation." Journal of Finance (March): 1-18.

RUTLEDGE, J. (1974) A Monetarist Model of Inflationary Expectations. Lexington, Mass.: Lexington Books.

Chapter 8

THE BASIS AND PRACTICE OF
TREASURY DEBT MANAGEMENT

CHARLES C. BAKER, JR.
U.S. Treasury

INTRODUCTION

In the years after World War II, the size and the management of the national debt, its potential for growth, and its effects on economic activity attracted the attention of a number of noted economists.[1] Despite this interest, however, little progress was made in developing a broadly acceptable theory of debt management on which practical debt management decisions could be based.[2] Given this unsatisfactory state of affairs, and with the further stimulus provided by the Treasury's advance refunding and "Operation Twist" activities, the 1960s and early 1970s witnessed still more efforts by a newer generation of economists to bring some order to the subject.[3] With perhaps the exception of Tobin's work, however, a usable theoretical or philosophical basis for debt management remained elusive. Consequently, in 1973 Nordhaus and Wallich (1973: 9) were still able to assert in introducing a discussion of the topic that "since World War II . . . no generally accepted philosophy of the public debt management has emerged."

Research has continued in the five or so years since that time, and fairly sweeping changes have taken place in both the size and the form of the Treasury's borrowing operations. Nonetheless, there seems to be little reason to contradict Nordhaus and Wallich's gloomy comment. In large part, the basis and objectives of debt management remain unclear. The likely quantitative effects of one or another action are largely unknown. And, as a result, debt management policies and operations have often appeared to be guided more by expediency and the desire to be an

AUTHOR'S NOTE: The author is an economist in the Office of Secretary of the Treasury. All opinions, analyses, and interpretations of fact, however, are those of the author and should in no way be construed as necessarily representing those of the Treasury Department.

economically neutral force than by analysis based on theoretical or philosphical ideas of what the role and impact of debt operations should be.

The blame for the current state of affairs cannot be laid at any particular door. This is because a major reason for the situation has been the overemphasis on detail by market and practical debt management experts, while theoretically inclined analysts have chosen to ignore those details in favor of useful, but largely impractical, generalizations.[4] As a consequence, there has been a parochialism in discussions of debt management reflective of incomplete understanding of one or another group of debt management's many levels of objectives, of the contraints on attainment of those objectives, and of the possible theoretical and operational options available for resolving conflicts and questions of priorities.[5]

The sections which follow attempt to correct this confusing situation by providing a detailed discussion of the major practical and theoretical objectives which have been proposed for debt management, and by examining the real or imagined barriers and limitations which may interfere with the attainment of those goals.

In brief outline, sections I and II are concerned with the technical goals of debt management, i.e., the financing requirements and interest minimization objectives. While these topics may be less interesting perhaps than debt management's stabilization or structural goals, they are vital for an understanding of why debt management must often choose to neglect other objectives. Section III is devoted to an examination of debt management's stabilization potential and the objectives which have been suggested as furthering that potential. These are considered both in general terms and in the context of several specific well-known analyses of the question. A fourth section reviews various structural objectives which have affected debt management operations in recent years. Finally, the debt managers' various objectives, operational goals and limitations are illustrated in a fifth section through a review of several significant operational changes of the 1970s: the use of auctions, the emphasis on regularization, and the use of Tax Anticipation and Cash Management bills. A concluding section seeks to summarize the discussion and to point to the areas where research would be highly useful.

I. TECHNICAL OBJECTIVES:
THE FINANCING REQUIREMENT

The basic *raison d'etre* for Treasury borrowing, i.e., debt management's justification in the narrowest sense, is to provide for the cash needs of the government which are not met from other sources of funds. This objective is so fundamental that in most analyses of debt management it is never examined in any detail. Because the requirement that the government's needs be financed is inescapable, however, this goal serves as the overriding constraint on all other debt management objectives. It cannot be ignored.

The importance and impact of the financing requirement on the debt manager's decisions is largely dependent on two considerations: its size and its expected market impact. As a general matter, of course, a large financing requirement will pose more problems than a smaller one. However, even a relatively small need can raise many difficulties if it is to be placed in an unreceptive market.

THE SIZE OF THE FINANCING REQUIREMENT

The Treasury's need to borrow funds arises from two sources. First, there is the need to raise money to refund existing securities at, or before, their maturity. Second, there is the need to cover the short-fall between the government's receipts and its expenditures, in a short-hand sense, the budget deficit. Stated in this way, measurement of the size of the Treasury's financing requirement would seem to be an easy matter. One would simply look up what outstanding issues are due to mature and add that amount to the deficit estimated in the President's budget. Unfortunately, the task is not so straightforward.

In the tradition of comparative statics, the majority of academic analyses of the debt management problem have been concerned solely with debt refunding strategies, holding the amount of outstanding debt constant and thus avoiding the question of the Treasury's net cash borrowing activities and any associated problems (see, for example, Okun, 1962:335). In terms of size, the Treasury's refunding task is typically far in excess of its new cash-raising operations because of the need for repeated refunding of short-term bills in the course of a given fiscal year. Even if bills are excluded from the calculation, the refunding obligation is often significantly larger than the cash activities, because the latter are roughly dependent on the size of the budget deficit.

At the beginning of any given fiscal year, measurement of the Treasury's refunding obligation is a relatively straightforward matter, especially as it applies to the note and bond sector. There may be some uncertainty about the volume of bill refundings which will be undertaken, however, since that amount will depend on the extent to which bills are used in the course of the year to meet cash needs. Looking beyond a single fiscal year, the dependence between the Treasury's cash and refunding activities is somewhat greater for each new issue, whether for cash or refunding, and creates a new refunding obligation at some point in the future. The importance of this relationship has been underscored by the use in recent years of a great many closely-spaced, relatively short-term notes to meet heavy demands for cash. Without a subsequent reversal of the budget situation and with continuing heavy cash needs, the result of these earlier actions has been that the Treasury is almost continually in the market for the purpose of refunding these or other maturing issues.[6] The point is, of course, that even from a purely technical viewpoint the Treasury debt managers must look to the future, as well as to the present, in considering the implications of their actions.

Returning to the question of the size of the financing requirement, measurement of the Treasury's cash borrowing activities is somewhat more complicated. There are several reasons for this. First, it is typical to measure that need by the unified budget deficit, but that figure is likely to be highly misleading since, on one hand, it is only an estimate and, on the other, it ignores the Treasury's need to finance so-called "off-budget" items.[7] The difference between estimated and actual unified budget deficits has often been substantial as the result of changes in underlying economic conditions, or in one or another of the assumptions on which the projections were based. And both shortfalls and overruns have been common. In the case of the off-budget requirements, the amount to be financed has risen from $0.1 billion in fiscal year 1972 to over $11 billion in fiscal year 1978.

The budget deficit, even when relatively accurate and augmented by off-budget amounts, may still give a misleading picture of the Treasury's borrowing requirement since the deficit represents only net amounts borrowed. That is, because of the ebb and flow of receipts and expenditures, subperiod borrowing requirements may substantially exceed net cash needs over, say, the entire fiscal year. Thus, for example, the Treasury's borrowing requirements have traditionally been very heavy in the latter half of the calendar year; but in the first half, heavy tax receipts result in a reduction in needs and often in debt repayment. Similar patterns arise from intramonthly and intraquarterly fluctuations in payments and receipts.

In large part, the Treasury's concern with the financing requirement is focused on its needs to borrow in the market, since that borrowing is more clearly related to other debt management objectives. Nonetheless, a substantial portion of the government's financing needs are met by nonmarket borrowing. One traditional source of such funds is the Savings Bond program. In addition, recent years have seen heavy purchases of Treasury securities, both marketable and nonmarketable, directly from the Treasury, i.e., outside of the market, by foreign official investors.[8]

Again, the budget deficit does not provide an accurate measure of the most important aspect of the financing requirement.

MARKET IMPACTS

It is clear that the market impact of the Treasury's need to raise funds for refunding maturing obligations or for raising new cash will depend primarily on market expectations of those activities. Projection of the Treasury's cash requirements, therefore, is a crucial activity for both the government and the market, and there are at the Treasury, at the Federal Reserve, and in the market a number of experts engaged in this task.[9] Using published as well as internal data, the Treasury's experts in this area have been able—at least in the near term sense—to produce highly accurate estimates of the volume and timing of the government's cash needs. For the most part, private estimating procedures have also been very successful in this area, although the lack of access to internal planning documents naturally has led to some inaccuracies.

If both the market and the Treasury can assume that they have reasonably reliable estimates of the Treasury's cash needs, then at least one aspect of the uncertainty of the market's response has been lessened, i.e., the need to place an entirely unexpected issue in the hands of surprised final investors. Attention may therefore be directed to the other characteristics of the projected financings that will determine market response—maturities, selling techniques, and so on—and to the achievement of other debt management objectives.

Basically the answers to these latter questions depend on the market's price elasticities and cross-elasticities of demand for the prospective issues—with "price" defined broadly to include the full spectrum of characteristics of an issue. In light of the importance of these elasticities, not only to the debt managers' technical financing goals but to the achievement of other debt management objectives as well, it is disturbing that there has been little or no definitive research to quantify them.[10] There are at least two important reasons for this situation. First, the concept of "price" is highly complex, involving maturity, method of sale, certainty of coupon, level of coupon, minimum available denomination, and so on. Modeling of these characteristics, which may be nonlinear in effect and which may be partially interdependent, presents major econometric problems.[11] A second reason for the paucity of empirical work on the elasticities of demand for Treasury issues has been the lack of detailed data on market response to individual issues. Since early 1973, however, the Treasury has collected individual tender data for all note and bond sales; and the absence of data can no longer be used to rationalize the lack of even rudimentary research on price elasticities.[12]

Lacking empirical studies of the price elasticity or cross-elasticities of demand for its securities, the Treasury has had to adopt a more pragmatic approach. In large part this has meant reliance on market advice and long-standing "traditions" about what can or cannot be done. The result has been a highly conservative approach to both refundings and to cash borrowing operations; and where possible, policy has been aimed at a neutrality of effect.

In questions of refunding maturing issues, this approach has tended to regularize operations and to insure that issues are in fact refunded, except in those instances where a budgetary surplus has clearly given rise to contrary market expectations. In the case of both cash and refunding operations, the lack of any quantitative estimates of demand elasticities and the resulting conservative approach to financing has generally meant that highly inelastic demand curves are assumed. One result of this assumption has been a hesitancy on the Treasury's part to increase the size of its offerings in a particular maturity area beyond what has proven successful in the past. Thus, in the early 1970s it was assumed that no more than about $1.75 billion of a five-year issue could be sold without substantial yield concessions above the outstanding market. Despite rapid growth in all financial sectors, and in the Treasury market itself, in the intervening years the size of a five-year note increased only to about $2.7 billion.[13]

Certainly, the debt managers' conservativism reflects market attitudes as well as Treasury assessments. Moreover, there is a greater willingness to vary both the size and other terms of an issue if a short-term, rather than a long-term, issue is under consideration.[14] Nonetheless, the major point remains: demand elasticities are presumed to be especially low in the short run and are assumed to change only slowly over time.[15]

This is not to say that some marginal increases in market response to an issue cannot be brought about. The Treasury's experiments with the "Dutch" auction were efforts in that direction. Such increases are sought, however, by changes in the more unusual dimensions of the price of the issue and are designed to have special appeal to one or another investor group.[16] And even in these instances, there is little firm, quantitative information about their success or failure in attracting those investors.[17]

SUMMARY

Neither of the Treasury's financing objectives can be avoided. By and large, maturing issues must be refunded, and the government's cash requirements must be met. In looking at these obligations it is important to remember two things. First, the near-term requirements of the Treasury, particularly its market borrowing needs, cannot be easily measured. Second, the borrowing decisions taken in the current environment can, and do, affect the flexibility and financing requirements of future debt managers.

Despite the difficulties that may be encountered in determining the Treasury's borrowing requirements, careful analysis by government and private experts has been able to produce highly accurate estimates and projections of those needs. The debt managers' problem is, therefore, how best to meet those needs. Unfortunately, those decisions require knowledge of the elasticity of demand for such issues, and that knowledge is sketchy at best. Lacking such information, the debt managers have typically chosen to assume the worst and have relied more on past experience and qualitative interpretation of that experience than on analytical research in their decisions.

The conservative approach to debt management that has resulted from the above methodology has meant that many characteristics of Treasury debt operations have remained static or have changed only very slowly over time; and such innovation as has occurred has been designed largely to appeal to special groups rather than to test, or to affect, the overall elasticity of demand for Treasury issues. It may be argued that this reaction, which underlies the debt managers' approach to other objectives as well, may have unnecessarily damaged debt management's ability to serve as a major policy instrument.[18]

II. TECHNICAL OBJECTIVES: INTEREST COSTS

Minimization of interest costs is one of the traditional objectives of debt management, the other being economic stabilization. A concern with interest costs is, of course, a natural one for the economist as well as for the politician for they serve as one measure of the "efficiency" of the Treasury's borrowing activities. Before turning to several theoretical and practical approaches to the problem that have been proposed, one must really ask if in fact it does matter if interest costs are *not* minimized. That is, if the burden of the debt itself is not a serious problem because it is only a transfer within the economy—as economists have argued for many years—then why should the associated interest payments, which are also transfer payments, pose an economic problem?[19] Or, put in another way, why should one concur with Tobin's statement that "from the taxpayer's point of view it is better for the Federal Reserve to enjoy . . . capital gains on [Treasury] longs than for the public to receive them" (Tobin, 1963:191f)? Are not taxpayers the public?

For most of the period since the mid-1940s, the answers to these questions would lead to the view that, while profligate behavior should not be condoned in debt management, the Treasury should not be overly concerned with cost questions.[20] In the 1970s, however, there have been two changes in the economic environment which suggest the need to pay greater attention to such costs. First, interest rate fluctuations have been far greater than at any time since the 1930s and have taken place from levels unseen in many decades. Second, the proportion of Treasury debt held by non-U.S. investors has risen markedly as a result of the balance of payments patterns that have developed in the mid-1970s, and foreign official dollar accumulations.[21] Thus, interest costs can no longer be ignored as having no significant intertemporal tax and debt service burdens. And, at least until the U.S. balance of payments problems are resolved, such payments on the debt can no longer be treated as entirely intra-U.S. transfers. In short, interest costs do matter.

Given that interest cost minimization is a reasonable debt management goal, one can distinguish several approaches to the problem. For purposes of exposition it is useful to divide these among two classifications, depending on whether their emphasis is primarily on theoretical or on practical considerations, although both will have elements of the other.

THE PRACTICAL APPROACH

It is generally conceded by term structure theorists and by market observers as well, that the "normal" shape of the yield curve is a rising one as maturity increases. The layman's reaction to this normal situation is then, that the Treasury should concentrate its financing operations in bills and very short-term notes where rates are "normally" lower. Arguing that it is impossible for debt management to have more than a transient effect on the term structure, proponents of the pure expectations explanation of the term structure would arrive at the same conclusion.[22]

While bill financing has certainly been heavily used by the Treasury in recent years, and the use of month-end two-year notes should probably also be considered as short-term borrowing, the extreme prescription of almost total reliance on short-term borrowing has generally been rejected. In part, of course, this may reflect the assumption that even in the very short term part of the maturity spectrum the elasticity of demand for Treasury issues is very low, and rate levels would soon respond to heavy supplies and would eliminate any original cost advantage of short-term issues. Even if such changes were short-lived, as advocates of the expectations hypothesis would argue, the possibility of some high-cost, short-term borrowing would exist; and it is difficult to assert that a net cost saving would occur.[23]

While the extreme version of this yield curve-based prescription for interest cost minimization may have been rejected by practical debt management, a variation has proved especially popular as a financing guide, particularly among economists and market observers advocating a "neutral" approach for Treasury debt management.[24] This variation may best be described by the advice to "finance where the market is beckoning"; that is, issues should be placed in those maturities where market irregularities have produced relatively lower yield levels.[25] It is not argued that the relative cost advantage of a given maturity will persist, only that at the moment of the financing there will be some cost saving by choosing a maturity for which, all other considerations equal, the yield is lower than that for alternative maturities.

A very sophisticated version of the "market beckoning" approach to interest minimization has been proposed by Tobin (1963:189-194). Given the decisions associated with achieving a desired degree of economic stimulus (to be discussed in section III), Tobin argues that borrowing should be in those maturities where costs are a minimum, *including* cost or savings expected to arise from capital gains due to changes in absolute and relative security prices. Unfortunately, as Cagan (1966:626) has pointed out, this gets the Treasury into the business of predicting interest rates, which is a dangerous and uncertain occupation even in the best of cirumstances. Not surprisingly, the Treasury has tended to agree with this objection.

THE THEORETICAL APPROACH

As the discussion has already indicated, several of the so-called "practical" approaches to the interest minimization question have been rejected on the grounds that they ignore important market and institutional considerations, and thus do not conform closely enough to reality to be truly practical. As will be seen, much the same difficulty arises in the major theoretical approaches to the problem.

The pure expectations theory of the term structure is perhaps the most general theoretical, as well as practical, framework relating to the interest cost minimization problem. As observed above, this analysis argues that Treasury debt management activities cannot affect the term structure, except perhaps in a transient way; and therefore cost may be minimized through borrowing at the lowest prevailing rates. For the most part, this will mean a concentration on short-term issues. The basis for the prescription is the assertion that, in perfect markets with uniformly-held expectations, arbitrage will soon remove yield variations that do not conform with underlying expectations.[26] Unfortunately, of course, markets are not perfect, and expectations are not uniformly held. Moreover, it seems clear that the term structure is affected by more than just expectations[27].

On the whole, it seems reasonable to suppose that Treasury borrowing operations can lead to changes in the term structure, not only in a short-run sense (which would still be important for interest cost calculations), but in a more lasting sense as well. That is, through their effects on the various factors determining the term structure, including perhaps expectations, the timing, volume, and terms of the Treasury's offerings will contribute to the determination of what constitutes a cost-effective borrowing strategy.[28]

Theoretical discussions of the determination of the term structure of interest rates are, of course, not aimed specifically at debt management questions. Among those analyses which are specifically concerned with debt management and with interest cost minimization, probably the most crucial are those by Rolph (1957, 1959), Tobin (1963), and Cagan (1966). Several characteristics are common to all. First, it is assumed that interest cost minimization is a secondary objective to broader economic goals. As expressed by Tobin:

> The problem of debt management, then, can be put in these terms: How are *long-run* interest costs on a given volume of federal debt to be minimized, given the contribution that debt management and monetary policy jointly make to economic stabilization? The proviso is, of course, crucial (1963:177, emphasis added).

Second, each tends to stress a dichotomous debt structure, composed of either short-term securities (bills) or very long ones (bonds). While the distinction may not be absolute, since each certainly recognizes the existence of a spectrum of debt maturities, it appears to dominate the analyses and thereby to lead to an unreality which lessens the usefulness of the arguments. Finally, in the apparent desire to present a simplified, and therefore more general, theoretical framework, each of these analyses introduces one or more "simplifying" assumptions about markets or the conduct of debt management, which have the effect of rendering them inapplicable to actual policy decisions. In the case of Rolph's work (1957:308-315), it is assumed that the marginal stimulative effect of variations in the composition of the debt are known and that the isoquants in his figures can therefore be drawn. As will be clear from the discussion in Section III, the problem is not so easy.[29]

While Tobin's discussion takes a somewhat more realistic view of the assessment of debt management's stimulative abilities, his discussion of interest cost minimization presumes a rather extraordinary prescience on the part of the debt managers with regard to future interest rate movements. That is, he indicates that cost minimization should consider, not only current yields, but the likelihood of capital gains and losses (Tobin, 1963:190-192). This same recommendation also assumes a greater degree of flexibility in the Treasury's timing of its borrowing than may in fact be the case. These problems were reviewed in section I.

Cagan's analysis sought to reconcile the apparent contradiction between the older view, proposed by Simons [55], that debt management should stress long-term finance in order to avoid creation of a potentially destabilizing stock of liquid assets and the newer view, represented by Rolph's work and that of Tobin, that a mixed composition should be sought to achieve minimum costs with the desired degree of economic stimulus. Again, however, the analysis introduces too many abstractions to be practical. For example, in addition to using a simplified long-term versus short-term debt dichotomy, Cagan assumes away all rate differentials arising from expectational factors, introduces liquidity premia that are invariant to the supply of bills, does not allow for retirement of long-term issues, and assumes that "bonds" have no liquidity (Cagan, 1966:625-626). Perhaps most damaging to the reality of his analysis, however, is the argument that the rate elasticity in response to a change in supply is significantly smaller for bills than for bonds because of "limitations of the supply of close substitutes for bills, whereas many corporate bonds appear to be good substitutes for U.S. bonds (Cagan, 1966:626). In today's markets, this statement is certainly at odds with observed rate movements and with investor reactions to the availability of CDs, Euro-dollars deposits, prime commercial paper, futures investment, options, and the like.

Other analyses of the situation could be examined; and even these three major discussions could be considered in greater detail. The conclusions that would arise from that additional review are already apparent however; the theoretical approaches to debt management which have also been concerned with interest costs have provided little practical guidance to the debt management process because of their use of often unreal, although theoretically elegant, abstractions in the attempt to provide a more generalized analysis.

SUMMARY

From both an economic and a political point of view, it is reasonable that the Treasury should seek to appear as efficient in its borrowing operations as possible. Minimal interest costs are one measure of that efficiency, and one that recent developments in markets and the ownership of the debt have made important.

Unfortunately, neither the major theoretical analyses of the interest cost objective in debt management nor those based on more explicit market considerations have been able to suggest a general approach to the problem that is superior to the highly eclectic view that financing should be undertaken in those maturities where prevailing yields suggest that the "market is beckoning." Even with this prescription, however, other debt management objectives should not be sacrificed to cost minimization. As expressed by two experts on the subject: The Secretary of the Treasury should not be over-impressed with the need to economize on interest, 1946:297.

> The minimization is not to be regarded as something to be precisely and continuously achieved. It indicates that direction in which adjustments of the debt structure should be sought (Tobin, 1963:191).

III. STABILIZATION OBJECTIVES

It is unlikely that Treasury debt management would have received more than polite passing attention from economists were its potential objectives limited to the largely technical goals described in the foregoing two sections. However, because of the size of the government's borrowing activities and the unique default-free character of its securities, the Treasury's debt management activities carry important implications for institutional and private portfolio management and, in turn, for real spending, savings, and investment decisions. Thus, it is generally conceded that debt management policy can serve as a means of achieving general economic stabilization goals alongside the efforts of the more familiar tools of monetary and fiscal policy.

Unhappily, general agreement on debt management's potential as a stabilization tool does not seem to have led to any clear-cut view on how that potential is to be realized. In the actual conduct of Treasury debt management a number of stabilization-related goals have been sought. The statements by various secretaries and under secretaries of the Treasury on the subjects of "crowding out," regularization, debt extension, twisting the yield structure, and so on, are clear examples of this concern.[30] Each of these topics, however, is highly specific and largely related to developments of the moment. They tend not to address directly the question of debt management's broader stabilization role, although of course each of these specific concerns carries implications for that wider impact.

The fact that debt management does not seem generally to have been conducted within any overall concept of what general goals should be sought should not be viewed as a condemnation of the Treasury's operations. Ascertainment of those goals has been especially complex for a number of reasons. First, and perhaps foremost, neither economists nor technicians have been able to agree on the theoretical channels through which debt management is supposed to have an impact on economic activity. Second, even when there is some agreement, there is rarely a consensus on the strength or certainty of the impact. Third, many of the proposed descriptions of debt management's effects are framed in the context of comparative statics and ignore both general equilibrium and dynamic considerations. And, finally, in those few instances when experience suggests a general operating proposition or a broad stabilization-related objective, data or econometric limitations have prevented confirmation of that suspicion.

Despite the problems just described, a number of analysts, including the author, continue to feel that debt management can and should pursue stabilization objectives; and they reject the notion that "debt management does not matter." It may be, however, that in pursuing those objectives one channel of impact may be more expedient under some conditions, whereas in different circumstances actions designed to affect markets and economic activity through other channels may be appropriate. The remainder of this section will be devoted to an examination of these various channels of impact, which for purposes of exposition have been placed in four broad categories: liquidity effects, rate level effects, relative rate effects, and flow of funds effects.[31] It should be remembered in the course of the discussion, however, that the classification scheme is often one of emphasis rather than exclusivity.

LIQUIDITY EFFECTS

The argument that debt management operations can affect activity by liquidity effects is based on two fundamental sets of assumptions. First, it is assumed that long-term securities have a greater degree of price risk than do shorter issues. Then, following Hicks (1946) and others, shorter issues have greater liquidity than long issues, and a shift in the composition of a given quantity of debt from longer to shorter maturities or, alternatively, a shortening of its average maturity, will increase its liquidity.[32] To this is then added the further assumption of a direct and positive relationship between the liquidity of the public's asset holdings and real expenditures, as described by the usual Keynesian-based income determination models.

If these assumptions hold, and experience and the results of a number of econometric investigations would suggest that they do, the Treasury's debt management strategy follows easily.[33] During periods when a stimulus to spending is desired the emphasis should be placed on issuing short-term highly liquid debt. When spending is getting out of hand and there are dangers of inflation and excessive demands, Treasury borrowing should stress long-term securities.[34]

For the most part, criticism of this approach to debt management stabilization objectives seems to have concentrated on the significance of the liquidity effects rather than their actual existence. One exception to this general types of criticism was proposed by Smith (1960:100), who asked, "Why should a person, who, because of the attractive terms offered, is induced to make a voluntary exchange of cash for long-term securities be thereby induced to change his expenditures on goods and services?" That is, the securities are substituted for idle balances, not for expenditures on real goods. In its extreme. Smith's criticism does not seem correct, for as pointed out in discussions on asset choice and in the many analyses of the demand for money in recent years, the economic unit must make choices among wants. Insofar as asset choice enters that calculus, the liquidity of the asset as part of the demand for money, goods, and earning assets must be weighed (Terrell and Frazer, 1972:9-10). Thus, while a policy of liquidity absorption through sale of long-term bonds may not be as straightforward an operation as the liquidity effect proponents would perhaps argue, some effect would likely occur as portfolio and other demands were balanced in light of the new supply of long-term securities (Tobin, 1963:154-162).

While the logic of debt management's liquidity effects may not have been subject to particularly severe criticism, the empirical importance of those effects has been seriously questioned and the effectiveness of any operations designed to affect liquidity called into doubt. That is, research on the demand for financial assets and the demand for money has established the importance of liquidity as a determining variable.[35] Nonetheless, even so mundane a question as how properly to measure, not only the average liquidity of a portfolio, but the changing marginal liquidity effects of a substitution of long- for short-term debt in that portfolio, remains largely unanswered empirically.[36] The one major effort in this area, by Van Horne and Bowers, devised a liquidity measure for individual securities and examined the changes in total liquidity brought about by the Treasury's debt management operations in the late 1950s and early 1960s.[37] They conclude that those operations had little effect; and, indeed, for a significant effect to have occurred, they argue that the Treasury's operations would have to have been so large that they would have been disruptive to capital markets (Van Horne and Bowers, 1968:533-534).

Unfortunately, the Van Horne and Bowers analysis does not entirely warrant their implied conclusion that debt management does not matter. First, there are significant data problems which are recognized in part, but which could substantially alter the results if corrected.[38] Second, their procedure of using the same time period for calculation of the liquidity measure and for testing the effectiveness of the Treasury's operations seems questionable. Finally, even if the liquidity effect of the Treasury's actions were small, there is the unresolved question of whether even a very small effect may have led to significant changes in economic activity.

Other analyses have examined empirical aspects of the liquidity-affecting role of debt management. Malkiel (1965), for example, has examined the rate implications of Treasury actions and the resulting liquidity implications; and Luckett (1964) and others have attempted to quantify reasonably the idea of the average maturity of the debt used in many discussions of liquidity effect. By and large, however, none of the discussions of debt management's ability to influence liquidity have taken the fundamental step of relating any changes in liquidity to economic activity beyond a very broad Keynesian outline. The result is then that small liquidity effects are presumed to be insignificant for stabilization. Until there is some resolution of this problem, judgment of the effectiveness of debt management's liquidity-affecting operations in economic stabilization must be withheld. In brief, the question is not one of logic or theory, but of data availability and econometrics.

RATE LEVEL EFFECTS

Debt management's effect on rate levels per se and on relative rate relationships are difficult to distinguish both logically and empirically since they are typically intermingled and occur simultaneously. Nevertheless, in both market and academic discussions of stabilization objectives for debt management operations the level of interest rates is generally presumed to impact economic activity in two distinctive ways: through investment costs and through their effects on price expectations. That is, the level of interest rates has been shown to have a significant effect on both corporate and non-federal governmental borrowing (1) through relative investment opportunity cost calculations, and (2) through expectations of future borrowing costs and the penalties involved in deferring borrowing.[39] Insofar as the level of Treasury rates is communicated through all markets, changes in that level will, therefore, affect economic activity through investment decisions. Second, for many investors Treasury market yields and Treasury borrowing rates represent "basic" interest rates and are reflective of a real, or inflation adjusted, rate of interest. Therefore, changes in the level of those rates may very well be built into the public's expectations of future price inflation, and will thereby influence spending.[40]

In the first instance, it is reasonable to assert that a new security issue by the Treasury will affect the level of interest rates in the maturity sector in which it is placed. Recognition of this first-order, and perhaps limited, effect leaves a number of important policy-related and operational questions unresolved however. First, and perhaps most important, the size of the rate effect, i.e., the elasticity of response to the increased supply, is not clearly known. This problem was also discussed in Section I. Second, despite the contributions to our knowledge of the workings of the economy by large econometric models, the effect of changing interest costs on investment and other expenditures is also largely unknown.[41] Third, the role of interest rate changes in determining price and other expectations, and the consequent effects of those shifting expectations on expenditures is still imperfectly understood and still less well quantified.

While clearly relevant to the problem at hand, the second and third of the foregoing problems have been examined in detail by a number of econometric model builders, as already noted; to review that work would be beyond the scope of this discussion. The first of the problems, however, is of more direct concern for the debt manager.

Despite the reasonableness of the assertion about first-order interest rate level effects, and substantial market testimony on the subject in a variety of contexts, it has proven especially difficult to quantify.[42] In particular, statistical tests designed to isolate that effect show virtually no significant supply-related rate changes (Baker, 1958). One interpretation of this result might be that the speed of adjustment of the market to a new supply is so rapid that the net rate change caught by the time frequency used in the models is nil. A second, and perhaps even more plausible, explanation is suggested by the discussion of Section I; namely that the market's broad knowledge of the Treasury's needs and the limits on its financing flexibility imposed by its own conservative approach to its operations allows the market to adjust gradually in advance of a new supply to the point where significant supply-related rate adjustments are unnecessary when the issue is actually marketed.

Whatever the hypothesized reason for the apparent lack of supply-related effects on the level of rates, it is clear that the debt manager is once again confronted by a situation of considerable uncertainty about the effects of his actions. Even with the evidence of very little net effect, there can be no assurances that such a result is not caused by special circumstances that may not prevail in the future.

The consequence of this uncertainty is that the conservative presumption of perverse effects is reenforced, and support for a policy of debt management neutrality is strengthened in order to avoid or lessen the possibility of economic error and the economic and political costs that might accompany or develop from such errors.[43]

RELATIVE RATE EFFECTS

An important part of the relative rate effect view of Treasury debt management's stabilization potential has already been covered in the discussion of term structure arguments about interest cost minimization. Briefly, the pure expectations hypothesis of the term structure argues that, under certain market conditions or assumptions, it is impossible for new supplies of Treasury issues to have more than a transient effect on relative rate relationships. However, the conditions assumed by that theory appear to be highly unrealistic for actual markets. Thus, it is argued that Treasury operations can have a significant and lasting effect on relative rates.

By and large, the argument presented by the term structure theorists, either for or against a relative rate effect, is framed in the context of a market for a single type of security. If not entirely true in purely theoretical discussions, this has certainly been the case for empirical testing. When rate differentials and relative rate relationships among different markets and type of securities or assets are involved, however, the problem takes on different aspects. In particular, it becomes one of portfolio or asset choice and, by extension, involves real spending and investment decisions, which are of course the final goals of stabilization policy.

Tobin has provided perhaps the best known and most thorough exposition of this area of the analysis of debt management's stabilization potential, basing his argument on the importance of the differential rate of return between loans and equity in influencing economic activity. To quote directly from the core of his analysis:

> What is the route by which management of money and public debt may affect economic activity? Ultimately its effectiveness depends on its ability

to influence the terms on which investors will hold the existing stock of real capital and absorb new capital. If investors demand a higher rate of return on capital than the existing stock can yield, given the state of technology and the supplies of labor and other factors of production, investment will decline and the economic climate will be deflationary. If investors are willing and anxious to expand their holdings of capital at a rate of return lower than the marginal productivity of the capital stock, investment will tend to outrun saving and the outlook will be inflationary. . . . The course of economic activity, then, depends on the difference between . . . the anticipated marginal productivity of capital . . . [and the] rate of return on capital equity at which the public would be willing to hold the existing stock of capital, valued at current prices. It is this rate of return, *the supply price of capital*, which the monetary and debt authorities may hope to influence through changing the supplies and yields of assets and debts that compete with real capital for place in the portfolios and balance sheets of economic units. . . . Lowering the long-term Government bond rate is not expansionary if the premium above it required for investment in real capital is at the same time commensurately increased. Increasing the long-term bond rate is not deflationary if the means that increase it at the same time lower in equal degree the equity-bond differential (1963:150-151).

In addition to its thoroughness and elegance, Tobin's analysis is of special importance from two practical points of view. First, it provides a detailed discussion of the specific linkages through which debt management operations are expected to affect financial markets, financial decisions, and eventually the course of economic activity. Of course, the quantification of these linkages had to await research such as that by Bosworth and Duesenberry; but Tobin's work at the very least provided a framework beyond the broad-brush, vaguely Keynesian context found in most debt management discussions. Tobin's work also for the first time underscored the complexity of any debt management policy decision designed to have economic stabilization effects. That is, his analysis shows that the policy prescription cannot be described in such simple terms as "short-term debt in a depression and long-term bonds in a boom." It is this complexity, of course, which has made debt management's stabilization potential and effectiveness such an intractable subject.

Turning from the theoretical discussions of the subject to practical attempts of the debt managers to affect relative rate relationships, the major focus of analytical attention has been on the Treasury's activities in the late 1950s and early 1960s. During that period, the Treasury attempted through use of advance refundings and other specific debt tailoring actions to achieve a significant lengthening of the maturity structure and, at the same time, to effect a "twisting" of the yield curve, lowering long yields, and raising short-term ones. These actions, and particularly the latter attempts to twist the yield curve, provided more grist for analytic mills than probably any other debt management actions in recent history.

In general, these analyses were concerned with the rate effect on the Treasury term structure, and changes in the rate differentials between Treasury and other securities were generally not considered.[44] Nonetheless, in dealing with the Treasury term structure, these experiments formed important tests of the immutability of the term structure to supply changes. As pointed out by Nordhaus and Wallich (1973:13-15) in their survey of the major work in this area, the econometric evidence in favor of a durable supply effect on relative rates is uncertain at best, and the conclusion of most of these analyses is that any Treasury attempts to bring about an effect were, and will be, frustrated.

This conclusion, and the econometrics leading to it, have been criticized on a number of grounds. In some instances, for example Wallace's (1967) critique of Modigliani and Sutch, it has been argued that the model and the tests have not been clearly enough specified to distinguish among possible alternatives. In other cases, the appeal has been more directly to expert market observation (Goodhart, 1973:27). Perhaps the most devastating argument against the conclusion that the Treasury cannot affect the term structure, i.e., relative rate relationships, has been provided by Culbertson by taking the argument to its logical conclusion; namely, that there would be no rate effects if the Treasury were to decide to issue all of its debt as short bills or as long bonds. Or alternatively, it makes no difference how much debt the Treasury issues in any maturity category (Culbertson, 1973:35).

It is clear that there are significant unresolved conflicts among theoretical, econometric, and market-based approaches to the question of the Treasury potential for affecting relative rate relationships. Given the importance of relative rate movements in both official and market discussions of debt management policy and operations, this is a highly unsatisfactory state of affairs. Resolution of this conflict would seem certainly to be a quantitative problem and is likely to depend on one or a combination of three needed areas of empirical research. First, a richer measure of the changes in the term structure and of changes in the composition of the debt should be sought.[45] Second, it is not clear that the models used for testing have accounted adequately for the many exogeneous factors that can affect the term structure; work to discriminate among term structure-influencing factors is needed. Third, the role of expectations and their potential for change, both before and after a financing, have not been thoroughly examined for perverse or econometrically confounding effects.[46]

While interest in the term structure effects of debt management operations continues, attention and analysis since the late 1960s has focused more on the relative rate effects of Treasury actions between Treasury securities and other earning assets and investment alternatives. A number of economic and financial developments appear to have been responsible for this change in analytical emphasis. In the area of short-term rate relationships, a number of new financial instruments have been developed since the late 1960s, and competition for funds by the issuers of those instruments has intensified. That competition has been complicated by the limitations imposed upon many of those issuers by regulatory ceilings on the rates that may be offered while, at the same time, market rates of interest were being pushed to record levels by inflation and the consequent response of monetary policy. In the long-term sector, economic recession and the fear that burgeoning federal financing requirements would compete with an already sluggish investment climate underscored concern with rate spreads between Treasury and other long-term instruments, much along the lines of Tobin's analysis. This concern was exacerbated by the fact that the Treasury's huge financing needs carried a danger of an undesired shortening of the overall maturity of the debt, leading to a structurally-related push by the debt managers to market a greater amount of long-term bonds.[47]

With the problem of undesirable debt management-related pressure on interest rate spreads present in both short- and long-term markets, but with the unavoidable requirement that the government's needs be met, the Treasury's response to the resulting dilemma was two-fold. First, there were direct attempts to discourage investment in certain Treasury issues; these actions, however, are more appropriately discussed in the subsection on flow-of-funds effects. Second, the Treasury sought to avoid selling its issues at rates that would exert a direct effect on rate spreads. This was accomplished by the adoption of auction techniques, for selling not only Treasury bills, but for setting the price on notes and bonds as well.[48] By so doing, the Treasury hoped that the resulting prices would be very little out of line with prevailing market levels and, given a program of careful consultation with the professional portion of the market concerning prospective Treasury requirements, abrupt and potentially disruptive changes in rate spreads among markets could be avoided. Section V will discuss these actions in somewhat more detail.

The Treasury's debt management response to the financial difficulties of the 1970s illustrates again a basic theme of this chapter. The theoretical basis for debt management operations, for whatever objectives, is largely unclear; and the empirical research that has been undertaken has typically muddied the picture even more. As a consequence, Treasury debt management has followed a policy of seeking "neutrality" in its impact on markets, on financial institutions, and on the course of economic activity. Under the circumstances, it is possible that that may have been the best course of action.

FLOW-OF-FUNDS EFFECTS

As discussed in the previous subsection, Treasury financing activities can and do exert an effect on relative rate relationships. While some actions may be taken to minimize or intensify the spread changes, e.g., use of auction or fixed price methods for selling the issues, there is still the possibility that new Treasury security offerings will attract funds from other borrowers. In the market for short-term funds, this phenomenon primarily affects financial intermediaries such as banks, savings and loan associations, mutual savings institutions, and other thrift intermediaries, and is known appropriately as disintermediation. In the long-term sector, competition from Treasury issues is spread more widely over a number of potential borrower categories, including corporations and state and local governments; and the phenomenon in this area has come to be known by the more general term "crowding out."

Thrift intermediaries serve as one of the major sources of housing finance in this country and are, therefore, directly related to one of the cornerstones of general governmental policy. In recent years, however, casual observation of the experience of these institutions suggests that the threat of large and disturbing fluctuations in their deposit flows has increased markedly.[49] Among the major reasons that have been cited for this development, two of the most important appear to have been the saving public's rising awareness of the corrosive effects of persistent inflation, and the fact that higher market rates and a number of market innovations now provide a small investor with the opportunity for higher-yielding assets than a savings deposit at a regulated institution.

Concern with the possibility of "crowding out" of private borrowers by heavy Treasury demands for funds, especially in the long-term sector, received particular emphasis by Secretary Simon at about the time that the U.S. economy was beginning to show signs of recovering from the recession of the early 1970s (Simon, 1975; 1976). At the time, the economic recovery was still somewhat hesitant, and it could easily be argued that much of the upswing was, and would have to continue to be, the result of government spending. Investment in new capital, although sorely needed, was particularly sluggish; and much of the private support for the recovery was derived from consumption expenditures. Thus, it seemed likely, as proved to be the case, that substantial federal budget deficits and Treasury borrowing requirements would continue, and would constitute a potential threat to the stimulation of investment expenditures needed for noninflationary economic growth.

In the 1970s, therefore, the Treasury was confronted by the problem that, whatever financing strategy it adopted, there were likely to be unwanted flows of funds to the government market. Unfortunately, quantitative work by neither the academic community nor the market was especially helpful in assessing the relative strength of alternative debt operations in stimulating or restraining such flows. Nor was there guidance on the question of whether such flows *should* be stimulated or restrained for achievement of general economic goals.[50]

Modeling of thrift flows and of related asset selection has taken place in a number of contexts, especially in the investigation of the financial decisions of households.[51] In terms of a broader approach, however, encompassing both short- and long-term asset flows, the most complete treatment is probably that by Bosworth and Duesenberry.[52] There are, in addition, a number of flow-of-funds projections—and by implication, theoretical models—used by major government securities dealers and by analysts within the government.[53] In most instances, however, the models underlying these projections are unspecified and appear to be based on highly subjective interpretations of economic relationships or on ARIMA-type analysis.

Whatever their underlying model form or elegance, all of these analyses are focused on broad economic relationships rather than debt management problems. Consequently, all of them, including that by Bosworth and Duesenberry, suffer from the same fault: they do not consider the problem of debt composition beyond the simplified assumption that the term structure, and by implication the compositional effects of the debt, may be represented by two, or rarely more than three, market yields. Thus, the debt manager's problem of assessing the potential flow-of-funds effects of an entire spectrum of maturity and pricing alternatives is never addressed.

Recognizing and potential attractiveness of its securities and the likely effect that heavy Treasury borrowing might have on the availability of funds to other borrowers, but lacking any empirical guidance for its actions, it is not surprising that the Treasury has chosen a somewhat prag-metic approach to its problems. Specifically, in order to cope with the threat of disintermediation into short-term Treasury issues, it chose to vary the nonprice terms of its offerings. Thus, when a sharp increase in bill rates in the fall of 1970 and the winter of 1971 led to long queues of small investors seeking to buy bills, the Treasury increased the minimum subscription size from $1,000 to $10,000. A few years later when two-year notes appeared to be attracting similar interest, the minimum subscription for those issues was raised from $1,000 to $5,000. Then, in the summer of 1974 when deposit flows at thrift institutions were already weak, the Treasury sold by price auctions two notes carrying 9 percent coupons. The response, said to have been from individuals, was extraordinary; and there were loud complaints from the thrift and housing industries. As a result, the Treasury adopted the yield auction in order to avoid the announcement effects of a high coupon. Section V discusses this and other auction decisions in greater detail.

In response to the potential for flow-of-funds problems in the long-term market, the Treasury's approach was less active. In general, the attitude seemed to be that structural considerations required continuation of long-term bond sales begun when the Congress granted an exemption to the 4-1/4 percent interest ceiling imposed by the Second Liberty Bond Act. In an even broader sense, it could be argued that the Treasury's attitude was similar to Ricks' response to Henry Kaufman's complaints on this matter; namely, that the purpose of markets is to effect a rationing of financial resources, and the fact that the government requires funds implies that there has been a policy decision that the underlying programs needing those funds are more important than the needs of the marginal, "crowded out" borrowers.[54]

SUMMARY

Consideration of the economic stabilization potential of its actions certainly plays a vital role in the Treasury's debt management decisions, although the expression of that concern is perhaps not as clear and as strong as some economists would desire. The stabilization effects of debt management, however, are complex and exert their effect in several quite distinct ways: through interest rate levels and spreads, through their influence of the liquidity of the public's asset holdings, and through the changing ebb and flow of funds throughout the economy. Any given debt operation will like be felt through all of these channels, but the impact through one or another may be greater in a particular economic environment.

Unfortunately, economic theory has provided the debt manager with little guidance, in even an abstract sense, for his actions. In those instances where a theoretical approach has attempted to focus on policy guidance, the reality of the underlying assumptions is open to serious questions or the advice conflicts sharply with other, inescapable Treasury debt objectives.

Empirical investigation of the effects of Treasury actions in an economic stabilization context have, if anything, only added to the confusion about the impact of debt management. Some lead to the conclusion that debt management does not matter, others suggest clearly that it does, and still others fail to reach any conclusive results whatsoever.

The Treasury's response to this highly unsatisfactory situation has been two-fold. On the one hand it has attempted to neutralize its operations' effects on markets, presuming that such a course of action reduces the risk of adverse economic reactions. The logical flaw in this presumption is obvious. Second, where direct action is necessary to avoid likely known adverse market reactions, a pragmatic approach of altering the nonprice terms of offerings has been adopted.

Whatever the rationale and form of the Treasury's response to the complex problems of its stabilization effects, one thing is clear: the quantitative basis and empirical analysis underlying those actions, or for analyzing their effectiveness, has been sketchy at best.[55] Thus, it is not clear that Treasury action was always needed or, if needed, that it produced the desired result (Roob, 1973:182-185). In the absence of that kind of information and research, there is little ground on which to fault the Treasury's choice of actions.

IV. STRUCTURAL OBJECTIVES

The final group of debt management's policy objectives is a mixture of a number of proximate goals relating to the Treasury's concern for the operation of the market for its securities and, by implication, for the overall financial fabric of the country. This concern was perhaps best outlined by Roob:

> It seems to me that from the standpoint of the Treasury many of our objectives in debt management revolve around a continuing effort to ensure that the U.S. Government security remains the best in the world. . . . This in turn requires that a smoothly functioning secondary market must exist wherein investors and traders can move freely into and out of them, from one to another maturity area and from issue to issue with a minimum of transactions cost. . . . [W]e hope the changes we have made have led or will lead to a better meshing of Federal financing operations with the market demands of other borrowers and to a continuing improvement in the functioning and efficient of the market [1973:179-180].

The key phrase in this statement is "smoothly functioning secondary market." In part, the Treasury's attempts to minimize the market impact of its operations may be considered within the efforts to promote this aim. Of greater importance, however, are two other areas of concern: the maturity structure of the debt and the institutional conditions in the market, especially as applied to the primary dealers.

MATURITY STRUCTURE

The Treasury's concern with the maturity composition, or structure, of the debt has focused almost entirely on the question of debt extension, i.e., with efforts to lengthen the average maturity of the debt.[56] Three major arguments underlie this emphasis. First, the shortening and need for frequent refinancing of the debt can involve undesirable administrative and economic costs. Second, in the tradition of accepted financial management, permanent or relatively permanent debt should be funded into long-term securities while short-term borrowing should largely reflect current or working capital needs. Third, there are important investor needs for a default-free long-term investment instrument and a market in which that instrument can be easily traded.

The maturity structure of outstanding Treasury debt will inevitably shorten with the passage of time unless offset by positive debt management actions. If such actions are not forthcoming and new cash operations are themselves concentrated in relatively short-term issues, both the size and frequency of the Treasury's refinancing obligation will increase, as discussed in section I. Under such circumstances, it may be argued that, as the premier borrower in the country's capital markets, those operations may very well overshadow demands for credit by private borrowers and may thus lead to adverse overall economic developments. In addition, it may also be argued that the need to retire and reissue a greater volume of securities to maintain a given level of outstanding debt would likely increase the administrative costs of debt management.

The fact that greater concentration of Treasury activity in short-term markets would leave intermediate- and long-term markets more to private borrowers, and the current use of computer-based records instead of physical securities for short-term Treasury issues, both pose fairly serious objections to the above arguments. Nonetheless, perhaps partly in the tradition of Henry Simons, both market and official experts continue to argue that *some* increased costs would be incurred if the shortening of the maturity composition of the debt were allowed to proceed unchecked.

Certainly the tenets of traditional financial management argued for Treasury efforts to extend the maturity of the debt. In fact, in light of the congressional recognition of a "permanent" amount of federal debt in its annual exercises to extend the total debt ceiling, it would not be unreasonable to advocate a program of truly permanent debt issues, i.e., perpetuities. Failing this, and interest in such a program has never received more than token attention, it is still reasonable that the Treasury should seek some lengthening of the debt through issuance of long-term bonds.

The third rationale for the Treasury's interest in debt extension is directly related to Roob's statement of structural objectives. That is, it is concerned with the provision of an efficient secondary market for Treasury issues in which investors can find securities to meet their needs and in which both investors and traders can move freely, and without undue cost, among maturities. In the early 1970s this need became especially crucial, for the rise in market interest rates meant that the yield on new bonds would have to be above the 4-1/4 percent ceiling imposed on Treasury bond rates by the Second Liberty Bond Act. Thus, with no new issues, the long Treasury market had failed to keep pace with investor demands; coupons on outstanding issues failed to reflect the income streams available on alternative investments; and as more and more issues became lodged in permanent, nontrading investor hands, the market for such bonds became increasingly thin and vulnerable to externally generated shocks.[57]

In the spring of 1971, Congress granted the Treasury an exemption to the interest rate ceiling for up to $10 billion of new bonds. In the years since then, the exemption has been extended and enlarged, and more than $35 billion in new long-term bonds have been sold. While these actions are said to have made considerable progress toward the Treasury's third maturity structure objective, i.e., revitalization of the long-term Treasury market's viability, little progress has been made on either of the other reasons for this objective. In fact, the average age of the public debt fell from 3½ years at the end of March 1971, when the exemption to the rate ceiling was first enacted, to 2 years and 11 months at the end of 1977. In addition to, and perhaps reflective of, this lack of debt lengthening progress, the Treasury's desires to extend the debt and to increase the size of the long market have also presented problems and conflicts for other debt management objectives, as discussed in greater detail in sections II and III.

It may well be that greater clarification of the bases and actual effects of the Treasury's attempts to pursue other objectives will lead to a greater success, or perhaps to a reassessment, in this area of its structural goals. For the time being, however, the empirical evidence—such as it is— suggests that debt extension may or may not be a successful policy as it can now be pursued.[58]

INSTITUTIONAL CONDITIONS

It is generally recognized that the U.S. government securities market is the country's largest. With the exception of recent rules for the trading of futures contracts, it is also entirely unregulated. In this market, probably the single most important institutional group is that composed of the primary dealers. These dealers act as the major underwriting group for new Treasury issues and in addition serve as the major market-makers for Treasury securities, standing ready to provide quotations for all issues and to buy and sell at those prices. Finally, the dealers are generally considered to be a vital informational link to the demands and attitudes of final investors.

In light of the role played by the primary dealers, it is not surprising that the Treasury's institutional concerns in pursuing its structural goal of an efficient, freely-functioning secondary market should focus on the performance, on the health, on the standards, and on the advice of these firms. Contact with the dealers is therefore frequent and probing; and their advice is sought on a variety of matters, including not only the timing but the maturities and other terms of the Treasury's security offerings.

A major forum for these discussions is the regular quarterly meetings of representatives of this group with Treasury officials at the time of the midquarter refunding and financing operations.[59] At those meetings, the Treasury usually discusses its prospective cash and refunding requirements over the remainder of the calendar quarter. Economic and general financial conditions are reviewed by both sides, and the meetings typically conclude with a presentation of recommendations for the forthcoming financing by the dealers.[60] The confidentiality of the proceedings is preserved by the fact that the dealers are precluded from returning to their respective firms until after the Treasury's financing announcement, and the data on the Treasury's prospective requirements has been made public. The reports and recommendations of the dealer representatives themselves are filed with the Library of Congress, in accordance with their role as chartered Federal Advisory Committees, and are publicly available after a suitable time lag.

In retrospect, a review of events shows that the Treasury has sometimes conducted its financing along the lines recommended by the advisory committees; at others it has not. This poses several important questions. First, if the information provided by the committees and their recommendations are not followed, how valuable to the Treasury are these groups? Then, by implication, are there not problems of propriety involved despite the confidentiality involved? And finally, should not these advisory groups be expanded to include representatives of other financial groups?

Some would answer each of these questions in a way highly critical of the Treasury's procedures. That point of view would not be reflective of the actual situation however. First, the information provided by the committees and their recommendations represent a concensus of views, often with strong arguments for a number of alternative courses of action. At times the Treasury's decision, reflecting perhaps far broader concerns than the market, has favored the alternatives. Second, the meetings with the advisory groups allow the debt managers to review industry-wide problems, to raise new and experimental ideas for reactions, and to respond to suggestions and criticism from the market as it is communicated through these crucial participants in its operations.

On the question of these meetings' having overtones of an improper relationship between a small market group and the Treasury, the Treasury's own actions on a number of instances would belie this. For example, the Treasury has steadfastly resisted any pressures, from the dealer community or from other financial organizations, to raise further the minimum denominations for its securities and thereby limit smaller investor access beyond present levels. In a positive direction, the Treasury has in recent years increased the maximum amount allowable for a noncompetitive subscription in its note and bond auctions, thus increasing the appeal of those sales to unsophisticated investors or those with limited resources. Finally, the Treasury's experiments with the "Dutch" auction were also designed to increase the appeal of its securities to the smaller or less sophisticated investor, despite the well-recognized disadvantages of such sales for professional market participants.[61]

It may be argued that some expansion in the number of Treasury financing advisory groups would be useful. Indeed in past years, there were such groups from several sectors of the thrift industry. However, those groups did not represent a group of market professionals with continuous contact to many investor groups, but instead groups of final investors primarily concerned with their own financial status. To admit some such groups to an advisory status would only encourage other investor groups, large and small, to seek a similar position to the end that a lobbying situation rather than an advisory situation would be created.

SUMMARY

The Treasury's concern with promoting a smoothly functioning secondary market for its securities is, of course, interrelated with many of its other objectives. In a more purely structural sense, however, it is possible to identify two more specific sets of goals: those associated with the maturity structure of the debt and those concerned with institutional conditions in the market.

The former of these has been devoted largely to attempts to effect an extension of the average maturity of the debt and to revitalize in the process the market for long-term Treasury issues. The latter has primarily emphasized the role and operations of the dealer community, stressing the need for communication between the Treasury and that portion of the market for new ideas, for financial information, and for criticism and surveillance.

The Treasury's success in its efforts to extend the maturity of the debt and restore the viability of the long-term market appear to have had been mixed, apparently due in large part to conflicts and limitations arising from other, higher priority financing requirements and stabilization objectives. In the areas of ensuring that the institutional conditions of the market assisted in its other goals, the continued efficient and unregulated operation of the market and its ability to handle smoothly the government's burgeoning needs for funds is ample testimony to the Treasury's success.

V. POLICY AND OPERATIONAL RESPONSES—ILLUSTRATIONS

Throughout the discussion of the four preceding sections, specific examples of Treasury operations were used to illustrate the principles or difficulties involved in seeking complex and often conficting debt management policy objectives. Nonetheless, before concluding this chapter, it is useful to examine in a little more detail some major areas of operational change in debt management's activities in recent years with an eye to the complexity of the policy basis for those changes. There are innumerable examples which might be chosen for these illustrations, depending on the time frame selected or the degree of generality desired. In the 1970s, however, three such operational areas were cause for more than routine discussion, and all serve as clear examples of the policy difficulties and the operational constraints confronting the Treasury debt managers. These are the use of auctions for selling notes and bonds; the emphasis on regularity in note and bond financing; and the attempts to smooth out the wide fluctuations in the Treasury's cash needs by use of very short-term cash management securities.

AUCTIONS

Use of auctions is certainly not new to Treasuring finance. Treasury bills have been regularly sold by a purely discriminatory form of auction for many years. The initiation of public sales of Treasury coupon-bearing issues in the 1970s was, however, a new development.[62] The first such sale was in November 1970, when $2 billion of new eighteen-month notes were marketed by a price auction against a preannounced 6-3/4 percent coupon. In addition to noting that the auction was in terms of the price of the issue, not the yield, the fact that banks could pay for one-half of their awards by crediting Treasury accounts should also be stressed.[63] Given the advantage to banks and the fact that the coupon was somewhat above the market for similar issues, it is not surprising that response to the issue was enthusiastic (U.S. Treasury, 1971:20).

In assessing the policy basis for the use of auctions, the crucial question is, "Why was late 1970 chosen for a radical departure from the postwar tradition of fixing in advance the price and yield of Treasury notes and bonds?" Market conditions, and both technical and structural objectives, were the underlying reasons.

Throughout 1970, fluctuation in market interest rates had been relatively erratic and often very large. In addition, a number of international shocks had periodically unsettled the market. Such conditions posed considerable risks for the usual form of Treasury financing in which a fully-priced issue was announced by the Treasury, to be followed several days later by a subscription period of two or three days. Not only did this procedure expose the Treasury to dangers of mispricing an issue in a fast-moving market, but even if correctly priced at announcement time, subsequent market movements could lead to a souring of the issue and heavy losses by already-committed investors or, alternatively, to undue speculative gains should the market move be favorable.[64] Auction pricing, in contrast, eliminated the awkward delays in pricing and subscribing for the issue, allowed the market itself to determine the price, and thus removed the Treasury from the necessity of having to guess the price and the likely course of the market until the financing was complete.[65]

In the context of debt management's objectives, the auction appeared to accomplish several things. By appealing to competitive price determination, it insured the best cost to the Treasury. In addition, it encouraged the market to utilize its own knowledge and efficiencies in absorbing the new issue. And, as a result of the market's participation in the process, one should not ignore the fact that the auction was consistent with the Treasury's attempts in late 1970 to minimize the disturbing effects of its financings on an already sensitive market (U.S. Treasury, 1971:9-10, 17-20).

Note auctions using price bidding against a fixed coupon were clearly regarded as a successful marketing method by the Treasury, and the techniques found repeated use in the following years. Then, in the winter of 1973 and in late summer of 1974, two important variants of the auction method of marketing Treasury notes and bonds were introduced: the uniform-price or "Dutch" auction, and the yield auction with the coupon rate and security price set after the fact.

In a uniform-price or "Dutch" auction, bids are submitted just as they would be in a purely discriminatory auction of, say, Treasury bills. The bids are then arrayed to determine awards and a minimum acceptable price (or maximum yield) is set. In the purely discriminatory auction, of course, all successful bids are awarded at the price or yield actually bid, and the Treasury expropriates the buyer surplus. In the "Dutch" auction, however, all awards to successful bidders are made at the last-accepted, or stop-out, price or yield. *Ceterus paribus*, the total interest cost of the issue will be greater for the Treasury under a "Dutch" auction. Proponents of the method, however, argue that the prospect of higher yields, of less price/yield uncertainty, and of less immediate trading risk immediately following the auction will all stimulate greater demand for the issue than would have been the case; and the resultant shift in the demand schedule will lead in fact to lower interest costs for the Treasury.[66]

Despite the distinguished history of the idea, the "Dutch" auction had not been tested as a marketing method for Treasury securities until the Treasury's announcement in December 1972 that in January it would use a price-based "Dutch" auction to sell $675 million of 6-3/4 percent twenty-year bonds. As described in the Annual Report of the Secretary, this action was designed "[to continue] to improve the maturity structure of the debt, reestablish a viable market for long-term Treasury obligations, and finance Treasury's cash requirements in a manner supportive of the administrations' economic policies" (U.S. Treasury, 1973:21). In terms of the objectives discussed in this chapter, it was hoped that the "Dutch" auction would lessen the interest costs of the issue; that it would increase general investor interest in the long-term market by removing some of the uncertainty about yield levels; that it would stimulate sufficient interest that the Treasury's need to rely on possibly inflationary short-term finance would be lessened; and that it would continue the Treasury's program of providing newer and more tradable issues to the long-term market.

Just as a single swallow does not make a spring, the success of the single "Dutch" auction sale, in comparison to alternative auction methods, could not be judged. On the basis of largely subjective interpretation of the results, the "Dutch" auction did not seem to be a failure, and the "Dutch" auction was used for selling long-term bonds until the middle of 1974.[67] Since that time, both price and yield based discriminatory auctions have been used to market long-term issues, thereby providing something of a statistical basis for analysis of the effectiveness of the "Dutch" auction technique in stimulating a shift in demand and lowering the interest costs of long-term bond sales. Unfortunately, while some initial investigation of this problem has been undertaken, the question still remains largely unresolved (Tsao and Vignola, 1977).

As indicated, the early discriminatory note auctions and the "Dutch" auctions were conducted in terms of the price bids on the new issue with a predetermined coupon rate. This selling method poses two problems for the Treasury however, despite its general advantage over the completely fixed price offering. First, it does not completely remove an issue's pricing from the risk of an unexpected change in the market's leading to a sharp distinction between the coupon rate and the likely auction price/yield level. Such a situation not only carries the risk of confusing potential bidders, but can lead to serious tax-related limitations on the issue's tradability.[68] The second problem posed by the price-based auction is that the announced coupon, if attention-getting, may attract an undesirable interest in the issue from thrift deposits.

The first of these possibilities occurred in the summer of 1974, when a sudden deterioration of the market pushed the bidding for a new Treasury note to the limit of the price discount before capital gains treatment of trading profits would have been necessary. Despite the narrow escape from such a pricing embarrassment, the Treasury continued to use price auctions until the following summer. At that time, however, the Treasury's announcement of two 9 percent note auctions (an historical record) attracted heavy individual investor interest in the issue just at a time when thrift institutions were already concerned about the strength of their deposit flows (U.S. Treasury, 1975:16-19). With markets exhibiting increasing sensitivity and more erractic rate movements, and with heavy pressure from the thrift industry to avoid disintermediation pressure, both technical and stabilization debt management objectives argued for a change. As a result, the Treasury's next note sale, in late September, was sold by the then-new idea of a yield auction, whereby bidding in the purely discriminatory auction was in terms of the issue's yield with the coupon, and price to be set after the average awarded yield was established.

The yield auction met several objectives. It let the market entirely decide the yield of the new issue, totally removing the Treasury from the pricing process. It avoided any danger of tax-related price discount problems. And it removed the potential for disintermediation and market disruption that might accompany announcement of an especially attractive coupon, i.e., it worked to minimize the effect of the Treasury's financing operations on financial markets and financial flows (Baker, 1976:148-149).

REGULARIZATION

In the early 1970s heavy direct Treasury borrowing requirments, arising from a succession of large budget deficits, and the very rapid proliferation of near-Treasury obligations as the result of credit demands by federal agencies led to pressure for greater regularization and routinization in the Treasury's financing activities in order to cushion the market from the impact of those demands (Volcker, 1972). It was felt by both market participants and Treasury officials that the government's needs for funds could prove unsettling to the market, in the sense of leading to undesirably high rates of interest and of damaging the access of other borrowers to the capital markets. Moreover, there was a fear that the shocks generated by unexpected large Treasury offerings could damage the market's efficiency because of the risk and uncertainty market-makers would have to incur in positioning securities and maintaining viable trading inventories.

Like auctions, regularization was not a new concept in Treasury finance; regular, and largely routine, sales of Treasury bills have taken place on a weekly schedule for many years. In the coupon-bearing sector, it was proposed that regularization take the form of scheduled sales of known-maturity Treasury notes. Initially, the operation would involve end-of-quarter, two-year notes. Such scheduling, it was argued, would allow investors to plan their activities with more certainty, thereby potentially enlarging investment demand for such issues, while at the same time lessening the potential market impact such issues might have (Kaufman, 1973:155-156). If the number of these issues were eventually expanded, it was also argued that the Treasury would be able to effect significant variations in its borrowing activity through relatively minor adjustments in the size of these securities, much in manner it raises or reduces its cash by marginal changes in the size of the weekly bill sales.

The first such issue was a $2 billion, two-year note sold at the end of September 1972; a second two-year end-of-quarter issue for the same amount was sold in the following December. The type of problems that can arise with such attempts at regularity were demonstrated in the spring of the next year when heavy foreign purchases of securities directly from the Treasury so increased the Treasury's cash position that the spring and early summer two-year issues would have been superfluous and they were skipped. Whatever initial difficulties may have been encountered, the advantages of these "cycle notes," as they came to be called, for the Treasury's cash-raising operations soon became clear; and by mid-1976, two-year maturity note cycles were established at the end of every month, and four- and five-year offerings became a feature of the end or beginning of each calendar quarter.[69]

The fact that announcement and sale of these issues is typically accorded little more than passing attention is certainly one indication of their having achieved the objective of minimal market disruption. And, given the fact that their size has been increased—and on occasion reduced—without notable market impact points to success on other grounds. Nevertheless, as discussed in earlier sections of this chapter, these issues do pose debt management problems in the areas of refunding inflexibility and of the need for an almost continual Treasury presence in the market. It may be that the Treasury's policy efforts toward regularization and routine financing will prove to have been too much of a good thing.

CASH MANAGEMENT BILLS

The discussion of the Treasury's financing objectives in section I noted that one set of problems arises from the mere ebb and flow of receipts and expenditures, and the fact that those flows do not coincide. Thus, the Treasury's cash needs, while not necessarily large over, say, an entire fiscal year, may be extraordinarily heavy at certain times of a month or a quarter; at other times, cash inflows may prove an embarrassment if expenditures are slack, since the Treasury has traditionally been unable to invest excess balances.[70]

It is clear that the solution to the problem posed by these circumstances, i.e., the avoidance of nonearning idle balances insofar as possible, is for the Treasury to borrow the needed funds only for as long as they are needed, repaying them when net cash outflows reverse and inflows are heavy. An early approach to this prescription was the introduction of Tax Anticipation Bills, or TABs, in the latter part of the 1960s. These bills, which were dated to mature just after one of the quarterly tax dates or shortly after the major April 15 tax date, could be used by the holder at face value in payment of federal income taxes. Since the final maturity of the bill was after the tax date, the investory would enjoy an earnings boost equal to the difference between the (discount) price that would prevail that many days prior to maturity and the par value that could be claimed for tax payment.

It was generally presumed that the earnings advantage of the tax payment would lead to a slightly better price for the issues for the Treasury because of bidding competition. In addition, use of TABs for tax purposes would simultaneously repay the debt and lessen the Treasury's excess inflow of tax receipts. In fact, as has been observed by many market analysts and in a number of official comments on the subject, the yield advantage to the Treasury for these sales was never large, although it may have been boosted slightly by the policy of allowing payment for the awards to banks by crediting Treasury accounts. As the use of TABs continued into the 1970s, it also became clear that fewer and fewer of them were being used for tax purposes, and any cash-flow advantages from that aspect were nil.

At the same time that the "tax anticipation" characteristics of the TABs were fading, both the federal deficit and intraperiod fluctuations in the Treasury's cash position and needs were increasing marketly. Thus, need for a more flexible cash mangement security was apparent, one that would not be tied to tax date-related maturities and that could be issued at short notice. The solution was the Cash Management Bill, or CMB.

Carrying no tax advantages, these securities are often sold with minimal notice to the market and may have maturities of only a few days or as long as several months. In the case of the longer maturities, the sale of the CMBs is much like an ordinary bill offering; for very short-term issues, however, it has been common for a minimum subscription of $1 million to be specified and for the issue to be sold almost entirely to professional dealers for eventual distribution. There is no requirement that either long or short maturities correspond to the maturity of a regular three-, six-, or twelve-month bill, although in fact that has generally been true.

There can be little doubt about the effectiveness of the CMB in overcoming one of the problems faced by the Treasury in meeting its technical debt management objectives. However, use of the CMB has been somewhat hesitant in terms of any possible major program to smooth out the fluctuations and associated costs in the Treasury's cash position. Once again the question at issue concerning such a program would likely be the effect it might have on market stability and uncertainty. Moreover, one might well question any such program on the bais of its impact of liquidity, on flows of funds, and on other stabilization-related channels of debt management effect. Like so many other areas of debt management analysis, policy, and operational guidelines, however, the answers to these questions can be provided only in subjective terms because of a lack of detailed, extensive, empirical analysis.

VI. CONCLUSIONS

The overwhelming conclusion of the discussion of the foregoing sections is that there is at this point in time no general, usable theory of Treasury debt management. The subject is one of special pleading, of inapplicable abstraction, of statics instead of dynamics, of contradiction and confusion. The inescapable fact is that Nordhaus and Wallich were right: there is no philosophical basis for debt management as analysis of the subject has developed since World War II.

To say that a theory has not been found does not, of course, say that there is no underlying, albeit undiscovered, theoretical framework applicable to the mangement of the public debt. Nor, even more importantly, does the absence of such a theoretical model imply that debt management does not matter in the vital sense of its potential as a means of achieving economic stabilization goals.

What the lack of a debt management theory does tell us—especially given the existence of partial, abstract theories—is that interest in, and knowledge of, both the theoretical and policy possibilities and the practical and quantitative details of debt management has been missing in work on the subject. Added to that has been the weakness of the testing and empirical verification of the presumed effects of the Treasury's actions. Of course, in part, this has been a reflection of data problems and the need to develop even more sophisticated econometric techniques. Both data and better techniques are now available, however.

Clearly, there is ample room for both theoretical and empirical research in debt management. In the long run, the careful work of the knowledgeable theorist will probably have the greatest impact on the Treasury's operations. Nonetheless, there are many instances of operational or policy actions that could be tested for their impact even at this rudimentary stage of our knowledge. The effect and effectiveness of various types of auctions is one such area. The role of dealers and their reactions to various Treasury actions is another. Expanded modeling of the yield curve and its determinants would be highly useful. Explicit integration of debt management in the detail of flow-of-funds and other models of the economy could not help but provide guidance for Treasury operations.

As stated at an earlier point, the author firmly believes that debt management does matter. Given the size and characteristics of Treasury debt, that conclusion seems inescapable. But in the current state of our knowledge about either the theory or the effectiveness of debt management, the skeptic may well ask, "Yes, but how much does it matter?" Hopefully, the discussion in this chapter will at least stimulate research which will permit a response to that question.

NOTES

1. Among the more well-known discussions are those by Buchanan (1958), Hansen (1959a), Musgrave (1959), Rolph (1957), Simons (1944), and Wallich (1946).

2. This lack of progress was amply illustrated by Culbertson's statement that, "Debt management policy is in an unhappy state" (Culbertson, 1959:89).

3. As examples, see Gaines (1962), Hamburger and Silber (1971), Scott (1965), Luckett (1964), Malkiel (1965), Modigliani and Sutch (1967), Okun (1962), Smith (1946), Tobin (1963), and Van Horne and Bowers (1968).

4. Of course abstraction does have a place in debt management theory; however, it must bear in mind that the eventual goal of such theory is to provide practical guidelines for operations not to serve as an exercise in logic or mathematics. A particularly illustrative example of the abstract approach is Cagan (1966).

5. This has been recognized as a common problem by many contemporary model builders. Among their responses have been greater detail in models of the economy, interest

in analyses in a stages of production framework, and application of flows of funds analysis. All are designed to merge theoretical abstraction and practical detail. See Bosworth and Duesenberry (1973:42-46) for a discussion of one of these approaches.

6. Section V contains a more complete discussion of the events leading to this situation.

7. For a detailed discussion of off budget items, see U.S. President (1976:32-36).

8 Foreign direct purchases of Treasury issues are not necessarily helpful to Treasury objectives in other areas; however, see the discussion of regularization in Section V.

9. Among the market experts engaged in this task, two of the Treasury forecasts are prepared by the Office of the Fiscal Assistant Secretary of the Treasury. These latter projections are not made public, although a general picture of them is disclosed as part of the Treasury's quarterly briefings on its borrowing requirements; see U.S. Treasury (1973: charts entitled "Projected Cash Operating Balance").

10. Some work in this area has been done at the Treasury of course; see Baker (1976) for a report on some of the results. Nonetheless extensive work is needed and has not been forthcoming from either official or private sources. The policy and operational consequences of this fact are a central theme of this chapter.

11. See the discussions of flow-of-funds problems and the rationale for different auctions for illustration of the importance of these factors in Sections III and V.

12. These data cover every note and bond offering since early 1973 with one record for each submitted tender (successful or not). The tender profile includes amount tendered, price or yield bid in auctions, and investor class of the subscriber.

13. Just in the Treasury market, for example, total offerings of notes and bonds was $34.7 billion in fiscal year 1970 and $80.7 billion in fiscal year 1976. With new bill sales included the totals show an increase from $55.3 billion to $125.2 billion (U.S. Treasury, 1970:22; and 1976:14f).

14. This reflects the traditional view that short-term markets are more resilient than longer ones. In the Treasury's case, moreover, the long-term market was especially thin in the early 1970s as a result of the debt managers' inability to issue new long-term issues because of interest rate ceiling limitations; see Section IV.

15. This assumption of an inelastic demand function is, however, contrary to Treasury's concern about disintermediation and "crowding out." At least one market experience suggests that it may not be in accordance with general market reactions. This is the result of the 1976 offering of $3.5 billion of five-year notes fully priced to yield 8 percent at par, or about one-eight above yields in the market for outstanding issues of comparable maturity. The sale attracted a record $29.3 billion in orders, constituting from that standpoint the most successful offering in history. In any event, the size of the issue was raised to $6 billion, of which $2.3 billion was sold to individuals with the remainder awarded to other small subscribers. See U.S. Treasury (1976:21).

16. Later sections, especially Sections III and V, will discuss some of the nonprice methods used to encourage or discourage interest by one or another group in Treasury issues.

17. Given the background of the uniform-price, or "Dutch" auction (see Section V), the failure to examine in detail the Treasury's experiments with this selling method is an especially glaring example of this lack of empirical work. See, however, Tsao and Vignola (1977) for an initial effort at such an assessment.

18. Thus, there is little concensus on the vital policy question of debt management's usefulness, and experts of the subject are likely to argue, "Debt management doesn't matter," or, "Debt management matters very much." See, for example, Nordhaus and Wallich (1973), and Goodhart (1973) in comment on Nordhaus and Wallich.

19. This presumes no intertemporal problems or preemption of investment opportunities.

20. In a slightly different context this same point was made by Wallich in 1946; see Wallich (1946:297). However, Wallich also recognizes a contrary view (1946:299-301).

21. The average interest cost of the public debt in fiscal year 1969, for example was 4.89 percent; by fiscal year 1977, the average had risen to 6.42 percent. In the same period foreign and international ownership of public debt securities rose from $10.2 billion to $95.5 billion (U.S. Treasury Bulletin: tables FD-2 and OFS-2, respectively).

22. Goodhart (1973:27); also Culbertson (1957; 1973), Malkiel (1966), Kessel (1965), and others.

23. That is, would long-term gains of such a strategy be offset by occasional, or even frequent, high-cost short-term offerings? If the Treasury's flexibility of timing is sufficient, it may be able to avoid high short-term interest periods; and the answer would be that they would not. As indicated by the preceding section, however, there is not a great deal of such flexibility.

24. See Wallich (1946), Hansen (1959b), Simons (1944), and Kaufman (1973) as examples of this approach.

25. At one point, for example, the concentrated market demands of a large official foreign investor led to a marked dip in the Treasury yield curve in the three-year maturity area.

26. Kessel (1965), Lutz (1940), and others.

27. See, for example, Malkiel (1965) and Modigliani and Sutch (1967).

28. Modigliani and Sutch (1966; 1967), Okun (1962), and Baker (1978).

29. Even in the abstract context of Rolph's original argument, matters were not so simple; and determinate results cannot be guaranteed. See R.M. Friedman (1959) and Rolph (1959), as well as Musgrave (1959).

30. See Simon (1975a), Volcker (1969), Dillon (1962), Rossa (1961) and Yeo (1976). It should be noted that Yeo's statement represents one of the fullest accounts of many of the concerns of Treasury debt managers that is available.

31. Some would include market disturbance effects among these stabilization goals on the grounds that, as generated by Treasury operations, they can impede the smooth functioning of the savings-investment intermediation process; See Gaines (1962:272-276) and Hansen (1959b). In the context of this chapter, however, these effects are better described in the discussion of market structure goals in Section IV.

32. Hicks (1946:150-151, 164-170). In actual markets where demand at the going price may be less than perfectly elastic, a somewhat broader concept of liquidity than a time-oriented one may be appropriate; see Garbade and Silber (1976) and Baker and Vignola (1979).

33. That is to say, it follows easily in generalized terms. Unfortunately none of the research or major models that incorporates these general assumptions focuses on the need for greater detail for the practical implementation of their implications.

34. See Rolph (1973), Culbertson (1973), and Cagan (1966), for detailed expositions of this point of view.

35. See Hamburger (1968); also see Goldfeld (1973), including comment by Duesenberry (1973) and Bosworth and Duesenberry (1973).

36. It is common, for example, to assume a fixed or linear relationship between liquidity and the amount of short- or long-term debt. It is also usual to consider only a dichotomous debt structure composed of "bills" or "bonds" despite the obvious fact that debt management deals with an entire spectrum of maturities. This latter problem is not confined to discussions of the liquidity effects of the debt of course.

37. Van Horne and Bowers (1968:528-530). Also see Luckett (1964) on the general idea of the average maturity of the debt; Bowers (1965) is also a useful analysis.

38. Van Horne and Bowers (1968:536). For discussions of other problems with these and similar data, see Garbade and Silber (1976) and Baker and Vignola (1979).

39. Bosworth and Duesenberry (1973:70) and relevant equations.

40. Smith (1960). Unfortunately Smith needlessly limits his discussion to investment expenditures alone despite the fact that his abstract exposition does not require such a constraint (1960:91-99).

41. As noted above, many current large models of the economy provide some idea of the aggregate effects of changes in the government's borrowing requirements. However, in doing so, virtually all such models rely on two or three rates, instead of a more complete term structure, for such effects. Thus, they provide little guidance for practical debt management since, in terms of, say, Smith's analysis they do not provide enough information for the debt managers to assess, or even predict, a net expansive or contractive effect.

42. Gaines (1962:266-262), Kaufman (1973), and Ricks (1973), and many more elegant empirical studies too numerous to review here, are ample testimony to the existence of such effects.

43. Kaufman (1973), Wallich (1946), Nordhaus and Wallich (1973), Van Horne and Bowers (1968), Roob (1973), and others have expounded this view at one time or another.

44. That is, the models and tests did not explicitly deal with intermarket effects. Such effects were implicitly assumed in many cases by the mere evidence of research interest in the subject. In this regard, it is wroth noting that critics of the "success" of Operation Twist have asserted that it was not the Treasury that brought about any change in the term structure, but rather outside forces which were said by proponents of the operation to have *resulted from* Treasury actions. In short, the causality was not, and has not been, clarified.

45. Luckett (1964) and Van Horne and Bowers (1968), were efforts in this direction of course; see also Baker (1978) for a mathematical approach to the question.

46. The work of Wood (1964), Cargill (1975), Terrell and Frazer (1972), and others in the area of expectations' formation may provide fruitful ideas for resolving debt management questions of this kind.

47. This subject is discussed more fully in Section IV.

48. See Section V; also see Roob (1973) and Yeo (1976).

49. For a review of the history of these flows and the associated problems created for financial institutions, see U.S. Board of Governors (1972) and U.S. President (1971).

50. In fact, early judgments on the sources of funds for some offerings, attributing these flows to interest by individuals, later proved incorrect; see U.S. Treasury (1973; 1974), charts on awards by investor classes for a number of issues. Thus, not only was there uncertainty about the strength or desirability of an effect, the character of those effects which did occur was not well known.

51. See, for example, Hamburger (1968) and Hendershott and Lemmon (1975).

52. Of course, this problem is also treated extensively in the vast literature on portfolio selection and analysis. Unlike Bosworth and Duesenberry, however, these analyses often stop short of making the connection to overall economic activity.

53. A particularly well-known private analysis is produced regularly by Salomon Brothers; among government analyses, probably the best known is by the Federal Reserve (U.S. Board of Governors).

54. See Ricks (1973:178) for a similar comment in a slightly different context.

55. See Baker (1976) for some of the difficulties involved and a review of the work done at the Treasury; also see Tsao and Vignola (1977) for a beginning effort on one area of concern, the effectiveness of auction techniques.

56. See Yeo (1976); also see Luckett (1964) for a more thorough analysis of the idea of the average maturity and its uses, also Bowers (1965).

57. The interest rate ceiling came into being largely as the result of a legislative oversight in the 1920s at the time such a ceiling was removed from Treasury notes. The maximum maturity for notes has been extended several times, from five years to seven years and then, in 1976, to ten years, in efforts to circumvent the restriction. Despite continuing efforts by every administration to have the ceiling removed, there seems to be little sentiment in the Congress for doing so; and bonds sales remain at the mercy of successive enlargements of the exemptions permitted in periodic legislation raising the limit on the total amount of debt that the Treasury may issue.

58. For example, the average maturity of the debt has continued its declining trend, with only temporary interruptions, as the weight of heavy bill financing and the enlargement of the end-of-month two-year notes has been felt. Moreover, little effort has been made to revitalize what is known as the long-intermediate sector, i.e., ten- to twenty-year maturities; and that market continues thin and subject to problems from outside shocks.

59. Officially, there are two groups, one from the Public Securities Association and another from the American Bankers Association. The groups meet separately and the members are not allowed to exchange views. For an indication of the composition of these groups, see U.S. Treasury (1973, 1974). It should also be noted that meetings with these groups occur at times other than prior to the mid-quarter financing if Treasury financing needs warrant it.

60. See U.S. Treasury (1973, 1974) for illustrations of the topics covered and the detail of that coverage as indicated by the charts and the final committee reports.

61. Kaufman's complaints on this items are especially interesting as an example of market professionals' attitude toward this technique (1973:163, 169-170).

62. In 1962, two issues were sold by syndicate, i.e., limited participation bidding, with mixed results. See Banyas (1973:14-15).

63. Treasury procedures are such that most receipts from the public pass through Treasury Tax and Loan accounts maintained with the commercial banking system; Treasury payments, however, are largely made from its account with the Federal Reserve. Thus, monies are "called" from the commercial bank accounts to the Federal Reserve account; but such calls are not necessarily immediate, and the banks will therefore have use of the funds for lending purposes for the number of days between the Treasury's receiving the funds and its calling them. If, in buying a Treasury security, the banks may pay for half of their awards by an accounting increase in the Treasury's account on their books, those funds may be lent until they are called. Banks, therefore, will have a small incentive to bid at a higher price than other subscribers because of the temporary earnings potential. The result is that, in the first instance, the overwhelming part of an issue allowing tax and loan account credit was taken up by banks.

In recent years, the Treasury has followed the practice of immediately calling its deposits, thereby virtually eliminating any bank earning potential from the receipt/call lag. Consequently, Treasury use of tax and loan account credit as one of the terms of its financings has withered.

64. This problem was, of course, the basis for the Federal Reserve's policy of "even keel" during Treasury financing operations; see Struble and Axilrod (1973).

65. U.S. Treasury (1971:10) and Weidenbaum (1970:377).

66. M. Friedman (1959); also Goldstein (1962), Goldstein and Kaufman (1975), Smith (1960), and others.

67. See Roob (1973) and Baker (1976). Unfortunately, "Dutch" auctions were not used to sell shorter issues, nor were other techniques used for selling bonds. This led to a statistically confounding dichotomy which precluded any reasonable testing of the effectiveness of the two or three techniques until some years later when the "Dutch" auction method had been largely discarded (Baker, 1976:149-150).

68. For discussions of the importance of an issue's tradability, see Garbade and Silber (1976) and Baker and Vignola (1979).

69. Even the regular mid-quarter refundings assumed an air of regularity, with three issues typically offered at three-, seven-, and twenty-year maturities.

70. The Treasury is now able to place its balances in earnings accounts with the commercial banking system. This development has, of course, significantly eased the pressures arising from the need to hold nonearning balances if borrowing and expenditure patterns are significantly mismatched.

REFERENCES

BAKER, C. (1976) "Auctioning Coupon-Bearing Securities: A Review of Treasury Experience." Pp. 146-154 in Y. Amihud (ed.) Bidding and Auctioning for Procurement and Allocation. New York: New York University Press.

_____(1978) "A Model of the Changing Term Structure of Interest Rates." Unpublished manuscript.

_____and VIGNOLA, A. (1979) "Market Liquidity, Security Trading, and the Estimation of Empirical Yield Curves." Review of Economics and Statistics (forthcoming).

BANYAS, L. (1973) "New Techniques in Debt Management From the Late 1950's Through 1966." Pp. 1-75 in Joint Treasury-Federal Reserve Study of the U.S. Government Securities Market, Staff Studies—Part 3. Washington, D.C.: Federal Reserve.

BOSWORTH, B. and DUESENBERRY, J. (1973) "A Flow of Funds Model and Its Implications." Pp. 39-149 in Issues in Federal Debt Management, Monetary Conference No. 10. Boston: Federal Reserve Bank of Boston.

BOWERS, D. (1965) "On Maturity Measures of the Public Debt: Comment." Quarterly Journal of Economics (May): 317-321.

BUCHANAN, J. (1958) Public Principles of Public Debt. Homewood, Ill.: Richard D. Irwin.

CAGAN, P. (1966) "A Partial Reconciliation Between Two Views of Debt Management." Journal of Political Economy (December): 624-628.

CARGILL, T. (1975) "The Term Structure of Interest Rates: A Test of the Expectations Hypothesis." The Journal of Finance (June): 761-771.

CULBERTSON, J. (1957) "The Term Structure of Interest Rates." Quarterly Journal of Economics (November): 485-517.

_____(1959) "A Positive Debt Management Program." Review of Economics and Statistics (May, Part 1): 89-98.

_____(1973) "Discussion (of Nordhaus and Wallich)." Pp. 31-38 in Issues in Federal Debt Management, Monetary Conference No. 10. Boston: Federal Reserve Bank of Boston.

DILLON, C. (1962) "Debt Management Policies." Statement, March 14, before the Senate Finance Committee, 87th Congress, 2nd Session. Washington, D.C.: Government Printing Office.

DUESENBERRY, J. (1973) "Comments (to Goldfeld)." Brookings Papers on Economic Activity 3:639-641.

FRIEDMAN, M. (1959) Testimony in Employment, Growth and Price Levels. Hearings, Joint Economic Committee, 86th Congress, 1st Session (October): 3023-3026. Washington, D.C.: Government Printing Office.

FRIEDMAN, R. (1959) "Principles of Debt Management: Comment." American Economic Review (June): 401-403.

GAINES, T. (1962) Techniques of Treasury Debt Management. Glencoe, Ill.: Free Press.

GARBADE, K. and SILBER, W. (1976) "Price Dispersion in the Government Securities Market." Journal of Political Economy (June, Part 1): 721-740.

GOLDFELD, S. (1973) "The Demand for Money Revisited." Brookings Papers on Economic Activity 3:577-638.

GOLDSTEIN, H. (1962) "The Friedman Proposal for Auctioning Treasury Bills." Journal of Political Economy (October): 386-392.

_____and KAUFMAN, G. (1975) "Treasury Bill Auction Procedures: Comment." The Journal of Finance (June): 895-899.

GOODHART, C. (1973) "Discussion (of Nordhaus and Wallich)." Pp. 26-30 in Issues in Federal Debt Management, Monetary Conference No. 10. Boston: Federal Reserve Bank of Boston.

GRIGGS, W. and SANTOW, L. The Schroeder Report. New York: J. Henry Schroeder Banking Corporation.

HAMBURGER, M. (1968) "Household Demand for Financial Assets." Econometrica (January): 97-117.

_____and SILBER, W. (1971) "Debt Management and Interest Rates: A Re-examination of the Evidence." The Manchester School (December): 261-266.

HANSEN, A. (1959a) "The Public Debt Reconsidered: A Review Article." Review of Economic and Statistics (November): 370-378.

_____(1959b) "Debt Management: 1959." Review of Economics and Statistics (May, Part 1): 185.

HENDERSHOTT, P. and LEMMON, R. (1975) "The Financial Behavior of Households: Some Empirical Estimates." The Journal of Finance (June): 733-759.

HICKS, J. (1946) Value and Capital. Oxford: The Clarendon Press.

KAUFMAN, H. (1973) "Federal Debt Management: An Economist's View From the Marketplace." Pp. 155-174 in Issues in Federal Debt Management, Monetary Conference No. 10. Boston: Federal Reserve Bank of Boston.

KESSEL, R. (1965) The Cyclical Behavior of the Term Structure of Interest Rates (Occasional Paper 91). New York: National Bureau of Economic Research.

LANSTON, A. and Company. Weekly Report on Government and Federal Agency Securities. New York: Aubrey G. Lanston and Co., Inc.

LUCKETT, D. (1964) "On Maturity Measures of the Public Debt." Quarterly Journal of Economics (February): 148-157.

LUTZ, F. (1940) "The Term Structure of Interest Rates." Quarterly Journal of Economics (November): 36-63.

MALKIEL, B. (1965) "The Strategy of Advance Refunding." National Banking Review (June): 493-505.

_____(1966) The Term Structure of Interest Rates: Expectations and Behavior Patterns. Princeton, N.J.: Princeton University Press.

MODIGLIANI, F. and SUTCH, R. (1966) "Innovations in Interest Rate Policy." American Economic Review (May): 178-197.

_____(1967) "Debt Management and the Term Structure of Interest Rates: An Empirical Analysis of Recent Experience." Journal of Political Economy (August, Part II): 569-589.

MUSGRAVE, R. (1959) The Theory of Public Finance. New York: McGraw-Hill.

NORDHAUS, W. and WALLICH, H. (1973) "Alternatives for Debt Management." Pp. 9-25 in Issues in Federal Debt Management, Monetary Conference No. 10. Boston: Federal Reserve Bank of Boston.

OKUN, A. (1962) "Monetary Policy, Debt Management and Interest Rates." Pp. 331-380 in Commission on Money and Credit, Stabilization Policies. Englewood Cliffs, N.J.: Prentice-Hall.

RICKS, R. (1973) "Discussion (to Kaufman)." Pp. 175-178 in Issues in Federal Debt Management, Monetary Conference No. 10. Boston: Federal Reserve Bank of Boston.

ROLPH, E. (1957) "Principles of Debt Management." American Economic Review (June): 302-320.

———(1959) "Principles of Debt Management: Reply." American Economic Review (June): 404-405.

ROOB, E. (1973) "What is Debt Management All About?" Pp. 179-186 in Issues in Federal Debt Management, Monetary Conference No. 10. Boston: Federal Reserve Bank of Boston.

ROOSA, R. (1961) "Reconciling Internal and External Financial Policies." Remarks to a Joint Luncheon of the American Economic Association and the American Finance Association, December 28. Washington, D.C.: U.S. Treasury News Release.

SALOMON BROTHERS-HUTZLER AND COMPANY Comments on Credit. New York: Salomon Brothers.

SCOTT, R. (1965) "Liquidity and the Term Structure of Interest Rates." Quarterly Journal of Economics (February): 135-145.

SIMON, W. (1975a). Statement, February 5, to the Joint Economic Committee, 94th Congress, 1st Session. Washington, D.C.: U.S. Treasury News Release.

———(1975b) Statement, November 7, to the Joint Economic Committee, 94 Congress, 1st Session. Washington, D.C.: U.S. Treasury News Release.

———(1976) Remarks, January 23, to the U.S. Industrial Payroll Savings Committee. Washington, D.C.: U.S Treasury News Release.

SIMONS, H. (1944) "On Debt Policy." Journal of Political Economy (December): 356-361.

SMITH, V. (1966) "Bidding Theory and the Treasury Bill Auction: Does Price Discrimination Increase Bill Prices?" Review of Economics and Statistics (May): 141-146.

SMITH, W. (1960) "Debt Management in the United States." Study Paper 19, Employment, Growth and Price Levels. Joint Economic Committee, 86th Congress, 2nd Session. Washington, D.C.: Government Printing Office.

STRUBLE, F. and AXILROD, S. (1973) "Even Keel Revisited." Pp. 235-253 in Issues in Federal Debt Management, Monetary Conference No. 10. Boston: Federal Reserve Bank of Boston.

TERRELL, W. and FRAZER, W. (1972) "Interest Rates, Portfolio Behavior, and Marketable Government Securities." The Journal of Finance (March): 1-35.

TOBIN, J. (1963) "An Essay on Principles of Debt Management." Pp. 143-218 in Commission on Money and Credit, Fiscal and Debt Management Policies. Englewood Cliffs, N.J.: Prentice-Hall.

TSAO, C. and VIGNOLA, A. (1977) "Price Discrimination and the Demand for Treasury's Long Term Securities." Unpublished manuscript.

U.S. Board of Governors of the Federal Reserve. (1972) Ways to Moderate Fluctuations in Housing Construction: Federal Reserve Staff Study. Washington, D.C.: Federal Reserve.

_____(1975) Introduction to Flow of Funds. Washington, D.C.: Federal Reserve.

U.S. President. The Budget of the United States Government. Washington, D.C.: Government Printing Office.

_____(1971) Report of the President's Commission on Financial Structure and Regulation. Washington, D.C.: Government Printing Office.

U.S. Treasury. Annual Report of the Secretary of the Treasury on the State of Finances. Washington, D.C.: Government Printing Office.

_____(1973, 1974) Summary Reports of Treasury Advisory Committees, Volume 2. Washington, D.C.: U.S. Treasury.

_____Treasury Bulletin. Washington, D.C.: Government Printing Office.

VAN HORNE, J. and BOWERS, D. (1968) "The Liquidity Impact of Debt Management." Southern Economic Journal (April):526-537.

VOLCKER, P. (1969) Testimony, February 19, to the Joint Economic Committee, 91st Congress, 1st Session. Washington, D.C.: U.S. Treasury News Release.

_____(1971) "Problems of Federal Finance." Remarks, June 10, to the Municipal Bond Women's Club of New York. Washington, D.C.: U.S. Treasury News Release.

_____(1972) "A New Look at Debt Management." Remarks, March 7, to The Money Marketeers (New York). Washington, D.C.: U.S. Treasury News Release.

WALLACE, N. (1967) "Comment (to Modigliani and Sutch)." Journal of Political Economy (August, Part II): 590-595.

WALLICH, H. (1946) "Debt Management as an Instrument of Economic Policy." American Economic Review (June): 292-310.

WEIDENBAUM, M. (1970) Remarks, November 19, to the National Association of Regulatory Utility Commissioners. Washington, D.C.: U.S. Treasury News Release.

WOOD, J. (1964) "The Expectations Hypothesis, the Yield Curve, and Monetary Policy." Quarterly Journal of Economics (August): 457-470.

YEO, E. (1976) Statement, March 4, to the Senate Finance Committee, 94th Congress, 2nd Session. Washington, D.C.: U.S. Treasury News Release.

PART III

POLICY-MAKING IN AN OPEN ECONOMY

Chapter 9

FOREIGN EXCHANGE MARKET INTERVENTION

MICHAEL P. DOOLEY
Board of Governors of the Federal Reserve System

After three years of intermittent crises in foreign exchange markets and two major devaluations of the U.S. dollar, the major industrial countries abandoned the system of fixed parities for their currencies in March 1973. This policy change was not the result of general acceptance of the view that freely floating exchange rates were desirable. On the contrary, the governments of the major industrial countries were forced to abandon fixed exchange rates by the actions of the private sector. These actions, generally referred to as "speculation," reached their peak in March 1973 when the German Federal Bank purchased $2.7 billion in a single day in trying to defend a parity that had been established less than a month earlier.[1] Even in the rarefied air of international finance, $2.7 billion per day is an impressive rate for a government to accumulate foreign currencies.

Although fixed exchange rates were abandoned in March 1973, the volume of exchange market intervention has probably increased.[2] The United States, which had by presidential order ceased intervention after the exchange market crisis in August 1971, reentered the market in mid-1972 and has intervened frequently in the years that followed. While the volume of intervention initiated by the Federal Reserve System and the U.S. Treasury has been quite small relative to that initiated by other countries, their reentry into the intervention arena has generated new U.S. interest in this relatively unfamiliar policy tool. The U.S. interpretation of the system of managed floating rates has been summarized as follows:

> The basic philosophy of the new monetary system incorporated in the amended IMF Articles, in particular Article IV on exchange arrangements, is that international monetary stability cannot be imposed from without, but

AUTHOR'S NOTE: The views expressed herein are solely those of the author and do not necessarily represent the views of the Federal Reserve System. The author wishes to thank Allan Frankel, Dale Henderson and Frank McCormick for helpful comments.

must be developed by countries from within, through the application of sound underlying economic and financial policies.

In line with that concept, our program for assuring a strong and healthy dollar relies on fundamental economic performance, not on market operations to hold or attain a particular exchange rate or maintain a particular exchange rate zone. We do recognize, of course, that markets can become disorderly, subject to great uncertainty, dominated by psychological factors and speculation. We have made clear that we are fully prepared to intervene in the markets to counter such disorders. We have intervened, at times in large amounts, for that purpose (Solomon, 1978).

The purpose of this chapter is to describe the mechanics of exchange market intervention, and to discuss the role of intervention in a system of managed floating exchange rates.

Since exchange rate policy is a relatively unfamiliar branch of economic policy, it is helpful to make use of the familiar analytical framework in which policy tools, intermediate targets, and objectives are first defined and then relationships among these concepts are explained.[3] A fascinating aspect of exchange rate policy is that none of these apparently straightforward concepts is easily fitted with widely accepted definitions. In keeping with Professor Mason's long interest in helping insure that the participants in economic debates are addressing the same issues, we will try to establish a consistent framework for evaluating the place of exchange market intervention in U.S. economic policy.

DEFINITION OF EXCHANGE MARKET INTERVENTION

The initial transaction known as intervention in foreign exchange markets is simply a government purchase from the public of money (bank deposits) denominated in one currency unit in exchange for money denominated in another currency unit.[4] However, defining intervention as a policy which increases the supply of one type of money (e.g., dollars) and decreases the supply of another (e.g., marks) leaves little room for distinguishing between domestic open market operations, and exchange market intervention.

If exchange market policy is to have any substance independent of monetary policy then we must more carefully differentiate their respective policy tools, exchange market intervention and open market operations. In practice, governments recognize the potential conflict of exchange market intervention and domestic monetary policy, and routinely offset the effects of intervention of their monetary bases.[5] This is done automatically in most central banks, and, in general, offsetting the change in the monetary base has more the character of a technical procedure than a policy decision. The procedure is simple. The country whose money supply has risen sells securities to the public while the opposite open market operation is undertaken by the country whose money supply has been decreased by intervention.

This set of transactions, which might be called fully offset intervention, leaves money supplies unaffected but changes the currency denomination of the securities held by the public. Fully offset intervention is the policy tool that is considered in this chapter.

Since the policy tool is a set of transactions, it might be useful to trace through an example.[6] Suppose that the German mark is rising in value against the U.S. dollar and that the governments of the two countries agree that intervention is desirable in order to limit the change in the exchange rate. Since for every exchange rate there are two central banks, we need only one to initiate the exchange market intervention. We will assume that in step 1 the German Bundesbank initiates a purchase of U.S. dollars against marks. Dollar money in the hands of the "public," which includes U.S. residents, German residents, and residents of third countries falls while the supply of mark denominated money rises.

	Public	*Bundesbank*
Step 1 (a)	−$ money; +DM money	+$ money; −DM money

In step 2 the Bundesbank offsets the increase in the German monetary base by selling a mark-denominated security to the public. The decline in the U.S. monetary base is offset when the Bundesbank, with the assistance of the Federal Reserve, invests its dollar intervention proceeds in a dollar denominated security purchased from the public.

	Public	*Bundesbank*
Step 2 (b)	+$ money; −$ securities	−$ money; +$ securities
(c)	− DM money; + DM securities	+ DM money; − DM securities

If we add transactions a, b and c we discover the net result of intervention. The public's holdings of mark-denominated securities have risen and its holdings of dollar-denominated securities have fallen by a like amount. The public is now "long" marks relative to its position before the intervention. That is, a larger share of its security portfolio is denominated in marks. The Bundesbank has the mirror image change in its portfolio since it is now "long" dollars relative to its initial position. If the Federal Reserve or the U.S. Treasury had initiated the intervention the ultimate position of the public would be identical. The only difference would be that the Federal Reserve or the U.S. Treasury would be long dollars and short marks rather than the Bundesbank.

This way of looking at exchange market intervention has several advantages. First, it clearly separates open market operations, which are usually directed toward domestic targets such as interest rates or a monetary aggregate, from exchange rate intervention, which has as an intermediate target the exchange rate. Second, it considerably broadens the set of transactions that should be considered exchange market intervention. For example, a government can change the currency denomination of the securities held by the public by issuing foreign currency-denominated claims on itself rather than domestic currency claims in order to finance a budget deficit. Large issues of dollar-denominated securities by United Kingdom and Italy in recent years are examples of this.

Finally, this definition of intervention clearly isolates the risks involved in exchange market intervention. By altering the currency composition of the government's financial portfolio, exchange market intervention exposes the government to profits or losses due to exchange rate changes.

EXCHANGE MARKET INTERVENTION AND POLICY TARGETS

The effectiveness of intervention depends on whether or not changes in the relative supplies of government securities denominated in different currencies affect the conditions under which the public is willing to hold such securities. If securities denominated in different currencies are perfect substitutes in the portfolios of enough market participants, substitution by governments of one for the other will have no impact on exchange rates.

If this were the case, exchange market intervention as defined here is a trivial policy tool since it would have no effect on target variables.

In a world of certainty about future exchange rates it would be difficult to see why securities denominated in different currencies would be less than perfect substitutes.[7] If future exchange rates were known, the U.S. or German governments could stamp "payable in dollars" or "payable in DM" on their liabilities with no alteration in the public's willingness to hold debt denominated in either currency. If the public thought that either government might not pay off, then regardless of the currency denomination of the debt, it would sell at a discount as compared to a more trustworthy government's securities.

But future exchange rates are not known with certainty by either central banks or the private sector. It would seem that the private sector (and the government) would care if it were offered securities denominated in one currency or the other. In buying dollar-denominated securities from the public in exchange for mark-denominated securities, a central bank can be thought of as believing that the dollar will appreciate relative to the mark from its current level.[8] The public believes the opposite. The expected value of the transaction to the two parties depends on the difference between the spot (or current) exchange rate and the exchange rate that *each* party expects to prevail in the future. Changes in the opinions of central banks and the private sector will generate intervention transactions in the foreign exchange market.

Suppose, for example, that private speculators thought that the mark would be worth $.50 in a year's time, but that the Bundesbank thought that the mark would be worth $.50. If the spot rate today were $.50, the Bundesbank would be content but private speculators would prefer mark-denominated securities to dollar-denominated securities since they anticipate a 10 percent appreciation of the mark during the coming year. If the spot rate were $.55, private speculators would be content but the Bundesbank would want to sell mark-denominated securities in anticipation of a 10 percent depreciation for the mark over the year. The spot exchange rate will settle somewhere between $.50 and $.55, depending on how much each side is willing to bet on its forecast. Suppose that private speculators, as a group, were willing to buy an additional $100 million equivalent of dollar or mark-denominated securities for each one percent difference in their expected yields. The Bundesbank could influence the spot rate by fully offset intervention since each $100 million purchase of dollar-denominated securities against mark-denominated securities would require a fall in the dollar's exchange value of about one-half cent from the private sector's forecast of $.55.

Whether the public is willing to buy $100 million or $100 billion for each one percent difference in expected yield, depends upon the public's confidence in its own forecast and on its attitude toward risk taking.

OBJECTIVES FOR EXCHANGE RATE POLICY

If the central bank can influence exchange rates through intervention it must decide on policy objectives. If effective, intervention forces the exchange rate away from the path which would result from the actions of private speculators. In order to know whether this is desirable, we must first analyze the role of private speculation.

Speculation has acquired a bad name over the years, but it is a critical element in the functioning of a market economy. The basic role of speculation is to build information about future events into the current prices. For example, if it becomes known today that the wheat crop to be harvested in six months had been destroyed the currect price of wheat ought to rise. If it does not, current stocks of wheat will be consumed too rapidly and none will be available in the future.

The speculator who buys wheat today in anticipation of future shortages is doing the community a great service, although he has never been a popular fellow. People do not like the bearer of bad news, even if he helps them to prepare for the future. In a similar way, the private foreign exchange speculator provides a service to the community. If private speculators see an impending exchange rate change, they will react to that information immediately, and the spot price of the currency will change. For the currency that is falling in value this is generally regarded as bad news, particularly by the government that feels a responsibility for the "integrity" of its currency. For the currency that is rising in value the change is also considered bad news since the appreciation of the currency threatens export industries. In short, there is a ready-made constituency to oppose any change in exchange rates even though for the community as a whole adjustment is desirable.

If private speculators are not properly incorporating available information into current prices, they are doing the community a great disservice. If, for example, they buy wheat in anticipation of a poor harvest and a good harvest occurs, then too little of the current crop will be consumed now and too much later. Most people would prefer a smooth consumption path to enforced famine now and feast later—so the speculator is not doing a good job.[9]

In exchange markets the same it true. Speculation that is wrong, after the fact, is harmful to the community. Central bank intervention would have a clear role to play in a world in which private speculators were consistently wrong. Indeed, there is no shortage of statements by government officials that would lead to the conclusion that this is the policy goal of intervention—to increase the accuracy of the implicit forecasts of future rates that are incorporated in current exchange rates.

A popular explanation for the failure of private speculation to accurately reflect the future is that private speculative expectations are based upon the "price dynamics" of exchange markets. The price dynamics view emphasizes the importance of market psychology and perceived trends in exchange rates in the formation of private speculators' expectations. Expectations based on "fundamental factors" are said to be "weakly held" because the individual speculator can profit by anticipating what other speculators will do rather than by analyzing fundamental factors. Since private speculators profit from anticipating trends and "herd psychology," exchange rate movements are subject to speculative runs, bandwagons, and technical corrections.

For example, in 1973 when the dollar fell very sharply against European currencies, it was argued that the dollar had fallen to "ridiculously low" levels, "unjustified . . . on any reasonable assessment of the outlook for the U.S. (balance of) payments position" (Coombs, 1973). Reportedly, traders generally *believed* the dollar to be fundamentally undervalued, but were unwilling to "buck the market" in the short-run, and indeed found themselves jumping on the bandwagon for the short-term ride. Again, in 1978, it was argued that "the pressing need was to deal effectively with the disorder in the exchange market and thereby to provide breathing room for the measures (designed to reduce payments imbalances) to take effect and for market participants to take stock of fundamentals" (Holmes, 1978).

If exchange markets are dominated by this sort of behavior, there is a clear role for central bank participation in exchange markets. By acting in a more "rational" manner than private speculators, the central bank can reduce the deviations in market rates from equilibrium rates and make profits at the expense of private speculators.

An alternative to the price-dynamics interpretation outlined above is the theory that exchange rates are determined in an "efficient market."[10] The "strong" efficient market hypothesis is based on the assumption that market participants have equal access to, and act upon, available information relevant to the formation of expectations about future prices. As a result, at any point in time, relevant information is discounted in the present price. Price changes can be large and frequent in an efficient market if the determinants of prices change often. But if exchange markets are efficient in the strong sense there is probably no basis for central bank intervention as a supplement to private speculation.

A weaker version of the efficient market hypothesis holds that while not all information is available equally to market participants, trends or patterns in past price movements are known to a sufficient number of market participants so that profitable speculation, and profitable central bank intervention, based on such information are impossible. In a weakly efficient exchange market, central bank intervention might be justified if based on superior evaluation of the fundamental determinants of exchange rates, but bandwagons or market psychology could not be profitably exploited.

While it does not seem plausible that information contained in past price movements could be profitably exploited by central banks, the evidence from the behavior of exchange rates since early 1973 is not conclusive. Research carried out by the author and Jeffrey Shafer (1976) indicates that, particularly in the early days of floating exchange rates, simple trading rules based on past exchange rate changes, so-called filter rules, would have yielded substantial profits.[11] There was, however, a tendency for the profitability of these rules to decline over time as speculators presumably learned the properties of the new exchange rate system. One possible explanation for the remaining profits is that the risk of speculating in foreign exchange is judged by the public to be so great that a substantial expected profit is necessary in order to lure the marginal speculator into the game.

Another possible basis for intervention is that the central bank could do a better job of interpreting the funadmental determinants of future exchange rates. One of the important determinants of further exchange rates is certainly the future course of monetary policy. It seems reasonable that central banks would have inside information concerning the future course of this important policy. If the central bank's intervention policy is designed to move exchange rates in a manner consistent with future monetary policy, the presence of the central bank in the exchange market would convey information to the private sector. In effect, intervention would signal the market concerning future monetary policy and would have a powerful influence on exchange rates.[12]

Intervention could also be justified on the basis of superior information concerning the future course of other fundamental factors. If, for example, the central bank utilized superior economic analysis, it could intervene in order to move the exchange rate toward a better estimate of the future exchange rate. If the central bank were generally correct, the intervention account would show profits on its transactions; if generally incorrect, the account would show losses.

SCOPE FOR SUCCESSFUL
FOREIGN EXHANGE MARKET INTERVENTION

In reality, the government will never know with certainty if a given exchange rate change is justified by changes in fundamental factors or if the change is due to a miscalculation by private speculators. Under these conditions, the optimal response to a given exchange rate movement depends on the probability that the movement is generated by changes in fundamental factors as compared to the probability that the exchange rate change is due to private speculative errors. The probability that an exchange rate change is due to one of these two factors can be measured by the past variability of the two factors.

It is not surprising that those who argue for active intervention, (Bernstein, 1974; McKinnon, 1974; Coombs, 1976), claim that fundamental factors such as inflation differentials or trade flows show very little short-run variability, and at the same time argue that private speculation is subject to large errors in assessing the equilibrium levels for exchange rates. These observers argue that the probable costs in limiting exchange rate changes are small, because in most instances the government is simply offsetting unnecessary variability in market exchange rates.

The counter argument, (Willett, 1977), points to oil price increases, rampant inflations, and other fundamental shocks to the world economy since 1973 as the primary cause of exchange rate instability. This group tends to emphasize the evidence that exchange markets are weakly efficient.

The evidence on both sides is inconclusive, and the relationships between changes in fundamental factors and exchange rates as well as the efficiency of private speculation should be the subject of further research. But before we conclude that some middle road in which governments intervene to manage rates is probably optimal, a final warning is necessary.

While it is possible that exchange market intervention could help insure that exchange rates reflect underlying economic reality, there is no guarantee that governments will play this role. The problem is not that they are incapable of doing so. It would be possible for the government to use its inside information concerning monetary policy in making more accurate and, therefore, more useful forecasts of future exchange rates. In addition, the government would easily mobilize the resources necessary to formulate optimal intervention policies.

It seems likely, however, that other objectives besides efficient speculation are likely to influence a government's exchange market policy. The temptation to pursue inconsistent monetary and exchange market policies is likely to be very strong. At times, for example, the failures of policies designed to limit inflation are made painfully apparent by depreciation of the exchange value of the currency. It is awkward for the government to agree that such an assessment is accurate. Instead it will be tempted to buy time with exchange market intervention until it can "put its house in order."

On the other side of the coin, a country with a relatively low rate of inflation and perhaps a growing current account surplus might be unwilling to change its domestic policies—but also unwilling to admit that the competitive position of its export industry should be adjusted through exchange rate appreciation. This is particularly true of countries that have in part based their successful post war recovery on the rapid growth of export industries.

To the extent that such consideratons influence exchange market policy, it will fail to meet its objectives. Exchange market intervention cannot remove any of the policy conflicts that arise within or among countries, although it can for a time mask inconsistent targets for exchange rate and other policies. It is a policy which can affect exchange rates only to the extent that it changes private expectations about future exchange rates or temporarily moves the current rate away from the public's expectations. The power of governments to hold an exchange rate that is inconsistent with fundamental determinants will erode rapidly as private speculators become more confident that governments are acting on a forecast of future exchange rates which is incorrect.

NOTES

1. See Bundesbank (1973) for a discussion of this episode.

2. While estimates of gross intervention are not available, a rough measure of net intervention involving dollars can be inferred from changes in U.S. liabilities to non-OPEC foreign official institutions. In 1977, for example, such liabilities increased by over $30 billion. A detailed description of U.S. intervention is available twice a year in the report on "Treasury and Federal Reserve Foreign Exchange Operations" in the Federal Reserve *Bulletin*.

3. For an application of this framework see Friedman (1975).

4. Since these transactions involve the central bank they also generate changes in the monetary base of each country.

5. See Waight (1939) for an early exposition of offsetting operations.

6. The transactions can be quite complicated in an accounting sense, although a simple example is not in any important way misleading. For a more detailed exposition see Balbach (1978).

7. For a model in which imperfect substitution is assumed see Girton and Henderson (1976).

8. An interest rate differential would make one security relatively more attractive. Throughout this chapter it is assumed that expected yields have been adjusted for interest rate differentials.

9. The speculator who misjudges the future will lose money, which might not be cause for concern. As Johnson (1976) has pointed out, however, we generally identify the speculator as the loser after the fact. It is clear that the community as a whole is better off if speculative expectations are accurate.

10. See Cootner (1964) for a collection of studies testing the efficient market theory.

11. For a different interpretation of the data see Giddy and Dufey (1975) and Kemp (1976).

12. Meigs (1978) has pointed out that the central bank could simply announce its plans for monetary policy and save the trouble of intervening in foreign exchange markets. While this is certainly correct, the public might be more inclined to believe the central bank if its intentions are backed by intervention.

REFERENCES

BALBACH, A. B. (1978) "The Mechanics of Intervention in Exchange Markets." Federal Reserve Bank of St. Louis Review (February): 2-7.

BERNSTEIN, E.M. (1974) "The Experience with Fluctuating Exchange Rates, 1973-1974." EMB (LTD) Research Economists' Report No. 74/11.

BUNDESBANK (1973) Monthly Report of the Deutsche Bundesbank (March).

COOMBS, C.A. (1973) "Treasury and Federal Reserve Foreign Exchange Operations." Federal Reserve Bulletin (September): 622-640.

_____(1976) The Arena of International Finance. New York: John Wiley.

COOTNER, P. H. (1964) The Random Character of Stock Market Prices. Cambridge, Mass.: MIT Press.

DOOLEY, M. P. and SHAFER, J. R. (1976) "Analysis of Short-Run Exchange Rate Behavior, March 1973 to September 1975." Federal Reserve Board International Finance Discussion, Paper No. 76.

FRIEDMAN, B. M. (1975) "Targets Instruments and Indicators of Monetary Policy." Journal of Monetary Economics (November): 443-473.

GIDDY, I. and DUFEY, G. (1975) "The Random Behavior of Flexible Exchange Rates: Implications for Forecasting." Journal of International Business Studies (Spring): 1-32.

GIRTON, L. and HENDERSON, D. W. (1976) "Financial Capital Movements and Central Bank Behavior in a Two Country, Short-Run Portfolio Balance Model." Journal of Monetary Economics (January): 33-61.

HOLMES, A. R. (1978) "Treasury and Federal Reserve Foreign Exchange Operations." Federal Reserve Bulletin (March): 161-178.

JOHNSON, H. G. (1976) "Destabilizing Speculation: A General Equilibrium Approach." Journal of Political Economy (February): 101-108.

KEMP, D. S. (1976) "The U.S. Dollar in International Markets: Mid-1970 to Mid-1976." Federal Reserve Bank of St. Louis Review (August): 7-14.

McKINNON, R. I. (1974) "Floating Exchange Rates 1973-1974: The Emperor's New Clothes." Presented at the Conference on Economic Policies, Pittsburgh.

MEIGS, A. J. (1978) "The Role of Information Disclosure in International Monetary Policy." Pp. 49-72 in Federal Reserve Policies and Public Disclosure. Washington, D.C.: American Enterprise Institute for Public Policy Research.

SOLOMON, A. M. (1978) "Exchange Market Developments and U.S. Policy." Presented at International Herald Tribune/Forex Research Ltd. Conference on Managing Foreign Exchange Risk.

WAIGHT, L. (1939) The History and Mechanism of the Exchange Equalisation Account. Cambridge, England: Cambridge University Press.

WILLETT, T. D. (1977) Floating Exchange Rates and International Monetary Reform. Washington, D.C.: American Enterprise Institute for Public Policy Research.

Chapter 10

SUBSTITUTABLE MONIES AND THE MONETARY STANDARD

LANCE GIRTON
Board of Governors of the Federal Reserve System

DON ROPER
University of Utah

INTRODUCTION

The history of money in this century has been one of progressive destruction of the link between paper money and gold, the dominant monetary commodity.[1] National currencies are not now convertible into gold either internally or externally. The elimination of the gold convertibility of national currencies and subsequent disintegration of the system of convertibility of national currencies into one another at fixed rates of exchange has given national authorities wide latitude to direct monetary policies at various domestic objectives.

The world has now completed the transition to a system of managed paper monies.[2] But experience under the paper money standard has not been particularly satisfactory. Conflicting monetary objectives, external events, and ineptitude have caused this century to be characterized by violent price movements and monetary instability. It is instructive to compare the experience in the nineteenth century of those countries convertible into gold, where prices—while not constant—moved only in gradual swings, with the experience of many countries which have suffered large price movements in this century. Even the price revolution of the sixteenth century, with the quadrupling of gold and silver prices of goods, involved by modern standards, only a gradual annual increase in

AUTHORS' NOTE: The views expressed herein are solely those of the authors and do not necessarily represent the views of the Federal Reserve System. In a volume of essays to honor Will Mason, it is appropriate that the monetary standard be discussed. Professor Mason has probably done more work on the monetary standard question than any other modern economist. It is Mason's work that stimulated us to address the question of the monetary standard with substitutable monies.

the price level.[3] The experience of the last decade is not reassuring as inflation continues to be a widespread problem.

The disappointing experience with a paper money or policy standard has led to several proposals or rules for the conduct of monetary policy. Perhaps the most famous is the Simons-Friedman proposal that the money supply should grow at a steady annual rate (Friedman, 1959). Other proposals have involved the pegging of one or another price index or focusing on some other objective. These proposals reflect the conviction that central banks have pursued objectives that are in conflict with the maintenance of stable valued monies.

A striking aspect of these proposals for monetary rules is that they have been suggested and supported mainly by economists that in other areas of economic policy have strongly supported the free market. Friedman, for example, suggests an arbitrary rule for the conduct of monetary policy, while in other situations he argues that the free market should be allowed to work unfettered by government controls.

The thesis of this chapter is that money balances can be provided by the free market without government controls. Competition in money issue provides a rule of behavior enforced by the market, and a monetary standard that is attractive compared to current monopoly paper money standards. Problems of inflation and deflation that have plagued the world since the widespread use of paper money would be eliminated. And this is achievable while maintaining the aspect of paper money that is the reason for its ascendance in the face of problems of control over its issue—its efficiency in production and use, as compared to commodity money.

In this chapter we will argue these propositions, building on recent work on competitively issued substitutable monies.[4] Monetary theory, whether Classical, Marxian, Keynesian, or Monetarist, has traditionally assumed that a single money is used in each country. The political authority in each country is assumed to create an environment in which one bank, the central bank, has monopoly privileges over the issuance of money. Consideration of the concurrent circulation of substitutable monies forces consideration of monetary economies where the behavior of money issuers is conditioned by competitive pressures in the market for monies.

The chapter is organized as follows: First, we develop a view of how a system of competitively issued substitutable monies would work and the kind of monetary standard that would result. Implications of substitutable monies for the revenue from printing money and the optimum quantity of money are then discussed. Next, it is argued that a competitive market issuing substitutable monies would supply money to meet the needs of trade. While this suggests the competitive monetary system would suffer from the defect ascribed to the real-bills doctrine, we show that it does not. The final section contains a summary and concluding comments.

THE THEORY OF MULTIPLE MONIES

Money is useful only in so far as it has command over goods and services. Money does not satisfy human wants directly. It is held to purchase goods and services, and its usefulness depends on the amount of goods and services it will purchase. This is true of commodity money as well as paper money, though commodity money has nonmonetary uses.

If the denomination of all money was multiplied by ten, e.g., a one dollar bill was altered to be a ten dollar bill, and all prices, including the money value of all debt, were multiplied by ten, nothing of any real consequence would be changed. A person that had been satisfied to hold ten dollars before would now be satisifed to hold one hundred dollars, since one hundred dollars would now have the purchasing power that ten dollars had before.

The fact that money is only useful if it has command over goods, together with the (stylized) assumption that *paper* money can be provided at zero marginal cost, has led to the view that a competitive market in paper money is not viable. The argument is that for any good with a zero marginal cost of production competition will drive the price to zero. For a normal good or services with a zero marginal cost of production a zero price would be efficient, marginal cost would equal marginal benefit. But money that has a zero price is useless as money; it has no command over goods and services. Therefore, for a paper money to be useful its supply must be controlled or monopolized so that the quantity will not be extended to a point where money has a competitive (zero) price.

While this argument has intuitive appeal, it rests on a faulty conception of the kind of paper money that would be produced. In this section we argue that a competitive market would produce monies that were differentiated by issuer. With distinguishable monies it is the cost of holding money and not the price of money that competition would drive to zero.[5]

The point can perhaps be seen most easily by reference to another type of financial asset, corporate bonds. It costs next to nothing to print a corporate bond certificate. But competition in the issuance of corporate bonds does not drive the value of pieces of paper representing claims on corporations to zero. Competition between corporations for loanable funds does drive the rate of return on corporate bonds up to the market rate of interest such that at the margin there is no profit to be made in issuing corporate debt.

Privately issued money consists of certificates (currency) or book-keeping entires (deposits) representing claims on banking corporations. Competition will tend to drive the profits from issuing money to zero. Banking profits will be zero if the rate of return on the monetary liabilities of the banking system is equal to the rate of return on assets the banking system holds. If the return on money is less than the rate earned on bank assets then banks will be earning profits. With competition and free entry into banking, existing banks will expand and new banks will enter the market. The way that new banks get their monetary liabilities held and existing banks expand is to offer more favorable terms to holders of money balances. This process will force the rate of return on money to the the rate earned on bank assets.

Since standard monetary theory assumes each country or region uses only one money, and on this money no explicit interest is paid, we need to explore the structure of a monetary system consisting of substitutable monies issued competitively.

MARKET STRUCTURE OF SUBSTITUTABLE MONIES

We assume the following institutional structure which is needed to facilitate a system of competitively issued monies. People may hold any money they choose without any constraints imposed by national governments. Banks are free of all legal requirement to denominate or make convertible their monetary liabilities, whether deposits or currency, into any national money or commodity. Banks are free to pay interest on money in any manner they choose and without any legal limit on the level of the interest rate. There are no legal reserve requirements. The ability of banks and money holders to enter into and execute contracts is assumed with the normal recourse to the courts in case of disagreement or fraud. Normal brand name protection is enforced, i.e., a bank can uniquely identify its currency.

This market structure is radically different from the situation as it exists today, and as it has existed since the advent of monopolized government paper money. Banking law has required banks to make deposits and currency convertible into government money, and, in the last forty years in the United States, banks have been restricted on the amount of interest they can pay on deposits.

How would private banks act under the new regime? First examine the deposit business of the private banks. If national monies had exhibited high rates of inflation and inflation rates were hard to predict, deposit holders would be interested in holding deposits denominated in terms of something with a more stable and predictable value. Banks would compete for customers by offering deposits denominated or convertible into different bundles of goods.[6]

Banks could only prudently offer goods value assurances on deposits if they held short-term assets denominated in the same units as their monetary liabilities. Banks could be expected to make loans to the same sort of customers as they do now—short-term consumer and industrial loans—but instead of denominating loans in terms of national monies they would insist on denominting loans in terms of goods or in terms of monies that were fixed in value to goods.

As far as the deposit business goes, banks could pay out and accept government paper, but the rate of pay out would be determined by a price index of a basket of goods. That is, a deposit holder could be paid in dollars but the number of dollars received when drawing a check would be determined by the latest estimate of the relevant price index. The medium of exchange could remain government money but the unit of account would be goods.

The situation is somewhat more complicated for hand to hand currency. Currency could also be denominated in terms of goods and have a flexible value with respect to government-issued currency and other bank currency denominated in terms of different baskets of goods. However, as the number of different currency denominations gets large, the efficiencies of a money economy are lost. This would limit the number of currencies of different denominations that would circulate in a region.

It is unclear how much should be made of the economies of scale in having a small number of different currencies. Countries now have a single national money because governments have used the printing of money to produce revenue. The government revenue from printing money is protected by requiring that all money in a country be denominated in terms of the government issued money.

Since government actions have restricted the concurrent circulation of monies, there is little evidence on the number of currencies that would be used in the absence of government restrictions. However, there are a large number of national currencies in existence now. Probably a number of these would remain. And as long as money holders were free to hold any denomination of money they wanted, these national currencies alone would offer individual holders and private banks a wide range of alternatives. If the performance of government monies did not improve, commercial banks would have an incentive to develop superior alternatives.

Even if the number of currencies that could circulate concurrently was small, there would be market pressure on the institutions issuing standard currencies to maintain their currencies at a stable or increasing value. In the absence of legal restrictions, the lead bank in a region would be loath to loose the confidence of money holders in the value of its money, because once lost, its business could vanish overnight as smaller banks shifted en masse to another unit of account.[7]

BRAND NAME IDENTIFICATION

It is in the market for hand to hand currency that many economists have assumed a competitive supply of money could not work. Since paper currency is assumed to be costless to produce, it has been asserted that banks would continue to issue paper until its value was driven to zero. This would be correct if monies were not distinguishable. But people would only hold monies that were identified by issuer, since only then could individual issuers be held accountable for changes in the value of the money they issue. The right to the exclusive use of brand names and logos for easy identification of a product is protected by law. In the market for currency, brand name identification would be important, as it is for most consumer durables, and issuers of monies would be forced by market pressure to offer brand name monies. There would be the normal problems with brand name pirating, called counterfeiting when applied to currency, but the problem is not unique to currency.[8]

VALUE GUARANTEES AND CONFIDENCE

What kind of assurances would banks of issue give to holders of their currency? How definite would these assurances be and what degree of confidence could the holders have in the issuers to live up to their pledges? It seems clear that banks would be under market pressure to give assurances that their monetary liabilities would have a predictable value in terms of goods. When choosing among different currencies, holders would be interested in the goods the assurances were given in terms of and the degree of confidence with which the assurances could be believed. Banks could acquire customer confidence by entering into legally binding contracts and/or by conducting their business so as to make explicit assurances believable.[9] Banks would make the assurance believable and make it possible to meet their commitments by holding short-term assets that had stable values in terms of the bundle of goods their liabilities were denominated in terms of. They would lease inventories of goods to businesses and make other types of loans, denominated in terms of goods, to businesses and consumers.

CONSTANT RATES OF MONEY GROWTH

One type of assurance that might seem appealing to holders of currency as an alternative to real value assurances is for banks to obligate themselves to supply new monies at predetermined (low) rates. This would be a simple extension to substitutable currencies of the Simons-Friedman constant money supply rule. However, there is a problem with constant money growth guarantees with substitutable monies that would make them unattractive to holders of money.

In a market with several substitutable currencies, shifts in demand between currencies or against goods could lead to cumulative movements in the value of any single money. A decline in the demand for a currency, with a fixed supply, would lead to a fall in its value. If this created expectations of a further drop in the value of the money, people would try to reduce their holdings of the money. The induced drop in demand from an initial shift in demand would push the value of the money down further. And with high degrees of substitutability between monies, the value of the money could drop to zero. Hence guarantees on the rate of issue could prove to be largely worthless.[10]

FIDUCIARY VS. COMMODITY MONEY

Governments have not proven themselves able to provide stable valued fiduciary money. There is no reason to expect private issuers of paper money to be any more deserving of trust. But a competitive market would force individual private banks to give believable assurances on the value of their monetary liabilities. Banks would make their assurances believable by holding claims on goods or in terms of the goods on which the assurances were based. Competitive paper money would be backed by goods. Given the highly developed state of the legal and financial system, there would seem to be little need for banks to hold actual commodities in their vaults. A competitive monetary system with substitutable monies would produce monies that provided predictable standards of value without losing the efficiencies of paper money.

IMPLICATIONS OF COMPETITIVELY ISSUED SUBSTITUTABLE MONIES

Typically, a single bank in each country, the central bank, has been given a monopoly over the issue of the standard money into which monetary liabilities of all other banks must be convertible. The introduction of substitutable monies would undermine the monopoly position of central banks. Greater competition would lead to lower rates of inflation and more nearly optimum holdings of real money balances.

There is a large literature on the real revenue that can be acquired by issuing paper money.[11] There is also recent literature on the optimum quantity of real money balances.[12] The literature on the revenue from printing money has focused on the amount of real resources that a monopoly issuer of paper money can extract from the economy for different rates of monetary expansion, while the optimum quantity of money literature focuses on the welfare implications of different rates of monetary expansion and derives the conditions for a welfare maximum level of real money balances. One of the interests in studying competitively issued substitutable monies is that it brings together these two strands of literature.

We will show in this section that profit maximizing banks issuing substitutable monies competitively will supply optimum quantities of real money balances. It is the monopolization of the production of monies by governments that has prevented the market from functioning so as to produce optimum quantities of monies.

REVENUE FROM PRINTING MONEY

The demand for money balances is assumed to be negatively related to the cost of holding money balances. This money demand relationship is plotted in Figure 10.1 as the negatively sloped D_m line. The demand for real money balances (M/P) is measured on the horizontal axis, and the real cost of holding money balances per time period (r_N) is measured on

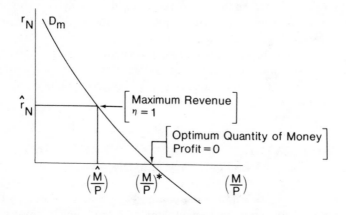

Figure 10.1: Maximum Revenue and Optimum Quantity of Money

the vertical axis. The higher the cost of holding money balances the smaller will be the demand for real money balances. The cost of holding real money balances is equal to the real rate of interest on alternative assets (r) minus the real return on money. The real return on money is equal to any nominal interest paid on money (i_M) minus the rate of inflation (π). In symbols:

$$r_N = r - (i_M - \pi).$$

A monopoly supplier of money would maximize revenue by setting r_N at the point on the demand curve where the elasticity of demand for money with respect to the cost of holding money (η) is equal to unity.[13] This point is indicated on Figure 10.1 by $\eta = 1$ at $\hat{r}_N$ and (M/P).

OPTIMUM QUANTITY OF MONEY [14]

Given the assumption that money balances can be costlessly provided, an optimum quantity of money, from a social welfare viewpoint, exists at the point where the marginal cost of holding money balances (r_N) is equal to zero.[15] At any r_N greater than zero, holdings of money balances will be suboptimum since the marginal cost of holding money is above the marginal social cost of providing money balances.

A zero marginal cost of holding money balances is a zero profit position for the banking system. At a cost of holding money above zero, profits to the banking system will be positive. If there is free entry into banking and banks competitively issue distinguishable but substitutable monies, then at any r_N greater than zero banks would compete by offering better terms to the holders of money balances until profits were competed away.[16]

When r_N equals zero the real return on money balances is equal to the real rate of return on alternative assets in the economy. This position is consistent with stable prices and an explicit real rate of interest on money at a rate equal to r, or, if explicit interest is not paid on money balances, a deflation at the rate r.

Banking profits would be zero when r_N equals zero because all the revenue acquired from printing money would be used in providing money holders with an assured real rate of return of r. If explicit interest is paid on money, and the value of money is guaranteed in terms of goods, then all interest received on bank assets would be required to pay interest on money, and all revenue received from printing money to meet growth in demand for real money balances would be used by the bank to purchase assets to insure that interest could continue to be paid on the increasing level of money balances.

If, instead of paying explicit interest, banks provided a real return on money by deflation, the profit position would be the same. With no growth in demand for real money balances, banks could engineer a deflation at the rate r by using revenue received as interest on their assets to retire their monetary liabilities at the rate r. With growth in demand for real money balances, in addition to retiring old money at the rate interest revenue is received, banks would print new money at the rate of growth in demand. The revenue received from printing the new money would need to be invested in real assets in order to provide funds for retirement of monetary liabilities in the future at the rate required to continue the deflation. With either method of paying a return on money, banks would use up all the revenue acquired from printing money in providing a rate of return on money equal to the real rate of interest.[17]

While the competitive rate of return on money balances could be provided either by explicit interest on money or by a steady deflation, other considerations might dictate which way the return would be paid. The suppliers of substitutable monies would have an incentive to tailor the method of paying the return on money balances to people's tastes.

The role of money as a standard of value might provide reason to pay explicit interest on money. A standard of value that was relatively constant over time might be preferred to a standard of value that appreciated against goods at a steady rate. If people preferred a constant standard of value, then monies that paid explicit interest at the real rate of interest and which had capital value assurances at a constant price in terms of goods, would be preferred by holders of money. It might be awkward to pay explicit interest on hand to hand currency, but banks could compensate holders of currency in other ways. For instance, businesses that agreed to mark prices in terms of currency issued by a particular bank could receive special consideration when using other services of the bank. Banks would compete on currency pick up and delivery service to business customers that made frequent deposits and withdrawals of currency. There are many other ways that banks of issue could compensate holders of currency if forced to do so by competitive pressure.

CURRENCY SUBSTITUTION AND
THE REAL-BILLS DOCTRINE

The real-bills doctrine held that banks should supply money to meet the needs of trade. Advocates of the doctrine argued that if banks discounted short-term commercial paper (real-bills) they would automatically supply money to meet the needs of the economy. The banking system would be sound because its liabilities would be backed by assets that were self liquidating. Mints pointed out the fallacy of the real-bills doctrine: the system had one nominal magnitude (the supply of commercial paper to the banks) controlling another nominal magnitude (the supply of money).[18] The problem is that if prices increase, then the nominal value of commercial paper tendered to the banks for discounting would rise with the price level and the money supply would be increased. This would tend to ratify and under some conditions exacerbate movements in prices.

Would a competitive monetary system issuing substitutable monies be subject to the real-bills problem? Banks issuing substitutable monies in a competitive market would increase loans and discounts as long as it was profitable to do so. If an individual bank could issue money that was indistinguishable from money issued by other banks, it would always have a profit incentive to do so. But the competitive market would force banks to issue distinguishable monies and to give assurances of the future value of monies in terms of goods. Banks attempting to issue money that could not be distinguished from that of a competitor would be subject to legal sanctions. And distinguishable money that did not carry assurances of its value in terms of goods could not be sold when people had superior monies available. Banks issuing distinguishable monies with assurances of value in terms of goods would have to contract the issue if price levels started to rise. Increases in the demand for real money balances though, would be met by increases in the supply of monies as banks tried to capture the new demand and keep the value of their monies from changing. The competitive banking system would act to satisfy changes in demand for real money balances and counteract any tendency for price levels to change.

SUMMARY AND CONCLUSIONS

We have argued in this chapter that if the banking system were freed from government controls and people were allowed to hold monies of any denomination, banks would offer distinguishable monies and would compete by offering monies with goods value assurances and competitive rates of return. Competitive pressure would force the banking system to respond to the tastes of the public as to the kinds of assurances that were acceptable and the method used to produce returns on monies. The resulting monies as standards of value would reflect the desires of holders of monies. Competitive pressure on the returns offered on monies would result in optimum holdings of the monies. A competitive monetary system would supply monies to meet the needs of trade at stable price levels.

The competitive system of substitutable monies we have discussed here would be radically different from the existing monopoly system of money issue, both in terms of its market structure and in terms of the nature of the monies that would be provided. It is probably not possible to foresee all the difficulties in a situation that is so much different from what we are accustomed to. However, it does seem that it is incorrect to think that a competitive paper money system would not function. It also appears that a competitive system of money issue would have several advantages over the present system. Even though a competitive system of providing monies would be radically different from the present system, it should not be rejected out of hand.

NOTES

1. Girton and Roper (1978) discuss the movement from commodity money to paper money in more detail than will be done here. See also Manne and Miller (1975).

2. The use of the supply of paper money to try to meet various policy objectives has led Mason to characterize the current paper money standard as a policy standard. See Mason (1963, 1978) for a discussion of the shortcomings of the policy standard as it has worked in this century.

3. Hamilton (1934) and Flynn (1978) analyze the price experience in the sixteenth century in Europe as gold and silver was imported from the Americas in large quantities.

4. The literature includes the following works: Hayek (1976), Klein (1974, 1976), Tullock (1975, 1976), Girton and Roper (1976), Vaubel (1977), and Calvo and Rodriguez (1977).

5. Klein (1974) has a very useful discussion and criticism of the view that paper money cannot be produced by the private market. Also see Hayek (1976).

6. Hayek (1976) has an excellent discussion of the market pressures that would compel competitive issuers of money to offer stable valued monies.

7. Vaubel (1977) discusses problems that would result from economics of scale in money production.

8. Klein (1974) emphasises the importance of distinguishable monies. See also Vaubel (1977).

9. Klein (1974) argues that some amount of bank deception would always be profitable if information is costly to acquire.

10. Girton and Roper (1976) present an explicit model of currency substitution and use it to derive the stability conditions with monies in fixed supplies. They also discuss the indeterminacy problem of substitutable monies that are fixed in nominal supply and that have interest paid on monies denominated in terms of the monies themselves.

11. Work that deals with the government revenue from printing money includes Newcomb (1865), Friedman (1971), and Auernheimer (1974).

12. The literature on the optimum quantity of money includes Tolley (1957), Tobin (1968), Marty (1968), and Friedman (1969).

13. This analysis follows that of Auernheimer (1974). In order to obtain this result, we need to assume the purchasers of money balances know the price, i.e., the issuer of money

does not deceive the public, and the real rate of interest and the rate of growth in the demand for real money balances are independent of time and the cost of holding money. The earlier literature of the profit maximizing rate of money expansion assumed a different set of conditions. See for example Friedman (1971).

14. Friedman (1969) has a detailed discussion of the concept of an optimum quantity of money.

15. This assumes the marginal conditions are met in all other markets. If there is no nondistorting source of government revenue, the marginal conditions will need to be violated in some markets for governments to obtain revenue. In this situation, the optimal tax on money balances would be positive. See Phelps (1973). But this should not be taken to imply that a tax on money balances has to be an inflation tax. Direct wealth taxes on money balances would produce revenue without some of the unfavorable aspects of an inflation tax.

16. If wealth holders at the margin always prefer money to real assets then an optimum quantity of money would be equal to the total physical wealth of the community. If this were the case, in providing an optimum quantity of money, the banking system would hold claims equal to the total value of the physical wealth of the community.

17. Auernheimer (1974) and Girton and Roper (1976) have more formal statements of the implications of providing competitive rates of return on monies.

18. The standard work on the real-bills doctrine is Mints (1945). See also Girton (1974).

REFERENCES

AUERNHEIMER, L. (1974) "The Honest Government's Guide to the Revenue from the Creation of Money." Journal of Political Economy (May/June): 598-606.

BAILEY, M. (1956) "The Welfare Cost of Inflationary Finance." Journal of Political Economy (April): 93-110.

CALVO, G. and RODRIGUEZ, C. (1977) "A Model of Exchange Rate Determination Under Currency Substitution and Rational Expectations." Journal of Political Economy (June): 617-626.

FLYNN, D. (1978) "A New Perspective on the Spanish Price Revolution: The Monetary Approach to the Balance of Payments." Explorations in Economic History 15 (September): 388-406.

FRIEDMAN, M. (1959) A Program for Monetary Stability. New York: Fordham University Press.

_____(1969) The Optimum Quantity of Money and Other Essays. Chicago: Aldine.

_____(1971) "Government Revenue from Inflation." Journal of Political Economy (July/August): 846-856.

GIRTON, L. (1974) "SDR Creation and the Real-Bills Doctrine." Southern Economic Journal 41, (July): 57-61.

_____and ROPER, D. (1976) "Theory and Implications of Currency Substitution." Federal Reserve Board, International Finance Discussion Papers No. 86.

_____(1978) "The Evolution of Exchange Rate Policy." In B. Putman and S. Wilford (eds.) Monetary Approach to International Adjustment. New York: Praeger.

HAMILTON, E. (1934) American Treasury and the Price Revolution in Spain, 1501-1650. Cambridge, Mass.: Harvard University Press.

HAYEK, F. (1976) Denationalization of Money: An Analysis of the Theory and Practice of Concurrent Currencies. London: The Institute of Economic Affairs.

KLEIN, B. (1974) "The Competitive Supply of Money." Journal of Money, Credit and Banking (November): 423-453.

———(1976) "Competing Monies: A Comment." Journal of Money Credit and Banking (November): 513-520.

MANNE, H. and MILLER, R. (1975) Gold, Money and the Law. Chicago: Aldine.

MARTY, A. (1968) "The Optimal Rate of Growth of Money." Journal of Political Economy (July/August): 860-873.

MASON, W. (1963) The Clarification of the Monetary Standard: The Concept and Its Relation to Monetary Policies and Objectives. University Park: Pennsylvania State University Press.

———(1978) "The Monetary Rule: Whence It Came and Where It Went—And At What Cost Was It Lost?" Unpublished Manuscript.

MINTS, L. (1945) A History of Banking Theory in Great Britain and the United States. Chicago: University of Chicago Press.

NEWCOMB, S. (1865) Financial Policy During the Southern Rebellion. New York: Greenwood Press.

PHELPS, E. (1973) "Inflation in the Theory of Public Finance." Swedish Journal of Economics (March): 67-82.

TOBIN, J. (1968) "Notes on Optimal Monetary Growth." Journal of Political Economy (July/August): 833-859.

TOLLEY, G. (1957) "Providing for Growth of the Money Supply." Journal of Political Economy (December): 465-485.

TULLOCK, G. (1975) "Competing Monies." Journal of Money Credit and Banking (November): 491-498.

———(1976) "Competing Monies: A Reply." Journal of Money, Credit and Banking (November): 521-526.

VAUBEL, R. (1977) "Free Currency Competition." Weltwirtschaftliches Archiv: 435-459.

ABOUT THE AUTHORS

CHARLES C. BAKER, JR. is currently a Senior Economist at the United States Treasury Department. Prior to his current research position, he was Assistant Director of the Office of Debt Analysis at the Treasury and Senior Economist at the Federal Reserve Board of Governors. Dr. Baker has also taught at Harvard University. He has written extensively on the capital and money markets.

WILLIAM J. BAUMOL is Professor of Economics at Princeton and New York Universities. He is author of numerous books, among them: *Economic Dynamics, Welfare Economics and the Theory of the State, Economic Theory and Operations Analysis, Performing Arts: The Economic Dilemma* (with W. G. Bowen), and *The Theory of Environmental Policy* (with W. E. Oates). He is President of the Eastern Economic Association, President-Elect of the Association of Environmental and Resource Economists, member of the Research Advisory Committee of Resources for the Future, Inc., the Nominating Committee of the American Stock Exchange, and the American Economic Association Committee on Honorary Members. He is an Honorary Fellow of the London School of Economics, a Fellow of the Econometric Society and member of the American Philosophical Society.

ROBERT W. CLOWER, Doctor of Letters (Oxford University), is currently Professor of Economics at the University of California, Los Angeles. A former Rhodes Scholar (Washington, 1949), Nuffield College Student (1950-1952), and Guggenheim Fellow (1965-1966), Clower has held visiting posts at the University of the Punjab, Markerere College, Monash University, and the University of Western Ontario, and, before joining UCLA in 1971, held permanent teaching posts at Washington State University, Northwestern University, and the University of Essex. His publications include books on mathematical economics, economic development, microeconomic analysis, and monetary theory, as well as numerous articles in leading professional journals. Clower is currently Managing Editor of *Economic Inquiry* and a member of the Executive Committee of the American Economic Association.

MICHAEL DOOLEY received his Ph.D. from Pennsylvania State University in 1971. He has since been a member of the staff of the Federal Reserve Board and currently is chief of the U.S. International Transactions Section. Mr. Dooley was a visiting faculty member at the University of Texas in 1974 and the University of Chicago Graduate School of Business for the 1976-1977 academic year. His reseach interests include the Euro-currency markets and exchange rate determination.

LANCE GIRTON is currently a Professor at the University of Utah. He was an economist in the International Finance Division of the Federal Reserve Board in Washington, D.C. from 1971-1978. He has been an Adjoint Associate Professor at George Washington University and a Visiting Professor at the University of Utah. His research speciality is international monetary theory and finance and he has published in numerous professional journals on topics in this area.

THOMAS HAVRILESKY is Professor of Economics at Duke University. He has held visiting professorships at Monash University, Rice University, Erasmus University (Rotterdam), and Simon Fraser University. He has also taught at the University of Maryland and was a research fellow at the Federal Reserve Bank of Chicago. Professor Havrilseky has published numerous articles in the theory and practice of monetary policy in the *Journal of Political Economy*, the *Journal of*

Finance, and the *Journal of Money, Credit and Banking*, among others. He is coauthor of several popular textbooks and books of readings in monetary theory and policy and money and banking. He is an associate editor of the *Journal of Economics and Business* and the *Social Science Quarterly*.

THOMAS M. HUMPHREY is an economist with the Federal Reserve Bank of Richmond. He has taught at Tulane University, Auburn University, the University of Virginia, and Wofford College. Dr. Humphrey is the author of numerous papers and has published extensively in the Federal Reserve Bank of Richmond's *Economic Review*.

EDWARD J. KANE occupies the Everett D. Reese Chair of Banking and Monetary Economics at Ohio State University. Previously, he taught at Boston College, Princeton University, and Iowa State University, and held visiting professorships at Istanbul University and Simon Fraser University. He has consulted for the Federal Deposit Insurance Corporation, the Federal Home Loan Bank Board, the Department of Housing and Urban Development, the National Commission on Electronic Funds Transfer, and various components of the Federal Reserve System. Professor Kane is President-Elect of the American Finance Association and was a Guggenheim fellow in 1969-1970. He has published in more than twenty different professional journals and serves currently on the editorial boards of the *Journal of Finance, Journal of Money, Credit and Banking, Journal of Bank Research*, and *Review of Social Economy*. He serves also as a Trustee of the Teachers Insurance Annuity Association of America and as a member of their finance committee.

HERBERT M. KAUFMAN is an Associate Professor of Economics at Arizona State University. Prior to his position of Arizona State, he was an economist at the Federal National Mortgage Association in Washington, D.C. He has published in the *Review of Economics and Statistics, Journal of Money, Credit and Banking*, and *Economic Inquiry*, among others.

RAYMOND E. LOMBRA is an Associate Professor of Economics at Pennsylvania State University. Prior to his position at Penn State, he was a senior staff Economist at the Federal Reserve Board of Governors in Washington, D.C. He has published in the *Review of Economics and Statistics*, the *Quarterly Journal of Economics*, and *Economic Inquiry*, among others.

DONALD ROPER is currently a Professor of Economics at the University of Utah. He was previously an economist in the International Finance Division of the Federal Reserve Board of Washington, D.C. from 1969 until 1975. He has taught at the University of Stockholm, the University of Texas at Austin, the University of California at Berkeley, and the Australian National University. His research speciality is in international monetary theory and he has published in numerous professional journals on topics in this area.

ROBERT WEINTRAUB is Staff Director, Subcommittee on Domestic Monetary Policy of the House Banking Committee of the U.S. Congress. Prior to his current position he was Senior Economist for the Senate Banking Committee and for the House Banking Committee for various periods of time. He has also been an Assistant Professor at Northwestern University, an Associate Professor at the City University of New York, and a Professor at the University of California. He has published extensively in professional economics journals including the *American Economic Review*, the *Journal of Political Economy*, and the *Journal of Money, Credit and Banking*. He is the author of *Monetary Economics* and *The Impact of the Federal Reserve System's Monetary Policies on the Nation's Economy*.